# LEARNING SUPPORT SERVICES

Please return
on or before
the last date
stamped below

 City College
NORWICH

A FINE WILL BE CHARGED FOR OVERDUE ITEMS

ALSO BY ALICE WALKER FROM THE WOMEN'S PRESS:

Fiction and poetry

Essays

THE SAME RIVER TWICE

Honoring the Difficult

A Meditation on Life, Spirit, Art, and the Making of the Film
The Color Purple Ten Years Later

ALICE WALKER

Published in Great Britain by The Women's Press Ltd, 1996
A member of the Namara Group
34 Great Sutton Street, London EC1V 0DX

This edition published 1998

First published in the United States of America by Scribner, 1996

British Library Cataloguing-in-Publication Data
A catalogue record for this book is available from the British Library.

Please refer to page 301 for photograph and text permissions.

ISBN 0 7043 4573 0

Printed and bound in Great Britain by Cox & Wyman Ltd

For my beloved family
ancestral and present
to whom the persistent
audaciousness of
Art
has kept me close.

And to Steven Spielberg and Quincy Jones
Magicians
Changelings:
the knock
at the
door.

THE LABYRINTH AT CHARTRES CATHEDRAL

Once we enter [the labyrinth], ordinary time and distance are immaterial, we are in the midst of a ritual and a journey where transformation is possible; we do not know how far away or close we are to the center where meaning can be found until we are there; the way back is not obvious and we have no way of knowing as we emerge how or when we will take the experience back into the world until we do. There are no blind ends in a labyrinth, the path often doubles back on itself, the direction toward which we are facing is continually changing, and if we do not turn back or give up we will reach the center to find the rose, the Goddess, the Grail, a symbol representing the sacred feminine. To return to ordinary life, we must again travel the labyrinth to get out, which is also a complex journey for it involves integrating the experience into consciousness, which is what changes us.

—JEAN SHINODA BOLEN,
    Crossing to Avalon

Contents

I belong to a people so wounded by betrayal, so hurt by misplacing their trust, that to offer us a gift of love is often to risk one's life, certainly one's name and reputation. I do not mean only the Africans, sold and bought, and bought and sold again; or the Indians, who joyfully fed those who, when strong, gleefully starved them out. I speak as well of the shadowy European ancestor, resentfully denied, except that one cannot forget the thatched one-room hovels of old Europe, put to the torch by those who grabbed the land; and the grief of the starving, ashen ancestor, forced to seek his or her lonely fortune in a land that seemed to demand ruthlessness if one intended to survive.

I belong to a people, heart and mind, who do not trust mirrors. Not those, in any case, in which we ourselves appear. The empty mirror, the one that reflects noses and hair unlike our own, and a prosperity and harmony we may never have known, gives us peace. Our shame is deep. For shame is the result of soul injury. Mirrors, however, are sacred, not only because they permit us to witness the body we are fortunate this time around to be in, but because they permit us to ascertain the condition of the eternal that rests behind the body, the soul. As an ancient Japanese proverb states: when the mirror is dim, the soul is not pure.

Art is the mirror, perhaps the only one, in which we can see our true collective face. We must honor its sacred function. We must let art help us.

ACKNOWLEDGMENTS

A book like this, that takes a lingering look backward at a dangerous crossroad in one's life, requires the unequivocal support and
love of many people. After all, there is significance in the vernacu-
lar expression "Don't look back, the past may be gaining on you." I
thank my friend, filmmaker Pratibha Parmar, for offering to read
the manuscript immediately, and for comprehending its relevance
to the world of films, and to women's films in particular. I thank
Gloria Steinem, whose sisterly loyalty was never more evident
than in her ruthless trimming of extraneous sprouts of the narrative; in an earlier incarnation I think she was a farmer whose yam
patch lay in the path of kudzu. I thank Robert Allen, who, upon
reading the manuscript, cheerfully acknowledged my description of
some of his earlier behavior, and said, "You caught me with my humanity showing!" Such a free and fearless response to memories
that have been painful to us both made me value our long years of
partnership even more, as well as the decades we have been friends.
I thank my chosen sister, Belvie Rooks, for all her patience with
me; for reading the manuscript and feeling comfortable about her
place in it.

For their work in bringing the book to its present completion I
thank my agent, Wendy Weil, my editor, Leigh Haber, and my ad-
ministrative assistant, Joan Miura. I also thank Greer Kessel and
Marla Stutman.

ALICE WALKER AND STEVEN SPIELBERG
ON THE SET OF *The Color Purple*.

FISH

AND

BIRD

COME

TO MY

HOUSE

I SWIM AWAY WITH THEM*

Journal Entry
February 21, 1984

Last night Quincy Jones and Steven Spielberg arrived. Steven looking rather like some kind of bird, perhaps a parrot—he says he broke his toes against his parrot's cage: two fingers were broken last night, from falling downstairs, now in a cast. Quincy first, in an enormous limousine that had difficulty turning into my lane. (Well, Galilee Lane, of course it would be narrow!) Quincy beautifully dressed and hair done just so. And Steven, who arrived later, casually and in (partly) someone else's clothes. Quincy had talked so positively about him I was almost dreading his appearance—but then, after a moment of near I don't know what, uneasiness, he

---

*Quincy Jones, born under the sign of Pisces the fish. Deep, mysterious, cool. Intuitive. Shimmering through life. Steven, Sagittarius, both owl (open-eyed and aware) and parrot (vari-plumed, skilled in mimicry), courageous: will fly anywhere, outside and inside himself. Me: Aquarius, the water bearer.

came in and sat down and started right in showing how closely he had read the book. And making really intelligent comments. And Quincy beamed.

Robert and Rebecca and Casey were with me. Rebecca amused and Casey looking for something to munch. Robert quite charming too. Well. I left them, waving, as we went out to Ernie's for dinner, where Quincy and Steven and I got slightly tipsy and energetic in our thoughts of a movie about Celie and Shug and Nettie. And after three hours they brought me back to my humble abode and rode off into the night in their enormous limo en route to the Warner Brothers jet and then home to L.A. and to bed. Quincy claimed not to have slept the night before because leaving L.A. at nine in the morning was so early.

Anyway.

It is agreed that Steven and I will work together on the screenplay. I will write it and confer. Write and confer. I feel some panic. I want so much for this to be good. Something to lift spirits and encourage people.

Back in bed. Reading *Prevention Magazine* and wishing I didn't have to get up and take my vitamins. I do.

June 18, 1984

I finished the draft of the screenplay a couple of weeks ago. Got it back from the typist yesterday and sent it off to L.A. today. There is nothing like relief! And I've told my agent to tell Warner Brothers that I'm not signing the chain-resembling contract they're offering. Far too many clauses and restrictions. I am too happy thinking of nothing but the colors I will be using to paint my little round house.

"Fame" exhausts me, more than anything else it does. I am still tired from being "recognized" by the Pulitzer Prize. I am sent countless manuscripts to read, books to endorse; there are invitations and awards offerings that I couldn't begin to accept. More mail than I thought existed. How rare too, now, to get a letter from someone I actually know. But I am slowly getting back my strength and in the country, at Wild Trees, I am very, very happy. The days are long and golden—they seem almost endless. And the full moons are astonishing. (What a sentence!) There is hay stacked neatly in the neighbors' fields, and everywhere we look there's beauty.

I've painted the pillar that holds up the main corner of my house a deep, dusty lavender/blue and the door sky blue. There's orange and poppy yellow in my buckets waiting to be called forth.

It occurs to me I haven't watched T.V. news in weeks, maybe months. Perhaps I'll wheel out the telly (I'm back in the city) and see what the world as many people know it is coming to.

Disasters (disconnection from the stars). I am oddly fascinated by the dead matter of T.V., and appalled that for so many it is the liveliest thing in the house.

Quincy sent more roses and a moving note. I love him already, and Steven too. Whatever happens or doesn't. Love is the way to feel.

THE

RIVER
HONORING THE DIFFICULT

To create today is to create dangerously. Any publication is an act, and that act exposes one to the passions of an age that forgives nothing. Hence the question is not to find out if this is or is not prejudicial to art. The question, for all those who cannot live without art and what it signifies, is merely to find out how, among the police forces of so many ideologies (how many churches, what solitude!), the strange liberty of creation is possible.

—ALBERT CAMUS

Since my book *The Color Purple* was filmed ten years ago, I have been asked innumerable times about my opinion of the result. I have found it one of the most difficult questions I have ever tried to answer. For many years I began my response by talking about the headache I got the first time I saw the film. Peter Guber, a producer, had warned me that on first viewing, I might be shocked. I was to be grateful for the warning. I saw the film in a huge theater with only two other people, and everything about it seemed wrong, especially the opening musical score, which sounded like it belonged in *Oklahoma*. After reciting this experience I would launch into my tale about buying the magic wand that I took to the premiere in New York City, and how, thanks to its magical powers, and a packed theater of enthusiastic viewers all sobbing and guffawing in my ear, I was able to critique the film for its virtues rather than its flaws. Sometimes I would simply say "I love the film." Other times I would say "I have mixed feelings." Occasionally I would say "It is a child with at least three parents: it looks like all of them." Most frequently I said "Remember, the movie is not the book."

It has taken me a while to realize that attempting to respond honestly to this question has kept me from examining the ones I've continually asked myself: "What did I learn from this extremely thrilling, challenging, and ultimately liberating experience? How was I changed during this period in my life? In what ways did my personal life and the filming of my book connect, so that looking back I am able to chart real learning, satisfaction, suffering, and growth?" I was late getting around to these questions because from the moment word went out that there would be a movie, it was attacked by people who loathed the idea. The attacks, many of them personal and painful, continued for many years, right alongside the praise, the prizes, the Oscar award nominations. I often felt isolated, deliberately misunderstood and alone. This too is the writer's territory; I accepted it with all the grace and humor I possessed. Still, there is no denying the pain of being not simply challenged publicly, but condemned. It was said that I hated men, black men in particular; that my work was injurious to black male and female relationships; that my ideas of equality and tolerance were harmful, even destructive to the black community. That my success, and that of other black women writers in publishing our work, was at the expense of black male writers who were not being published sufficiently. I was "accused" of being a lesbian, as if respecting and honoring women automatically discredited anything a woman might say. I was the object of literary stalking: one black male writer attacked me obsessively in lecture, interview and book for over a decade, to the point where I was concerned about his sanity and my safety. In the country north of San Francisco, where I had always sought peace and renewal, I regularly found myself the target of hostile, inflammatory comments by the editor and publisher of the local paper. Because I was the only black woman resident in the community, I was highly visible and felt exposed and vulnerable. This feeling prevented my working at the depth of thought at which I feel most productive. I eventually sought temporary refuge in Mexico, where I was able to work in peace. By then I had grown used to seeing my expressions taken out of context, rearranged, distorted. It was a curious experience that always left me feeling as if I had ingested poison.

Of all the accusations, it was hardest to tolerate the charge that I hated black men. From infancy I have relied on the fiercely sweet spirits of black men; and this is abundantly clear in my work. Nor did these spirits fail me as I sought to stay on my path to health, wholeness, truth and creativity. Bob Marley, Ron Dellums, Nelson Mandela, Black Elk, Jesse Jackson, Randall Robinson, James Baldwin, Crazy Horse, Langston Hughes, and a host of black and red men living and dead walked with me. As did the spirits of Walt Whitman, Leo Tolstoy, John Lennon, and Howard Zinn. But even more important, I felt close to, and always affirmed by, the black male spirit within myself. This spirit's indomitable quality is fierceness of emotion, tenderness of heart, and a love of freedom so strong that death is easily preferable to imprisonment of any kind. Out of respect, I worked hard to reassure my nephews, uncles, brothers, friends and former lovers that the monster they saw being projected was not the aunt, niece, sister, woman who loved them. I was not guided or accompanied by the spirits of black men who embarrass and oppress us, or by those of assorted "gangsta" rappers for whom the humiliation and subjugation of women is the preferred expression of masculinity: I feel no regret for this.

What the question about my response to the film could not address, I realized only belatedly, was the hidden trauma I endured during its creation, of which these attacks were only a part, trauma not always noticeably connected to the making of it. The reason the question itself seemed so exasperating was because I knew a comprehensive response would be long. It would not be simple. It would be, in order to have meaning for me, about deeply painful issues that were literally the "behind the scenes" struggles of one of my life's most complex public events.

For instance: at the time the movie was being made, I thought that I, and my mother, were dying.

In the beginning, at the end of the seventies, my mother had small strokes that left her barely marked, but shortly after *The Color Purple* was written in 1981 she suffered a major one. I flew to Georgia to see her and to consult with my family and her doctor about what should be done. Her X rays showed carotid arteries so blocked with cholesterol that almost no oxygen was getting to her brain. Though this blockage was removed, she remained largely paralyzed. There followed many months of trying to make life better for her, a temporary, hopeful period when she felt well enough to make the journey out to California to visit me. As I had suspected, she loved the redwoods, the ocean, the hills, and valiantly lurched along, leaning on my arm, her face radiant; but then, ultimately, there was a decline brought on by many smaller "afterstrokes." For over a decade, until her death in September 1993, my mother was completely incapacitated physically. She had not read *The Color Purple* before her stroke, beyond the first few pages, though it was deliberately written in a way that would not intimidate her, and other readers like her, with only a grade school education and a lifetime of reading the Bible, newspapers and magazine articles. Because of her inability even to sit up in bed, she would never be able to read it.

From the moment I realized my mother would never again be the woman I knew, something fell inside of me. It did not fall with a crash, but was rather a slow, inexorable collapse. There was a strong green cord connecting me to this great, simple seeming, but complicated woman, who was herself rooted in the earth. I felt this cord weakening, becoming a thread. My legs seemed to be going out from under me. My heart felt waterlogged. My spirit lost its shine. My grief was kind enough to visit me only at night, in dreams: as I felt it wash over me, I did not care that I might drown. I knew that, awake, the unshed tears of rage and irremediable loss I was suffering would surely kill me. I had only known my mother as active, heroically so, and strong. This does not mean she was never sick; she was, from time to time. But she was never one to lie in bed past seven in the morning, even after her eight children were out of the house for good. After raising all of us, and being a full-time worker and housewife, she was often up at dawn managing her house and garden, honoring her religious obligations and hastening to her duties to her friends. She was stronghearted. Which, indeed, she remained. Her doctor marveled that even though the rest of her body failed to obey her most minor wish, her heart remained that of a lion. This was also true, amazingly, of her spirit. Eventually, all that was left of my mother was her smile, radiating out of a body that already seemed, in her bed, settled into its final resting place. There was not a day, all those years, that I did not feel the emptiness left by my mother's absence, particularly as she gradually lost the ability to talk, beyond a slurred greeting, which, true to her spirit, she slurred cheerfully.

I loved the way my mother talked, which was always fresh, honest, straight as an arrow describing anything. When I sat on the set of *The Color Purple*—and as controversy raged even over whether my characters "degraded" black folk speech—it was this kind of speech that I tried to make sure the actors expressed. For me the filming of my book was a journey to the imagined and vastly rearranged lives of my mother and father and grandparents before I was born (among other things); it was a re-created world I hoped desperately my mother would live long enough to enter again through film. I used to amuse myself, on the set, watching Steven work, and thinking of the gift he was preparing for a woman he had never seen.

My own trial was different from my mother's, but coincided with and to an extent echoed portions of it.

It is my habit as a born-again pagan to lie on the earth in worship. In this, I imagine I am like my pagan African and Native American ancestors, who were sustained by their conscious inseparability from Nature prior to being forced by missionaries to focus all their attention on a God "up there" in "heaven." Unknown to me however, sometime during the late seventies and early eighties, the earth tired of people, worshipers or not, taking her for granted. I was bitten by three of the ticks that cause Lyme disease. I pulled off the ticks casually, as I had done all my life, and thought no more about it, although I later noticed the marks on my stomach, large, red bull's-eyes. I felt soreness and swelling. I did not even realize I was sick for most of 1983, even though my mood swings, always precipitous because of PMS, became increasingly dramatic. I found myself one day ranting at an old friend whose ineffectual efforts to colonize me and my work—she insisted in public gatherings and in private that she comprehended the significance of both me and my work far better than I did—suddenly became intolerable (I'd suffered uncomplainingly for years). I noticed I was always tired.

It was not until I flogged myself onto a flight to China, where I hoped to exchange ideas with Chinese women writers, and once there found it a challenge even to think, that I realized something was very wrong. Pictures of me from that trip show a gray, puffy-faced woman, much older and heavier than I would later be, pitched blankly toward the camera. On the train from Shanghai to Hong Kong I began to hemorrhage. By the time I reached Hawaii, I was barely able to put one foot in front of the other. By the time I reached California, I ached in every muscle and joint. I couldn't raise my arms; I could barely move my legs. My eyes ached. My ears. I felt a weariness so profound, it disturbs me to remember it. Though the pain for the most part left, eventually, the weariness and weakness remained. For the next three years I would require a walking stick to keep me upright. And in fact the one memorable item I purchased in China was an elaborately carved dragon-headed cane.

In the early eighties nobody knew about Lyme disease. There was however a rumor about something else that eventually became known as Chronic Fatigue Syndrome; I latched on to that, desperately needing some label to define what was happening to me. It was known to be a condition that afflicted mainly women, women who were active politically and socially, women who were "creative." I read that most of these women spent their days weeping and depressed, scared and often unable to move. It had no cure (and still doesn't), though Lyme disease does—if caught early. I went to doctor after doctor, but there was, as far as they could see, nothing wrong with me.

It felt exactly as if I were being attacked from the inside at the same time I was being attacked from the outside. Would I survive it? I thought not. And then, just when I was feeling this, my partner of many struggling but overall happy years informed me that because I had been "distracted by my work and sexually inattentive" he'd had an affair a year or so earlier with an old girlfriend from the past. Having felt more secure in our relationship over time, I'd had no inkling of this, and had blissfully helped plan our future as if it were assured. I felt completely foolish and naive. Though we were in a committed, monogamous relationship, which I, after many hesitations, honored, I did not blame him so much for the infidelity. I recognized that our bond was complicated by my need to live in my own space most of the time, by my periods of creative and/or depression-driven moodiness. It was also complicated by my bisexuality, which my partner joked about—"I am alcoholic, you are bisexual, we cancel each other out"—but which caused both of us a degree of anxiety. I knew he often wondered if I really loved him, and for how long. At times my deep love of and reverence for women felt like ambivalence to both of us.

It was the timing of his confession that sent me reeling. Although his revelation came before there was public awareness of AIDS, I worried there might be a connection between his infidelity and my inexplicable illness. As my trust dissolved along with my health, I became horribly conscious of my vulnerability: I began to make arrangements to leave the relationship. My partner however blamed his behavior on alcoholism, a disease that had caused us much suffering before. He was someone whose sweetness, intelligence, love of the moon, and refusal to be inducted into the Vietnam War I cherished, someone I deeply loved. He was also a person who would try to do what he said. I stayed. But in fact the relationship had lost its numinousness, especially sexually: without a sense of the sacred in our physical connections I began to slowly starve. Though we continued together for many more years, and though he tackled and successfully overcame not only his addiction to alcohol but other addictions as well, what remained of the life we'd constructed together was only its shell.

I also stayed because I was too weakened and confused by my illness, and by my mother's illness, to make such a painful break. The humiliation of being in this position with a black man, at a time when I was being publicly and venomously accused of "attacking" black men, was especially enervating. These accusations seemed singularly crass and simpleminded, but they found their target just the same.

In a filmed interview around that time my partner, looking embarrassed but determined, bravely talks about the pain of envying my success, and of our struggle to talk out and understand his feelings so that I would not be sabotaged by his behavior without even knowing it. But I had, by then, already been sabotaged. In this film I am studying my partner as he speaks with a look of horror, for I am fearful he will speak of his affair as an example of his undermining behavior, and I feel trapped to still be trying to stay with him and not be ashamed. This is the feeling of being deep in the messy stuff of women's secret lives, that place from which unscathed survivors are so rare.

Because she was a black woman of humor and spunk, I had responded affirmatively to Elena Featherston's request to make a film about my life during this period of illness. I still had no idea what was wrong with me. Nor was I even able to talk about it, since it had no name. I still leaned on a stick everywhere I went. I think I wanted a witness, through this film. (Reading through my journal from that time I am amazed at how upbeat I sound, with remarkably little mention of my fear. I just omitted any mention of health. Occasionally I admitted to being *tired*. I seemed to focus most of my attention on present and former relationships with lovers, teachers, and siblings: I wrote often about my father. Not knowing what is wrong with you is silencing, even to yourself.) Always chronically short on funding, the filming of *Visions of the Spirit* (an ironically apt title) took nearly four years to complete. It is clear to me at least how sick I was the first years I was filmed in the countryside and at my writing shack in Mendocino. There is a heavy, stoic quality of resignation that reminds me of those days when it took everything I had simply to sit upright and respond to Elena's questions. I can see that I was somewhat better, not as puffy or as absent, when she filmed me a couple of years later on the set of *The Color Purple*, and that by the end of the film the puffiness is gone, my color is normal, and I have begun the long journey back to myself. I will always be grateful to Elena for providing this record, though the first time I viewed her film I saw mostly my own and my mother's suffering and went into mourning for my mother's lost strength, my own weaknesses and failures. My mother, in Elena's film, is typically happy to be alive, though she can move neither foot nor arm, and though there seems little possibility she ever will again. By then she had seen the film of *The Color Purple*; she was carried to the theater on a stretcher in an ambulance. She liked it very much. She said it reminded her of her mother's life.

My mother was less frightened of movies than of books; seeing the characters of *The Color Purple* in the familiar way she'd always seen movie characters soothed her, as did feeling the overwhelming acceptance of the movie by the people in the audience. I understood that part of her resistance to having my book read to her was based on things she had heard about it, or been told. She must have had terrible fears about what I had created, given the vehemence of some of the opposition; but that she could see even a glimmer of her mother's life in our film deeply comforted me.

She adored her own mother, Nettie, whose name I gave to the character most longed for, most consistently loved and missed, in my story. In real life her mother, unlike Nettie who goes to Africa, never went anywhere, and was battered unmercifully by my grandfather. She died, still sweet, but broken, when I was two. A lament of my weeping mother—"My mother was *good*; and he still mistreated her!"—has haunted my life. I am sitting next to my mother in Elena's film, trying gallantly to put up a good appearance, and not to mention to her or to my sister that my own legs and arms are a little hard to move. For with my mother's collapse I have suddenly become "the strong one." Certainly the primary one to be counted on financially, however extended that long haul might be.

When I think of Steven Spielberg's "version" of my book, my first thought is of Steven himself. His love of and enthusiasm for my characters. His ability to find himself in them. I also think of what he says about me in Elena's film: he says that I am "otherworldly." That I always seem to be somewhere else. That there is something "apparitional" about me. That I am "very haunting." When I saw this I realized that perhaps Steven intuited that I was extremely fragile as our film was being made, walking some days as if in a dream; as, perhaps, many of the cast and the crew also sensed. For even though I was present on the set every moment I could drag myself up from my couch, I was also not there. As I watched each scene unfold I felt more like a spirit than a person. Sometimes a couple of the male characters would move my director's chair to a new location, with me in it. Whoopi and Oprah, Danny and Akosua, Margaret, Desreta and Willard, carried on splendidly; I sat under a tree and offered speech lessons and tarot readings, painfully conscious of my fuzzy thinking and blotchy skin, my soul-deep exhaustion and an almost ever-present nausea. I was unequal to the task of pointing out to Steven every "error" I saw about to be made, as my critics later assumed I should have, or even of praising the exquisite things he constantly thought up, which moved me to tears each evening as we watched "dailies." This pained me; I felt it an unexplainable and quite personal failing.

My inability to speak up further prostrated me. I was moved by the way the actors themselves often saved the day, and of how receptive Steven was to them. I was amazed to see how true to the character Oprah and Margaret played Sofia and Shug; and how incredibly *sweet* and gracious they were as themselves. I cheered inwardly to see Whoopi stand toe to toe one day with Steven and insist that Celie would not age the way he was envisioning her, but would look more like colored women do as they age. A matter of posture and gait, not of wrinkles and a white wig. Because Oprah reminded me of my mother as she was when I was small, I could barely resist sitting beside her as I worried about what was wrong with me and about my mother, and putting my head in her lap. Of all the women in the cast Oprah was most loving and protective toward my daughter, Rebecca (at fifteen the youngest production assistant on the film), spending time with her on the set and inviting her to visit in Chicago. Days when I could not be there I considered Oprah the "aunt" whose presence meant Rebecca would feel "looked out for," more at home.

Throughout the filming Quincy Jones was the older brother/father/beloved figure everyone responded to with simple adoration, longing, and love. Though I would never like the *Oklahoma*-sounding opening score, I would help choose the music for the rest of the film, and it would feel right. The song "Sister," written by Quincy, Rod Temperton and Lionel Richie, which I immediately imagined as a signal of affirmation that women could hum to each other coast to coast, is an immeasurable gift to the bonding of women. And, because men of a certain kind wrote it, it includes them, necessarily, in that bonding. In Elena's film Quincy "sees," affirms, and praises me with an abandon unknown to me previously. This "seeing" of what I am as an artist and a person was to heal some of the pain I felt when other black men attacked me. It also served to remind me that I and my work could be loved without envy—creative "distraction" could be recognized and honored—and that I did not have to fear, as I sometimes did, that there were no black men who were healed enough to value the truth of my work. Or to publicly affirm it.

Although I have wanted to publish this book for a number of years—as a record of this process, which I consider especially useful for women, anyone who is fascinated by film, and people of color—I have hesitated. I certainly could not attempt it while my mother was alive. Even after her death it is painful to dwell on her over-a-decade-long immobility; there was the task, as well, of seeking to understand, and not be hurt by, the not-so-noble parts of her that her sickness sometimes revealed, and my efforts to "forget" those parts, while attempting to address them in my art. Nor could I put my relationship with my former partner into perspective while still sharing a life with him. When I finally began to get well again, and leave the relationship, I experienced a return of energy, of clarity and groundedness in reality, that I'd missed for a long time. A gift of a well-earned, just, separation. I was also aware that throughout all my struggles, my feelings at various times to the contrary, I had never been truly alone. Always with me was the inner twin: my true nature, my true self. It is timeless, free, compassionate and in love with whatever is natural to me. This was the self that came in dreams, to be pursued in the essays I was writing at that time. And as always the sight of trees, the scent of the ocean, the feel of the wind and the warmth of the sun were faithful to me. In fact, as my body became less dependable over the three years I was most ill, my spirit became more so; my sense of humor sharpened, and I frequently had dreams, visions and spiritual revelations of extraordinary power. There was developed in me a spontaneous way of knowing that seemed more like remembering than learning. There were things I just suddenly seemed to know, about life, about the world. As if my illness had pushed open an inner door that my usual consciousness was willing to ignore. I found myself in easy contact with the ancestors, a condition I relish, and I seemed to spend long, delightful seasons in a time before this one. I recorded some of these experiences in my book *Living by the Word*, and in the novel I wrote after *The Color Purple*, *The Temple of My Familiar*.

I understand that, oddly, the experience of making a film of my work, as bewildering and strange as any labyrinth, and as unpredictable as any river, was an initiation into the next, more mature, phase of my life. Harsh criticism, especially when it is felt to be unjust, is at first very painful. After that, there is numbness. After that, as Emily Dickinson wrote about grief, "there is the letting go." I discovered that "the letting go" is actually a state that can be survived, lived in, and treasured. I am a different, more flexible and open person now than I was before. Slower. More maternal about the world.

Both more committed and more detached: I recognize solitude as my most necessary private room, yet I now find I am *always* glad, eventually, to welcome guests. I know now that my religion is love and that I practice it by hugging, something I did spontaneously from babyhood. My mother used to tell me, with an incredulous expression, "You would always go to just anybody!" Perhaps I was initiated, via collaboration on the film, into how such trust could feel as an adult. I admit that, as in a fairy tale, when suddenly in the midst of my peaceful life there comes an unexpected knock at the door, I am happy to go off in strange conveyances with odd people I've never met before; this suits the wondrousland quality of life to which I was apparently born attuned.

Certainly much that concerned me before, does not. I lost what attachment I had to the image others might have of me, since I learned decisively that this is an area over which I have little control. I was called "liar" and "whore" and "traitor" for no other reason than that people who have been made to depend on the approval of the powerful grow afraid of criticizing themselves, because the powerful may hear, amplify their distress, and hold them up to censure and ridicule. The powerful can also manipulate people, and pass horrible, repressive laws, based on the negative images that are permitted to proliferate. This is the reality. And yet, until we can criticize ourselves, and feel safe doing so, there is no hope of molding better values in our children, or of increasing the respect we feel for ourselves. I am not interested in being a role model, or in fulfilling the expectations of others. I know I am of most use to others and to myself by being this unique self: Nature, I have noticed, is not particularly devoted to copies, and human beings needn't be either.

During my time on the labyrinthine river of high-risk collaborative creativity, private illness and public praise and censure, everything I understood as a child was reinforced. The world *is* magical; there *are* good people in it. *Inherent in life is fun.* What I may never know is why my initiation involved tick bites and illness and Steven Spielberg. Nor do I need to know. To me the world seems filled with an endless stream of miracles and wonders; some feel better than others, but I am amazed by them all.

At the heart of the most mysterious labyrinth lives the greatest mystery. Because I followed love and joyous curiosity through the twists and turns of the labyrinth, because I managed not to be turned back, or battered too disastrously by the boulders rising up in the river, I did find all the women in *The Color Purple*, who together are the sacred feminine that, because of the accessibility of film, can be beamed across a world desperate for its return. They also suggest infinite possibilities for women, and for myself. Womanist women. I also found Quincy and Steven, two green and supple men; also much longed for by the world. But even more calming to my heart, I found again the old imperfect sinner and pagan I love so much, my grandfather. Surely doing his part, after a sorely misguided youth spent in dissipation, confusion, and cruelty, to represent, as a grandfather, an old man, the sacred masculine. It broke my heart that so few people were able to really see him, in the much maligned character of Mister. But *irregardless*, as he used to say (meaning, *in spite of everything*: an "incorrect" word I carry with me everywhere; it is on my license plate), there he sat at the end of the day, the end of the film, the end of the journey, in the small wooden chair he sat in for so long it began to look like him. Waiting. For me to finish taking him completely apart, for me to share his failings with all the world, for me to understand him as well as a granddaughter can. For me to know that my love and appreciation of his life is even more sturdy than my grief. Waiting for me to bring him back home, back inside my heart, secure, in myself. Unlike Danny Glover, who played Mister in the movie, my grandfather was small, and, as an old man, decidedly impish. I always understood there were layers and layers of him: to think of him reduced to one layer, and that of brutality, was a torture I survived only because I knew he would understand it was my intention to render him whole. I felt no condemnation from his spirit.

I especially have wanted to publish the script I wrote for the film. I read in magazines after the film opened that I started a script but couldn't finish it. This would have been, it was said, like "giving birth to the same baby." I started a script, under conditions of debilitating illness, single motherhood, betrayal and nearly unbearable grief, and I completed it to my own satisfaction. It was however not the script that Steven loved. It was quieter than the one by Menno Meyjes, which was filmed, and which I was happy to find I liked a lot. There was not so much music in mine. It was clear the women loved each other. It was clear that Shug is, like me, bisexual. That Celie is lesbian. Do I regret my version of my book was not filmed? I have accepted that it wasn't. But to balance this experience, I have felt a need to share what I did attempt.

What I discovered in any event was interesting. An old idea: you really cannot step into the same river twice. Each time it is different, and so are you. Though it hurt to see in Spielberg's film that Celie ceases to be a writer, which she is to her very soul, when I had sat down to re-create her, it bored me to make her a writer, and so I too thought of something else. When people criticized the movie for not being more true to the book, I understood how difficult it is for a creative person to stick to one way of doing things. Though why Harpo keeps falling through the roof, among other odd inventions; why it rains inside the juke joint, I will never understand. Perhaps Harpo is Steven, falling down the stairs of his life at the time, breaking his bones against his parrot's cage, needing to rattle his own. Or maybe Steven assumed Harpo was named with Harpo Marx in mind. He wasn't.

When I read my script, I see that in some ways it is also different from the book. What I have kept, which the film avoided entirely, is Shug's completely unapologetic self-acceptance as outlaw, renegade, rebel, and pagan; her zest in loving both women and men, younger and older. When Shug says in the book *The Color Purple* "I believe God is everything that is, ever was, or ever will be," she is saying what I too believe; she is also quoting Isis, the ancient African goddess, a precursor of the Virgin Mary, mother of Christ, although I did not know this at the time. I have also kept Celie's grasp of the concept that what is holy is the whole thing, not something above it or beyond it, not something separate from herself; as well as her complete bafflement that there could be anything wrong with loving another woman. Especially a woman so loving, brave, and sweet-smelling as Shug. And that the earth itself produces all the wonders, along with the sorrows, anyone could want. I have kept Albert's awakening to the fact that *it is attention to the details of tenderness* that supports and encourages life, which he learns under the guidance of a child.

After nearly three years of feeling almost dead, I decided I would live as if I were really alive. I heaved myself onto yet another plane and went to Custer, South Dakota, where Dennis Banks, a Native American I believed in, was on trial for defending himself and other Indians against the F.B.I., the contemporary cavalry of the Federal Government. I was still so weak that I spent most of the time outside the courthouse lying on the ground. Only dogs and children approached me, and the drumming of nearby Buddhist nuns and monks kept my pulse going. But it was that journey that marked the clear beginning of my return to health. My decision to continue to live as myself, regardless of how tedious it might be to get around. Later on, I would read that what I had done was exactly what a person with Lyme disease should do: something that seems impossible. Apparently such behavior is a kick to the immune system. I would one day run into Dennis Banks again, as we delivered medicines to the children of Cuba, and I would tell him what he, a bound prisoner in South Dakota, had done for me; he would tell me that the copy of *The Color Purple* I managed to slip him during the trial was the only reading matter he had, and that in prison, that same copy passed from hand to hand among the prisoners until it fell apart. Knowing I must have been stung by the harsh criticism of the character Mister, Dennis said: "There's a little bit of Mister in all of us." We rejoiced to find ourselves connecting on hard and often amazing paths through life, held each other, banged on the ceremonial drum he always carries and prays with, and thanked the Universe we had survived.

If one factors in the time difference between Georgia and Cali-

fornia, my mother died on my father's birthday. That is, in any
event, when she died for me. Knowing how deeply she loved him
and that he loved her as much, for all their struggles and failings,
made me feel this was a special message to me about loving and
healing, about remembering and honoring the love. When I think
of my parents—my father died in 1973—both of them are green.
Both rooted in the earth. Both faithful to their love of Nature, the
beauty of the seasons, the magic of this heaven we are in. My
mother was given a splendid farewell ceremony, to which hundreds
of people came. Generations of children, other than her own, she'd
raised. People of all ages she'd inspired, encouraged, helped. There
was an endless cortege, pickup trucks filled with the flowers she
loved. My daughter and I stood beside her coffin and thanked her
for the blessing her life had been to us. We asked her as well to take
our greetings and our thanks to a long list of other warriors of good
who had preceded her into the spaciousness. Since my mother's
burial, according to my sister who visits her grave regularly, the entire cemetery has been carpeted, in each season, with flowers. I am
not surprised.

My former partner is someone who has for many years counseled
other men and boys about the physical and emotional violence
they inflict on women and children, and on other boys and men,
and about how this behavior destroys everything: families, communities, relationships and themselves. We have known each other
all our adult lives, since I was a student at Spelman College, in Atlanta, and he was a student at Morehouse, across the street. We
were lovers for thirteen years and friends for thirty. The dramatic
way that "success" strikes in America is extremely stressful and destructive of certain areas of a relationship. Perhaps, this being so,
there is no way we could have survived as a couple. On the other
hand, I accept that I am of a particular character, prone to distraction and content to think of my body and my sexuality as my own;
my autonomous behavior need not invite betrayal, sabotage or attack. At least we were able, after staying together and steadily
working our way toward the next honest place for us, to separate

with increased humility before the imponderables of coupledom, whatever its status and configuration, and with vastly reduced rancor and pain. We are able still to talk, to joke, to laugh and go on walks together; we are hopeful of honoring both the difficult and the good, and especially that place where they meet.

A few days ago a friend, the director Pratibha Parmar, came to visit me in the country. I have, since the movie *The Color Purple* and the astounding bestsellerdom of the book, moved from my writing shack into a house I had built on a hillside overlooking a valley. This I call my writing temple. The way that I understand my work is that it is a prayer to and about the world. Pratibha and I have made a film together called *Warrior Marks: Female Genital Mutilation and the Sexual Blinding of Women*, about the prevalence of female genital mutilation in many parts of the world, and she came over from London to visit and to apprise me of how well it is doing, though attacks on it have often been as painful and as vicious as those on *The Color Purple*. Indeed, after the showing of our film in London, there were death threats against the courageous African woman, Efua Dorkenoo, who'd helped us make the film, and who directs Forward International, a health organization for African women. Pratibha and I were accused of sensationalizing an issue that doesn't concern us, since neither of us is African, though she was, in fact, born in Africa. I would have been born there, given a choice; but alas, my African ancestors were sold into slavery in the West. I was accused of attempting to restore my place in a surely mythical "limelight," as a writer whose "star" has begun to fade. It was also suggested that the eye I turned on the suffering of my African sisters—not a blind one, fortunately—was marred by its "colonial gaze." The attitude of our accusers was only too familiar. I thought of how, when *The Color Purple* was published, and later filmed, it was a rare critic who showed any compassion for, or even noted, the suffering of the women and children explored in the book, while I was called a liar for showing that black men sometimes perpetuate domestic violence. It is harder, in a way, to know that my image, and attacks upon it, have been used to distract attention from a practice in Africa, and other parts of the world, that endangers the health of literally millions of people every day.

Pratibha brought friends with her whom I found I was unable to see. I tried to explain to her why this was so. Why I could relate at the moment to only one other person, her. At first I thought it was the grief I was feeling about the O.J. Simpson case, which was all over the news. This hit me harder than almost anything in months. I was in mourning for his former wife, Nicole Brown Simpson, her friend, Ronald Goldman, also murdered, and for the Simpson children, by both first and second wives. For O.J., whether guilty or innocent. It hurt that he was a batterer of women; that his opinion of women is, if police records, eyewitnesses and a recorded tape of him breaking in his former wife's door are accurate, so backward, so low.

It was heartrending to see that when every policeman in L.A. was after him, he went searching for his mother. She raised him all alone, apparently because his own father had also been violent. As a mother, I understood why her response to the nightmare of his life was to have a heart attack. My own heart felt as if a giant boulder were sitting on it. That a man so very graceful and beautiful could be so ugly and so wrong, if only in his language about women, his brutality and need to control, caused all the women I talked to about it to suffer. It is a tragedy, whether he murdered a woman or not. Men too have been affected deeply, their present sadness equal to their former pride. It was painful to realize that many men rarely consider reading what women write, or bother to listen to what women are saying about how we feel. How we perceive life. How we think things should be. That they cannot honor our struggles or our pain. That they see our stories as meaningless to them, or assume they are absent from them, or distorted. Or think they must own or control our expressions. And us.

There is also the case of Taslima Nasrin, a Bangladeshi feminist writer whom I have been reading about. She has been sentenced to death by Muslim fundamentalists because she has said the Islamic laws that oppress women should be revised. They are unjust laws that hurt the entire people, and she is right. Still, there is a price on her head. If she is captured, she may be hanged or stoned to death for blasphemy. Societies all over the world fear woman's critique, a critique now crucial to the survival of the planet; the methods used to silence us, whether verbal or physical, are as crude today as they were during the Renaissance, a time, ironically, when men boasted of being enlightened and women were still being burned as witches all over Europe. Truly all the ages of the world exist simultaneously, and all the postmodern thought in the West could not save Taslima Nasrin from destruction, until she was spirited out of her country. She is a prophet, a teacher her country needs; its citizens alone can fight for and truly save her, because they are one. And because they are the reason she risks her life to write.

But as I was relating these two things to Pratibha, I realized there was something else. That I was in fact letting go of something, perhaps of many things, that I no longer needed; that I was in the throes of change. I'm growing a new skin, I suddenly said to her. She immediately understood. But then later, when she asked about my work, I talked about this book: about how I felt publishing it would release me into another cycle, freeing me to swim in other rivers; and about my resistance to "looking back" long enough to finish it. She said: "But obviously it is part of the old skin."

So it is.

Working with Pratibha, working with women, loving and being partners with women, but also recognizing, loving and honoring men who can "see" and affirm women, men who can write true songs about women and attempt to make true movies, is much of the new skin. As is returning to my rightful and accustomed relationship to Nature. The morning after Pratibha left, I took out my computer and thought of what I would say to you, the reader, from whom I've felt so much support in the past—and surprisingly little distance. Having a film made of one's book is an agonizingly complex gamble, with hundreds of people having something to say. Though *The Color Purple* is not what many wished, it is more than many hoped, or had seen on a movie screen before. It still moves me after all these years, as I relive the feeling of love that was palpable daily on the set. This does not, however, prevent me from cringing at the same spots in the film that originally seemed bizarre to me. (The bluntness of Celie's erroneous statement that she has been raped and impregnated by her "daddy" in the opening scenes of the film was a horrible shock to me, destroying as it does the mystery of what has really occurred, and effectively obscuring the fact that her biological father was forcefully heroic. It was also disturbing to see Shug pretend not to know why Celie can't "speak up" after Shug leaves her alone with Mister to go back on the road.) Some things are simply absurd. (For instance, the scene in which Mister doesn't know where the butter is kept or how a fire is started.) I still regret that Mister was not as "forgiven" by Steven as he was by me, and that Shug and Celie don't have the erotic, sensuous relationship they deserve. I always wonder if viewers (or readers, for that matter) ever realize that Sofia is named after the goddess of wisdom: for it *is* wise, however painful, to stand up for one's self, to have one's laughter and one's say, no matter how long one's tongue has been tied. I wonder if viewers realize that Olivia is named not after Oliver Twist (as implied in the film) but from a line in Virginia Woolf, "Chloe liked Olivia," which appears in *A Room of One's Own*, a book that made me happy to be a writer, and bolstered and brightened my consciousness about the role other women, often silenced or even long dead, can have in changing the world.

I have been glad to see how the issues of incest and domestic violence were opened up by the book, and more widely by the film. In letters and on visits women and men all over the world have expressed to me the power and transformation they've received from both. It felt clear to me however, as I watched O.J. being pursued by the police across L.A., that this was transformation and power he'd missed. Which depressed me, as a writer trying to communicate for so many years: violence to others is soul abuse; when you hurt others you hurt yourself. The most gorgeous man in the world who deliberately causes the suffering of anyone, but especially of a

woman or a child, becomes hideous. You cannot be beautiful
breaking down a frightened creature's door. I have always considered men of color brave and daring beyond compare; it is from
them I have learned much of what I know of gracefulness, of how
to love and how to fight. My grief has been seeing and experienc-
ing in them, as I have seen and experienced in other men, that
which destroys beauty in anyone: oppression of those over whom
one has power.

On the level where I most like to live, the level of contempla-
tion, I realize that during these ten years I have been involved in a
series of spiritual tests: a test of my love of and loyalty to my
mother, as I witnessed her decline over so many soul-whipped
years, and worried constantly about my ability to protect her and
provide for her needs, even as I felt myself to be in mortal danger.
A test of my loyalty to myself, in my relationship with a partner, as
I wrestled my way to the limits of my capacity for understanding,
forgiveness and acceptance. A test of my belief in the creative integrity of others, during my involvement with the collective creating our film. A test of my faith in Nature and my love of the earth,
which was, I now understand, what my illness was about.

Just as Muslims, Jews and Christians have crises of faith, when
their God seems to have hurt them or abandoned them or never
seems to be near, Pagans (people whose primary spiritual relationship is with Nature and the earth; people who have traditionally
been oppressed or destroyed by patriarchal religions) have crises,
too. This became obvious to me only this summer, when, after an
absence of many years, I began seriously to garden again. Kneeling
on the earth as I planted each small seed or set out each tiny plant,
I was shocked to realize how many years had passed since I had
done this. "This" being the prayer involved in planting that, I am
convinced, was one of the first acts of supplication, of worship, in
the world. When I asked myself why this absence from "service,"
from worship, the answer was: fear. Fear of tick bite, fear of disease,
fear of debilitation. Fear. The benign Goddess/God I had assumed
the earth to be had turned on me. My faith was battered by that be-

trayal. And yet, as with a lover, what can one really absolutely trust? Only that she or he will be themselves. And that, I see, is how I must love the earth and Nature and the Universe, my own Trinity. Trusting only that it will be however it is, and accepting that some parts of it may hurt. And so, with socks pulled high and sleeves pulled low to protect myself from tick bite and disease, I am back into the relationship with Nature that sustains my happiness and my faith. Back as well into sharing my work collectively with others. Open once again to love, intimacy and trust.

My daughter counseled me to make this book very small and to publish it very quietly. This seemed sound advice, but it isn't possible. The book is larger than I thought it would be because it has many parts that, together, create the necessary whole. I have included my script of *The Color Purple*, alternatively titled *Watch for Me in the Sunset*, as well as my synopsis for the film and all my notes, including notes for recordings of the film's musical score. Because I realize much of the excitement of the experience felt like something removed from me, I have included my favorite essays and interviews by other people, whose work gave me a second chance to experience what I partly missed. I've also included portions of my journals from the period, entries especially concerning my dreams, all of them vivid, most of them filled with anxiety about being robbed of something essential to my female spirit. Literally the spirit shaped by one's menstrual cycle, one's connection to the moon.

While criticism of the film still raged, I thought of publishing a book called *The Other Half of the Gift* (which is one way I thought of Steven's film, the book being the first half), a collection of other people's responses to the movie and the book. Letters, quite wonderful ones, came in from everywhere, and I asked permission of numerous of their writers to include them in a book. A few of those letters appear. There is also a letter to Quincy Jones; a letter I wrote to Danny Glover, who played Mister in the film; a letter to the critic Barbara Christian, who said she hated the film the first time we talked about it; and a letter to my daughter, Rebecca, who found my absences and scanty mothering during the writing of the script especially hard to bear. (She was not told of my illness; I didn't wish to frighten her. As a single mother, even before becoming sick, I worried that I could not offer the secure home life she had been used to while we lived with her father. There was also the problem of not knowing quite *what* to say. That I had become physically debilitated was obvious.) I include also some of the objections to and criticisms of the film, in the belief that we also learn from the misperceptions of others. Some of the more libelous charges and critiques I have omitted on purpose, just as I dropped them from consciousness when they occurred, in order to keep going. The silence of some of my family, friends and colleagues, and even of my partner, as I was being attacked was particularly trying: it has been helpful to see, over the past few years, that many of them have begun, out of their own experience, to speak out against violence and woman hating; to say aloud that it is not too much to ask that our homes, streets and communities be safe for women, children and men. And that love is not controlling but setting free.

When *The Color Purple* was published, the level of violence many people are living with today would have been unthinkable. Young black men, beautiful warriors without a cause and frequently without fathers, are killing themselves, each other, and our communities in a frenzy of despair. Who would have dreamed just ten years ago that black grandmothers would be sleeping in their bathtubs at night in an attempt to escape the bullets of armed male children on their streets? It is hard not to wonder what would have been the effect if young black men had been encouraged by other, older black men to listen to what black women writers, black women and girls, have been saying, and to understand it is not black men we want out of our lives, but violence.

We dare not lie to our children about what they are seeing with their own eyes. Understanding with their own minds. Feeling with their own hearts. They may love us still, if we do lie, but their trust will be destroyed. As for respect? Even Rosa Parks, the "mother" of the black freedom movement, has been assaulted in her home.

As people of color and as women, as non-establishment or politically disempowered people, we face an increasing challenge simply to stay alive on the planet. To be healthy, hopeful and committed to the future. Perhaps to our surprise, this condition now seems to be that of the entire world, though some may be in a position to buff their diamonds as they race their Jaguars over the cliff. Hatred of women and of women's autonomy is the most intimate of the psychic diseases that brings us down. As with Lyme disease, it can be years before we even recognize we are infected. More years pass before treatment is sought. Sometimes there doesn't even seem to be a name for the way one feels. All the while there is weakness, bitterness and pain. Violence, in word or deed, is often the only language familiar enough to express our confusion. To those who wish to shed a bit of this particular old skin of suffering, to swim more freely in the ever-changing, ever-multiplying rivers of life, I dedicate this book.

It is also dedicated with love and thanks to, in the order of their appearance in my life: Peter Guber, Quincy Jones, Steven Spielberg, Whoopi Goldberg, Kathleen Kennedy, Lucy Fisher, Allen Daviau, Danny Glover, Margaret Avery, Oprah Winfrey, Akosua Busia, Willard Pugh, John Patton, Desreta Jackson, Leonard Jackson, Adolph Caesar, Larry Fishburne, Rae Dawn Chong, Tata Vega, Lionel Richie, Rod Temperton, Kokayi Ampah, Ruben Cannon, Aggie Rodgers, Michael Riva and Menno Meyjes. And to my daughter, Rebecca Leventhal Walker, and everyone else who worked on The Color Purple with such faith and love and passionate intent; and with a special embrace for my sister, Belvie Rooks, on whom I leaned throughout the period of my illness. And to my former partner and present friend, Robert Allen, with whom I was often very happy.

I also send the spirit of this book to the spirits of my father, Willie Lee Walker, who loved a good story, and to my grandfather, Henry Clay Walker, a man who charmed, even mesmerized, me when I was a child. Though a sometime "drunkard" to the adults who knew him, to me he was intriguingly silent and mysterious, a man with a past. Out of his silence I have created fictional worlds.

Perhaps, as an adult, I was destined to fall in love with an alcoholic, a person who, in accordance with aboriginal wisdom, at least perceives there is another reality, but out of ignorance chooses a self-destructive means of accessing it. I send the book's spirit out to my mother, Minnie Tallulah Grant Walker, a woman from whom I still learn, in death as in life, a woman who loved movies and deserved to see some true part of her vibrant life on the silver screen. I also dedicate this book to my brothers Bobby and Bill, who never fail to meet the challenge of being on my side. And to my nephews Billy and Gregg, strong and tender black men.

BEING

THE

RIVER

Journal Entry
March 15, 1984

This is my third week in the country writing the screenplay. The first week went remarkably well. And the second. But now I feel stuck. I've been lying in bed reading and feeling less energetic than usual. Probably because of the sweet cookies and custard I had last night and yesterday.

George Gowan (a distant neighbor) just brought a nice half cord of dry wood and the fire I made is sputtering happily. It has been raining, but perhaps now it will clear? I'm stuck in the screenplay. But at least I've brought it to the place where Celie and Shug leave home. Now I must show Celie and Shug in Memphis and then the death of Celie's stepfather, then Shug's infatuation with the 19 year old, and Celie's return home and her and Albert's friendship, and then Shug's return and Nettie's—and it seems hard to do in 50 pages. But thank the Universe I have two and a half months to do a draft.

Meanwhile, Whoopi Goldberg is auditioning for the role of Celie and I go to L.A. to see her on Friday. One of Robert's friends, Joe B., was raving about her and suggested we catch her show at the Valencia Rose. I liked her right away. I like people who refuse to be victims and delight in showing everybody else how this is done. She was wonderful, dreadlocking, with an irrepressible, sly gleam in her eye. She makes it really clear there's no use actually trying to fit into this madness.

Journal Entries
March/April 1984, a "strong" period
The evening with Whoopi went extremely well. Quincy sent a jet for us and Steven's building (Amblin) is beautiful. Very Southwestern and Native American: real Navajo blankets and pottery. I'd been so worried it would all be plastic. Whoopi was terrific, and I've been typing the screenplay. Trying to get my taxes completed, the land (Wild Trees) in the country nailed down, and my garden started. I love that there will be lots of space to do all kinds of outdoor things and no one will see me! This is the way it often was when I was a child. I remember a garden I started out of sight of the house, down the hill. I tried to grow beans and corn in sand. Everything came up, but soon died. But at Wild Trees I just bought huge mounds of composted manure. And I feel so good having it. I've been double-digging a nice long bed for carrots and lettuce. Yum. And I'll plant mustard and turnip greens, and tomatoes and perhaps some kind of beans. Okra would be nice. Onions. Peppers. And I'm continuing to plant trees. Very slow on this. Waiting for the Harkleroads (neighbors from whom I bought land) to leave before I plant poplars in front of their house.

Susan sent hollyhocks which I'll plant this week.

• • •

Mike Reeves, who is to do the work on Wild Trees (carpentry, hauling, etc.), brought two beautiful willow chairs that he made. I bought them and now look at the view through their backs. I've just typed out 65 pages of the screenplay and feel better than I have in two weeks. I had worried that it was lagging—as I went off to Burbank, saw friends and movies and bought land and hired carpenters, etc. But I still have over a month and a half before it will be time to turn it in. And I feel good about this half. (Now to worry about the second half!) We've reached the point of Celie leaving home. And perhaps the second half should open with her busy and happy in her Memphis life with Shug.

It is a blustery, partly sunny day in the country. It rained all night, which should be good for the trees. I've still got a dozen trees and shrubs to plant. But I spent four hours weeding the garden yesterday; after feeling depressed and as if I had no support. But really, I have the support of the Universe. And if I meditated more I would feel less alone.

THE COLOR PURPLE
A Synopsis for Film

The story really begins circa 1903 with the lynching—by envious whites—of
Celie's father, a striving and beginning to be prosperous entrepreneur/farmer in
a small Southern town.* Celie's mother becomes mentally unstable but is wooed
by and marries a man more interested in her trim Victorian house, fields and
property than he is in her or her two daughters, Celie and Nettie. When Celie is
14 this stepfather, whom she believes (because nobody talks about the lynched)
is her father, begins to rape her, causing the birth of two children whom he gives
away to an old friend who has become a missionary. Celie's mother dies angry at
Celie and, because she's been warned by her stepfather not to tell anyone (but
God) who fathered her children, she dutifully writes letters to God.

Later, when her younger sister, Nettie, runs away from home, she comes to
the house Celie shares with Mr. ———, a mean-spirited, often brutal man
who, having been denied Nettie by her stepfather, married Celie so that she
would look after his children: his first wife, Annie Julia, having been murdered
by her lover. Because Nettie spurns his attentions he turns her out of his house
and Celie sends her to the same missionaries (Corrine and Samuel) who have
unwittingly adopted her children, Olivia and Adam. With them Nettie goes as
a junior missionary to Africa, where she remains, writing letters to but never
hearing from Celie for thirty years.

Beaten down for many years by her life of drudgery and abuse with Mr. ———
and his obnoxious offspring, Celie's spirit begins to rally when Shug Avery, a
blues singer and old lover of Mr. ———'s, is brought home by him, ill, for Celie
to nurse. Celie and Shug fall in love, and Celie leaves Mr. ——— to accompany
Shug to Memphis, where Shug makes a grand living singing (earlier she made her
living as a domestic) and where Celie begins a happy and independent life designing and sewing pants.

The last straw in Celie's life with Mr. ——— was the knowledge, provided
by Shug, that Mr. ——— had hidden all the letters Nettie had written her over
the years. In these letters, which she finally receives, Nettie's parallel life unfolds: She and Celie's children and Samuel and Corrine live among the Olinka
in a small village of thatched huts (some round, some square) in West Africa.
They all teach and nurse and Samuel preaches as well. Corrine gradually recog-
nizes the strong resemblance between her adopted children and Nettie and
(with help from a tropical fever) agonizes herself to death. After her death,
Samuel and Nettie marry. During this personal drama, the Olinka's village is
destroyed by an English rubber company, and the Olinka are forced onto an

*See *The Autobiography of Ida B. Wells*, 1970, edited by Alfreda M. Duster. Wells exposed
and documented the hundreds of lynchings, like that of Celie's father, that occurred in
the South from before the turn of the century through the 1920s.

arid reservation. Adam marries Tashi, an Olinka woman, and with her, the Americans return home.

Meanwhile, Shug has left Celie to have a fling with a cute boy of 19 who plays blues flute. They travel to the Southwest to meet Shug's grown children, one of whom teaches on an Indian reservation that is a mirror image of the one the Olinka now occupy in Africa. Celie, whose stepfather has died and left her real father's property to her, including a large beautiful house, forgives and becomes friends, for the first time, with Mr. ———, who has changed considerably and whom she now calls Albert. Though missing Shug, she is content with her friendships, her designing and her sewing. Naturally, at this point, Shug comes back.

With Shug and Albert by her side, Celie needs only one thing to make her life complete. Her sister, Nettie. One day, as they are all sitting companionably on the front porch, Nettie, Adam, Olivia, Samuel and Tashi arrive (after Celie has received a telegram saying their ship was sunk by German mines off Gibraltar).

About the Characters

CELIE

In rural and small town turn-of-the-century culture, through the forties, at least, the voluptuous, the portly, the stout female form was admired. Even a very fat female was admired if she was also good-natured and "light on her feet," i.e., a good dancer. Skinniness, boniness (though not slenderness, which was admired if the body was also curvaceous and perceived as strong), was considered, in a woman, to be almost a deformity.

Being skinny is Celie's major "fault," since when one was a woman and very skinny (with flat breasts), one's form was not considered "womanly." Hence Mr. ———'s frequent criticism of Celie that "You shape(d) funny." Today we would say Celie has a model's figure. Her other "ugliness" consists of a furtive, beaten down manner (she cowers), unkempt hair and poor and slovenly clothing (she has no one to teach her to care for herself and no one to buy her clothes or even to notice she's still wearing her dead mother's clothes, tattering, years after her mother's death). As she begins to create herself through her writing (and without her writing it is clear she would have remained unformed, even to herself) and her love of Shug and Nettie, she begins to take on an outer beauty that approximates her extraordinary loveliness of spirit: and we begin to see that "ugliness"—in Celie's case—was a matter of her physical environment and condition, and a state of mind that matched.

SHUG

Shug Avery is modeled after one of my aunts who worked as a domestic in the North most of her life. I could never believe this because when she came South to visit us—swathed in rhinestones (her diamonds) and furs (hand-me-downs from the woman she worked for)—you couldn't imagine her cleaning her own house, not to mention anybody else's.

She has the requisite "stout" shape to qualify as sexy and "womanly." The exact opposite of Celie's. In addition she knows how to dress (flamboyantly), carry herself (sometimes merely like a queen, sometimes arrogantly but always with self-possession) and she doesn't fumble verbally like Celie. She is a woman in control of her life (after the breakdown Celie pulls her through). She's gorgeous and knows it, with only positive thoughts about her very black skin— since during this period the black- and lighter-skinned black woman had about the same chance with black men. It was the stage shows and early movies produced by whites that began to use "high yellow" women exclusively in their cabaret and stage dance scenes, thereby encouraging the colorist sexism later exhibited by blacks. Shug looks like Pearl Bailey (and my aunt) and acts like one imagines P. Bailey would act in an all-black setting: assertive, funny, irreverent, unself-conscious and relaxed.

ALBERT

Albert is a small (physically and mentally), bitter, weak man at first. A man whose father has made the most important decisions of his life for him. Though married twice, with at least one longtime lover and two "sets" of children, he knows almost nothing about children or women. He's never really looked at either. He's the kind of person who really thinks women are a separate species whose feelings are as negligible as those of animals. What saves him from total failure as a human being is his irrational but sincere love of Shug Avery. It is because he loves Shug and *she* loves Celie that he can begin to *see* other women and to find something in them to appreciate. He is still following someone else's lead rather than his own, but unlike his father's blind alley of misogynism, Shug and Celie lead him to the source of love itself, i.e., wonder over the universe, existence itself.

The man who comes to treasure the fragility and beauty of seashells without having ever seen the sea is very different from the man who raped his child bride even though her head was bandaged.

SQUEAK/MARY AGNES

The most significant thing externally about Mary Agnes at first is her color. She is white-looking (like the early singer/actress Fredi Washington, for example), with gray or green eyes and light hair. She represents many light-skinned black women who found themselves pursued by black men and white men because of their color and because, as "mulattos," they were stereotyped in books and the media as wanton and easy (to the white man) and "desirable because nearly white" (i.e. closer to white standards of beauty) to the black. Many white-looking black women were lost to themselves because they were stereotyped by both societies. Squeak finds herself through her struggle with Harpo and Sofia and their children—and most of all, through singing, without which she would have gone under. The fact that she has a squeaky voice but sings anyway emphasizes black people's traditional view of singing: it need not be "pretty," but it must be sincere.

This sincerity comes out of the life lived and the struggle endured. Period.

HARPO

Harpo, like his father before him, and largely *because* of his father, thinks of women as a subservient race. Yet it is precisely Sofia's non-subservient nature that he fell for. He is a very slender young man when they marry, but by the story's end is quite portly. Since his father remains small and slender, Harpo, because of his size, begins to look like the father and his father like the son. And this mirrors their inner development; for Harpo matures and begins to become a real human being before his father does.

NETTIE

Nettie is neither skinny nor stout, but medium in size. She is brown, not black (Corrine is several shades lighter, as befits her bourgeois Atlanta status), and she wears her hair unstraightened in a neat Victorian upsweep, parted in the middle, at times, and twisted up at the back. She wears long, plain skirts and white blouses with bow ties. (Old photos of Spelman College missionaries may be viewed for this.) Lace-up shoes and short jacket. Hers is a plain, straight beauty that is due, partly, to her kindness. Unlike Celie (finally) and Shug, it would be hard to imagine Nettie angry, making her anger at Albert's assault all the more powerful. She is not by nature prim and proper; this is simply the way she has experienced life. Her true personality begins to develop (the sexual aspects) when she holds Samuel in her arms and "concern and passion runs away with them."

SAMUEL

Samuel is a large, black, kind and gentle man whose priestly look belies the ease with which he gets on with women. (This is his real look, contrasted with how he first appears to Celie, as frightening.) He is a "touching" person and a natural comforter. With Samuel women feel no need to appear other than themselves because they sense he is at least capable of loving them as they are. (Is Nettie plump and gray? Wonderful!) Though Nettie claims she never thought of him "as a man" before he cried in her arms, he is the kind of man women have fantasies about (erotic rather than pornographic) because the woman he is with generally seems so contented. He is a vulnerable man, capable of tears, of being wrong, of admitting failure. In this he is a success as a human being, as well as a success with women who desire a man who is human like themselves. Ironically, it is his trustworthiness that makes his wife so devastated by the thought that he (maybe) has actually deceived her.

SOFIA

Sofia is a "bright-skin," stout, spunky woman with "big legs" and plenty of hair, perhaps *the* ideal of early-twentieth-century country beauty. ("Bright skin" is brownish yellow and *alive*.) One of the first womanists. She can work and fight her own battles, enjoys men, the company of other women, sex, her children and her home. The sort of strong, hardworking woman who, once out of her overalls and into her lipstick and dress, makes a man blink not once but many times. Women also like her for her directness, humor, generosity and loyalty.

Notes for Quincy Jones

ABOUT THE MUSIC

If the movie starts (as it might) during Celie's happy baby life, before her father's death, the late 1890s–1900s, the music would be ragtime. Perhaps just a tinkle, to let us know there *was* something upbeat, before the fall. Almost anything by Scott Joplin.

For the rest, the songs made from the book and Celie's life (which would, as we said over lunch, illustrate how blues are made: "Celie *is* the blues," as you said), and then the traditional jook* women's blues (down at Harpo's, etc.) by the women on *Mean Mothers*** and Bessie Smith. Some of the early songs (in the film) could be typical "female as victim" songs, but they must develop into songs of self-possession and independence. The kind of songs Mde. C. J. Walker hummed to *herself*. And Shug Avery began to sing after her illness, when she gave up the idea of men as the center of her universe in favor of herself.

It is important to me that the suppressed independent women's music—music as sassy and free and devilish as the jazz the male musicians accompanying them played—be reintroduced to the world. We need it.

It might look like this (and my history is plastic):

1897–1903   Fading ragtime

1903–1914   Celie's period of silence (some church music)

1914–1925   Songs from *The Color Purple* (a great idea!)

1925–1940   Popular songs of the period from Bessie and *Mean Mothers*. Including for the Harlem section (1920s) whoever would have been playing: Duke Ellington, maybe. Just a riff, for sophistication, and church music. In the Africa section, traditional West African women's music. *Not* drums.

Two of my favorites from *Mean Mothers* are "There Ain't Much Good in the Best of Men Nowdays" (we'd bring down the house) and "Keep Your Nose Out of Mama's Business." The first is a Shug song; the second, a liberated Squeak/Mary Agnes song.

There's a wonderful song I'll find, about how you treat a no-good man:

> *You make him*
> *Stay at home*
> *Wash and iron*

*Jook, an African word meaning "place of sin," i.e., fun and good times, eventually became "juke" in America, with the introduction of the jukebox. Both words are used in this book.
**Mean Mothers, a collection of Black women's jazz, edited and compiled by Rosetta Reitz.

> Let the neighbors think
> He's lost his mind

In Bessie's mouth iron and mind rhyme.

IN AFRICA

Some of the most important scenes in "West Africa" are the ones about the building of the road, the starting of the rubber plantation and the destruction of the Olinka village. This happens, not just in Africa (where it has gone on for centuries), but in many places of the world: in all those countries where United Fruit, Firestone Rubber and Hershey's Chocolate need (and take) land for their plantations. Indigenous people's traditional housing in Central America, Africa and the U.S. is destroyed and replaced by the most rudimentary hovels, as the people gradually become mere workers on land now owned by people who live elsewhere. The article (below) on South Africa illustrates this. The "housing units" (really toilets) are forced on the people with an attitude that even this is more than they deserve. "Erasing a 'Black Spot'" could have come straight out of *The Color Purple*.

SOUTH AFRICA
ERASING A "BLACK SPOT"

By their homes the people of Magopa wept, and then they prayed. They had pleaded with the South African government. It turned them down. They had consulted lawyers. They had appealed to the Supreme Court. But after an all-night vigil in the village square last week, 2,000 members of the Bakwena tribe, captives of the South African government's apartheid laws, began to dismantle their modest homes and load their meager belongings onto trucks for the 80-mile journey to a "homeland" few had ever seen.

Magopa was no land of milk and honey. Its houses were built of stone or mud bricks. A few trees and scrubby brush dotted the desiccated countryside. But it was the only home the 300 families here have ever known. The Bakwena have owned the land since South Africa gained independence from Britain. For more than 70 years they maintained a remarkably self-sufficient community, building two schools and four churches, drilling wells for irrigation—all without help from the South African government. In the end, Pretoria identified Magopa as a "black spot" in an all-white area. The government bulldozed the village churches and schools, giving the Bakwena seven days to pull out. Bishop Desmond Tutu, general secretary of the South African Council of Churches, called the forced removal "as evil and immoral as Nazism."

Bantustans: The South African government has already "resettled" more than 3.5 million black South Africans—more than 10 percent of the population. Another 2 million people are scheduled for similar treatment. The aim is to group the country's 21 million blacks in 10 "homelands," or Bantustans, taking up only 13 percent of South Africa's land, leaving the remaining 87 percent of the land for 4.5 million whites.

Pretoria has an abundance of legal pretexts for carrying out its policies. Besides the Group Areas Act, which codifies the inequitable distribution of land, there are the various pass laws, which require blacks who do not live in their "homelands" to carry identity (pass) books at all times. The laws also prohibit blacks from dwelling in white areas except to work. According to the Surplus Peoples Project (SPP), a three-year survey of more than 1,600 households involving more than 10,000 people in 19 different areas, blacks who do relocate often face desperate conditions.

Onverwacht, located in the Orange Free State, is South Africa's largest relocation area. Built in 1979 on barren land near the Lesotho border, it is a sprawling slum, housing at least 60,000 people. New arrivals were allocated 98- by 49-foot plots, each consisting of a patch of bare ground with a prefabricated toilet whose number—painted on the door—became the new address. The newcomers were provided with tents and told to build their own shacks. Some sites were flooded; others had large boulders, and the tents—too small and offering little protection against the bitter cold—were a fire hazard. Inadequate sanitation led to an outbreak of typhoid in early 1980 (denied by officials in Pretoria). But burial facilities in Onverwacht appear to be excellent. By July 1980 the cemetery had 525 graves—269 of them for children.

"Resettlement projects must be considered an effort to improve the general standard of life," said Pieter Koornhof, the government minister in charge of the program. But the effects were anything but positive. Wives and children were stranded in relocation areas while husbands sneaked back to seek illegal work in the cities; children died of cold and disease; families were torn by separation and divorce.

Saul Mkhize, 48, was the elected leader of a black spot in the Transvaal. He led a campaign by the 5,000 residents to resist relocation, saying in a letter to Prime Minister Pieter Botha, "We do not wish to be rebellious in any way, but only to live our lives out in our own environment." Two days after writing the letter, Saul Mkhize was killed by police who tried to stop a local meeting. A constable has been charged with the murder. One woman in the SPP study was sent with her family to the Kammaskraal areas in "independent" Ciskei in the winter of 1980. In August her husband died; in December her youngest son died, and in July 1981 her only daughter died. "Nothing grows in this land," she said. "Everything dies. Flowers, animals, people."

Exodus: Worried by the international outcry, Pretoria dispatched Deputy Foreign Minister Louis Nel to talk with the Bakwena and present the government's case. Nel argued that a majority of the tribe supported the move and had already gone to Pachsdraal. He pointed to the new clinic at Pachsdraal, saying that Magopa had none. "Not one person has been forcibly removed," he said. A faction of the Bakwena has been in Pachsdraal since June. Still others chose to go to Bethanie 50 miles farther east. But the people who stayed back in Magopa claim that they are the majority. They charge that the government co-opted those who left, promising them all of the compensation money paid for the tribe's relocation. They say that they do not want to live together with those who betrayed them. "My husband lies buried here," said Elizabeth Kgatitsoe, who owns the local store in Magopa, "and I wish to be buried beside him. If they carry me out, I will walk back." But the forced exodus did benefit at least one man in Magopa. Lieb Niehaus charged the Magopans 300 rand ($250) a truckload to move them to their new "homeland." He is white.

D. D. GUTTENPLAN WITH PETER YOUNGHUSBAND IN CAPE TOWN NEWSWEEK/DECEMBER 12, 1983

AKOSUA BUSIA, GORDON PARKS, OPRAH WINFREY,
ALICE WALKER, QUINCY JONES, ROBERT ALLEN

WATCH FOR ME IN THE SUNSET,*
OR
THE COLOR PURPLE

BASED ON THE NOVEL *The Color Purple*
JUNE 15, 1984

INT. DAY   CELIE'S BED
CELIE
(*A peacefully sleeping form, CELIE, under a colorful, beautifully appliquéd quilt. Close-up on a square that depicts a white, prosperous little house set in a garden of vivid flowers under a happy sun. The year 1907 is embroidered in a corner.*)

EXT. DAY   1914
(*Front yard of same house depicted in quilt square. Except: paint is peeling; porch appears to sag; flowers are straggly and faded; it is drizzling rain. At end of walk stands a horse and buggy and TWO WOMEN about to climb into it. One of the women, CELIE'S MOTHER, is obviously ill. Her face is drawn and her movements slow. THE OTHER WOMAN keeps an arm under her elbow. PA, dressed in high-necked white shirt and vest and round rim hat, pulls CELIE'S MOTHER to him to say goodbye. There is something sexually suggestive in his embrace and she pulls herself out of it wearily. Two small children rush forward and bury their heads in her long skirt and she bends down to hug them. Then, she and 12 year old NETTIE embrace. Then 14 year old CELIE and MOTHER. CELIE watches as her MOTHER is helped into the buggy by THE OTHER WOMAN [midwife cum local doctor] and, holding the two little ones by the hands, watches as the buggy disappears along the path.*)

EXT. DUSK
CELIE
(*We see CELIE'S legs as she carries a three-legged stool along a plank walk that connects the main house to the girls' room. Behind her, at a somewhat more leisurely pace, walks [his legs] PA.*)

INT. NIGHT   GIRLS' ROOM
CELIE
(*Is cutting PA'S hair. We see her legs. Her white stockings. The snip, snip movement of the scissors. Hair falling. See the bottom of PA'S checkered bib. The hat and mirror he holds in his hand. Quiet. As CELIE moves gingerly—we should feel this is her first time doing this—in front of him.*)

---

*Some part of me was afraid that no matter how good his intentions, Steven's version of *The Color Purple* would not deserve the name. And so I created an alternative title for his film.

PA

(We see his hand move slowly up the side of CELIE'S dress. The hand suddenly seizes her at the waist as PA crams CELIE'S body between his legs. PA and CELIE struggle. Objects fly, fall and break, though there is still no sound.)

INT. NIGHT

PA

(Rises off a battered, disoriented CELIE, whose head is jammed between the leg of the bed and the wall. Her lip is bleeding, and she is crying. In her confusion she pulls the checkered bib off PA and covers her face with it.)

PA

(Fastens his pants. Jams on his hat and yanks the cloth from CELIE'S face. Then speaks first words of the film.)

> You betten not never tell nobody but
> God. It'd finish killin' your mammy.

INT.   SEVERAL NIGHTS LATER

CELIE

(A distracted CELIE on her knees beside her bed trying to pray. She turns her face upwards. She puts her hands prayerfully under her chin. She rocks, opens her mouth. Nothing comes. She drops her head to the bed and weeps in frustration. In her right hand she holds the soiled dress she was wearing when raped. She begins slowly ripping it apart.)

EXT. DAY

CELIE

(CELIE, hugely pregnant, unkempt, barefoot, carrying two large pails of water from the backyard pump. Her younger sister, NETTIE, prettier, neatly dressed, coming from school, puts down her books and comes to help her.)

PA

(PA, his back to us, is handing another man a bundle. We recognize him by his hat. When he moves away, we see it is a baby. On the cloth covering baby's head is a beautifully embroidered, brightly colored star.)

INT.   THE KITCHEN

CELIE AND NETTIE

(CELIE is cooking. NETTIE at table studying. Two small children, girl and boy [CELIE and NETTIE'S LITTLE SISTER and LITTLE BROTHER], playing with wooden spools on the kitchen floor. It is clear from this scene that CELIE has taken on the complete mother role.)

INT. AFTERNOON   CELIE'S MOTHER'S BEDROOM
MOTHER
(In bed, a quilting frame designed for the bedridden that stretches across the bed, in front of her. She is busy with her needle on a somber, intricately worked square. Resting her needle, she watches a pregnant CELIE hostilely as she lumbers about the room. Sadness, illness, hatred and betrayal vie for first place on her face. CELIE brings in a tray which she places first on the dresser [which is cluttered with medicine bottles and boxes of all description] while rearranging her mother's pillows and bed coverings, then places on her MOTHER'S lap after removing the quilting frame and helping her sit up straight.)

CELIE
(Looking down at her MOTHER'S face, hoping she will like the meal. Nervous, but waiting patiently for some sign that she has done things right. The food looks especially appetizing and she has even put a flower in a small vase on the tray. Her MOTHER slowly, weakly, removes the flower and lets it drop to the floor. She scorns the food and motions for CELIE to take it away.)

CELIE
(Her eyes, hurt, question why.)

MOTHER
(Long glance down CELIE'S body that says: You know why.)

CELIE
(Takes the tray, replaces the quilting frame, and lumbers out, crushed. In the doorway she meets PA. He is sharply dressed, and checks his reflection not in CELIE'S eyes, which he avoids, but in the looking glass that hangs beside the door. He runs his tongue over his lips, slicks down his mustache, composes his face, takes off his hat, and [with CELIE turning to watch him] enters his wife's room.)

MOTHER/WIFE
(CELIE'S POV)
(Holds up arms to him. As the door closes.)

CELIE
(Drops her head, continues toward kitchen with the tray.)

INT. NIGHT   CELIE'S ROOM
(CELIE is again on her knees beside the bed in an attitude of prayer. But she is not "praying." She is sewing. We see parts of the dress she was wearing when raped now cut into precise shapes. We also see pieces of PA'S checkered bib. We see a heavy black piece of cloth in the shape of PA'S hat. There is a replica of her baby's brightly

embroidered star, and likewise a flower like the one on her mother's tray. As she works, totally absorbed, cutting, placing, contemplating, sewing, we should have the feeling that in putting these poor scraps of her life together CELIE is in fact praying— and telling her story to God.)

EXT. MID-AFTERNOON   CELIE'S MOTHER'S FUNERAL
(At which point we see nearly all the characters in the film.)

> MUSIC:
> Will the circle
> be unbroken
> bye and bye, Lord
> bye bye
>
> There's a better
> home awaiting
> in the sky, Lord
> in the sky.

(An old-fashioned country farm wagon, with the wooden coffin, is going slowly down a narrow dirt road. It has a small homemade wreath of the same flower CELIE put on her MOTHER'S tray. PA, CELIE, NETTIE, LITTLE BROTHER and LIT-TLE SISTER. MISC. MOURNING RELATIVES [i.e., families with children]. Some dressed in black or dark colors, many not. MISTER, HARPO, TWO YOUNGER SISTERS, ONE YOUNGER BROTHER. MISC. OTHER MOURNERS. The appearance is of a slow, almost random trickle down the road from the small, white church, through the door of which now comes a young SQUEAK, HER MOTHER, and SISTERS. Their appearance in this setting would be startling to anyone not used to the white-looking colored people found so often in the South. Unlike everyone else—who is brown or black or yellow or tan— SQUEAK is white, with gray or green eyes. HER MOTHER is a medium brown-skinned woman, and they are holding hands.)

EXT. DAY   GRAVEYARD
                    PREACHER
(Standing over open grave.)
            Ashes to ashes, dust to dust.
(As he sprinkles dirt into grave onto coffin.)

EXT. DAY   GRAVESIDE
*(Two men are filling in the grave. PA, CELIE, NETTIE, LITTLE BROTHER
and LITTLE SISTER stand by. CELIE and NETTIE sad. People stop to offer con-
dolences, to shake PA'S hand, to embrace the children and CELIE and NETTIE.
Then, abruptly, the solemn mood gives way to one of relief for all except the family.
Someone laughs. People start to walk more loosely, to look at other graves, straighten-
ing flowerpots, pulling weeds; start to leave the graveyard and all thoughts of death behind them.)*

HARPO
*(Looks at SOFIA BUTLER, who is looking at a nearby marker. She is a solidly built
young woman who radiates health and vitality.)*

SOFIA
(Does not look at HARPO.)

HARPO
(Looks at her hard.)

SOFIA
(Glances up. Amused. Somewhat defiant.)

HARPO
*(Catches her eye. Gives her the kind of wink that practically makes you hear the
click.)*

SOFIA
(Tosses her head.)

MISTER
*(Is standing in a little clump of his children, who are dirty, knotty haired, with falling
socks and runny noses; stares at NETTIE, who is quietly weeping. He moves up to
PA, touches his shoulder. They shake hands. MISTER wears a black armband, as
does PA.
Speaking to PA but staring at NETTIE—who looks at the ground.)*
          My little ones sure could use a mother.
(He glances over at them. Back at NETTIE.)

PA
*(Notes how MISTER looks at NETTIE. Looks at her the same way. It is a frankly
sexual stare, and thorough. He clutches her arm. She jumps.)*
          Poor thing!

(Hugs her fake-fatherly.)

> She young and innocent. Don't know nothing
> but what you tell her. Smart though. Gonna
> make a schoolteacher out of her.

(Kisses her on the forehead. Then looks at CELIE.)

> That one'd make the better wife. She not
> good-looking like her sister, here, but she
> can work like a man.

MISTER

(Still looking at NETTIE.)

CELIE

(Looks at all of them quickly, then sidles off. NETTIE ducks from under PA'S arm and goes after her. Takes her hand. They walk among the graves. LITTLE BROTHER and LITTLE SISTER straggling at a distance behind them. They are moving nearer the main road.)

MISTER

(Still looking at NETTIE. He is clearly fixated.)

> I never really look at that one before.
> Don't she have two children?

PA

> God took care of that. And her too.
> Both her young uns died and she can't
> have no more. The Lord knows some women
> don't deserve children.

(As he says this, a very handsome horse and buggy passes directly in front of CELIE and NETTIE, who do not notice it, particularly, as NETTIE is comforting CELIE. PA and MISTER take a long look, however, for driving the stylish buggy and dressed to the nines is SHUG AVERY, going fast in the opposite direction from the mourners.)

INT. NIGHT   CELIE AND NETTIE'S BEDROOM

PA

(Is sitting on the edge of the bed holding NETTIE'S arm. She is lying under the covers and her eyes are wide with fear. She is slowly trying to pull back her arm.)

> You have to help take care of
> PAPA now.

CELIE

(Appears in doorway. Takes in what is happening in a flash. Quickly she ducks into her mother's bedroom. Appears in doorway again wearing her mother's nightgown,

false hairpiece, bedroom slippers, lipstick, powder, rouge—the whole schmeer. She looks ludicrous, like a "sexy" ghost of her mother, and the first impulse should be to laugh. But then, surprisingly, for such a meek, beaten-down person who has not spoken before, her voice carries absolute authority.)

Come to bed, PA.

INT. NIGHT   MISTER'S BEDROOM
MISTER
(Is fucking CELIE while looking at a photograph on the wall. CELIE is crying silently and there is a bandage above one eye. When MISTER moves his head to the other side, CELIE fastens her eyes on the large picture of SHUG AVERY, buxom, flamboyant, and gorgeous, on the wall. The inscription reads: To Albert, the man I love, Shug Avery. Signed with her full name. CELIE looks into SHUG'S eyes, sighs, and puts one arm over her new husband's shoulders.)

CELIE
a) (Combing a little girl's hair [one of MISTER'S daughters]. The little girl frowns, then pulls out of CELIE'S grip. When CELIE reaches for her, she bites CELIE'S hand, kicks her, takes the comb and runs and throws it down the well.)

b) (Washing clothes in a huge tin tub over a rub board. Mounds of clothes. In a big black pot in the yard [over a fire] the white clothes are boiling. The children sit on the steps not helping. Throwing rocks. MISTER sits on the porch smoking.)

c) (Chopping wood and carrying it inside and filling up the wood box. Then making a fire in the huge kitchen stove [which looks like a truck] and cutting up a chicken for dinner.)

d) (Serving dinner.) Gradually over these scenes, the household and children begin to look better. Shirts are white, noses dry, hair combed, socks up. There is order. Only CELIE fails to look better. In fact, she looks worse and worse, as the old clothes of her mother's she has been wearing become tattered and faded.

EXT. DAY   ABOUT A YEAR LATER
CELIE
(In a field, plowing behind a broken-spirited mule. Stumbling over the clumps of dirt, in her long dress.)

EXT. DAY
NETTIE
(On the path leading to the field. Carrying bundles, coming toward CELIE. When CELIE notices her, she drops her plow line. NETTIE drops her bundles and they run toward each other. They embrace.

NETTIE *pulling back, looks closely at* CELIE. *Notices a bruise on her cheek. Touches it.*)

CELIE

(*Embarrassed.*)
> You know how clumsy I is.

NETTIE

(*Puzzled, concerned, angry, looks her in the eye and takes her by both arms, as if about to gently shake her.*)

CELIE

(*Shrugging. Lamely.*)
> I fell.

EXT. DUSK   FRONT YARD AND PORCH OF MISTER'S HOUSE
(*Simple, L-shaped house, unpainted, weathered silvery brown. Two doors open onto porch; the chairs in which* MISTER *and* NETTIE *sit are between the doors. Through the door on the left we see* CELIE *cleaning up after supper, directing the children to bed. She holds a water bucket out to* HARPO. *He bangs it against the floor. Stalks out.* CELIE *picks it up. Goes out.*
There is the sound of crickets. A frog. The occasional flicker of fireflies.)

MISTER
> You sure do look good, Sister NETTIE.

NETTIE
> Why, thank you.

MISTER
> Your clothes fit you just right.

NETTIE
> Thank you.

MISTER
> Hair just as neat.

(*Beat.*)

NETTIE
(*Says nothing. Looks around for* CELIE. *Smiles nervously in* MISTER'S *direction.*)

MISTER
> Nice teef.

EXT. NIGHT

CELIE

(Through the open door we see CELIE return with two buckets of water, which she puts on the shelf. CELIE then comes to join NETTIE and MISTER on the porch. She is bushed. Dressed in rags. Looks like a slave.)

NETTIE

(Looks at her sister and smiles.)

You sure do look good, Sister CELIE.

CELIE

(Looks at her puzzled.)

Thank you.

NETTIE

Your clothes fit you just right.

CELIE

(More puzzled.)

MISTER

(Mouth tightens.)

NETTIE

(Looking tenderly at CELIE'S hoo-raw's nest of unkempt hair.)

Hair just as neat.

CELIE

(Catching on. Laughs.)

NETTIE

Nice teeth.

MISTER

(Face closes in, cold.)

EXT. DAY   MISTER'S FRONT YARD

CELIE AND NETTIE

(Hugging. NETTIE dressed as on first day in long black skirt and neat purple paisley blouse. Her bundles at her feet.)

CELIE

All I can tell you. Wherever you may
travel, go first to the house of the
Lord.

(HARPO and SMALLER CHILDREN stand looking.)

NETTIE
(Trying to be strong.)
I'm satisfied I'll be all right.
(She looks around at the house and yard. At HARPO. At the sullen children.)
It's like seeing you buried.

CELIE
Naw. If I was buried I wouldn't
have to work.

CELIE AND NETTIE
(Holding hands, begin to walk down the path together. Unable to let each other go.)

MISTER
(From the porch.)
CELIE! Git back in this yard.
(Precisely as he would tell his dog.)

CELIE AND NETTIE
(Stop in their tracks. Hug again. Kiss each other on the lips.)

CELIE
Write to me, now.

NETTIE
(Crying.)
What?

CELIE
Write me. You know. Letters.

NETTIE
(With feeling.)
Nothing but death could keep me from it.
(They part.)

NETTIE
(Starts on her journey. A path made by wagon wheels and feet. Trees, bushes, grass, sky, all we see. She turns. Comes back. Puts her bundles down. Puts one arm around CELIE'S waist.)
Watch for me in the sunset.
(They look at a glorious, purple-stained sunset.)

CELIE

And watch for me in the moonshine.
(Hugs NETTIE. Then turns and looks at the house, children, fields. Wipes her eyes. Picks up the brush broom at her feet and walks back into the yard. Begins sweeping the yard. The tracks left by the broom resemble the desert or the sea.)

INT. NIGHT   CELIE AND MISTER'S BEDROOM
(CELIE is on her knees beside the bed looking as if she's praying, again. But she is actually sewing. This time giving all of her love and concentration to where to place a small circle of fabric snipped from NETTIE'S purple blouse. In the appliquéd quilt square she is now constructing is a purple sun. Going down.)

EXT. DAY   SAME PATH A COUPLE OF YEARS LATER
CELIE
*(Standing on the porch steps, eyes shaded with her hand. Dressed as usual in ill-fitting castoffs: some remnants of her mother's old dresses. Some leftovers from MISTER'S dead wife. She is straining to see if someone is coming. We should feel she has been standing there waiting for NETTIE for two years.
HARPO and SOFIA BUTLER are coming toward the house. SOFIA in front. She seems to be marching. HARPO has to make an effort to keep up. We do not see enough of her to note her pregnancy.)*

MISTER, SOFIA, HARPO
(Are sitting down on porch. CELIE hovers near door, doesn't sit.)

MISTER

(With contempt.)

> You young womens today got your legs
> open to every Tom, Dick and Harry.
> Then, time you get in trouble you
> try to latch on to the first sucker
> you can git.

SOFIA
(Rearing back in her chair and running her hands along her hugely pregnant sides.)
> I ain't in no trouble.
> Big, though.

CELIE
(In doorway. Looks at SOFIA, amazed.)

MISTER
> You needn't think I'm gon let my
> boy marry you just for that. He

young and limited. A good-looking
gal like you could put anything over
on him.

SOFIA

(Waits for HARPO to speak up.)
(Beat.
While HARPO looks at his hands. Then at the floor.
SOFIA rises.)

Yeah, maybe you right. Anything I put
over on HARPO he probably couldn't
handle.

(To CELIE.)

I'd thank you for a glass of water,
Miss CELIE.

CELIE

(Always moves with the promptness of an abused servant. Speedily gets a glass from the kitchen, brings it to the water shelf on the porch, dips up a glass of water and hands it to SOFIA.)

SOFIA

(Downs the water in a gulp.)

Well, HARPO, me and the baby staying
with my sister, ODESSA, and her husband,
JACK. When you ready for us, we be
waiting.

HARPO

(Rises guiltily. Attempts to leave with her, or rather, behind her.)

MISTER

(Contempt.)

Aw, sit down, boy.

HARPO

(Sits.)

CELIE

(Sitting down herself. Deeply sad. To HARPO, but almost to herself.)

I never got a chance to talk to
her. I would have told her I got a
sister name NETTIE. I got a sister,
too.

MISTER
You *had* a sister, you mean.

CELIE

(Softly.)

NETTIE not dead.

MISTER

(Taunting.)

Why she don't never write you, then?
If "nothing but death could keep her
from it"?

CELIE
(Used to this. Stands. Reaches down for HARPO'S hand. Drags him up.)
Come on, HARPO. Time for me and you
to git to the field.
(They stumble off.)

CELIE AND HARPO
*(Backs to camera. Heading toward the field with mule. CELIE and HARPO carry
hoes.)*

MISTER
*(On porch. Leaning back against the wall. Holding his pipe. Brings chair down
slowly. Spits over the railing.)*

INT. CHURCH   SUNDAY 11:00 A.M.
*(Camera pans congregation. We recognize some of the same people who were at
CELIE'S MOTHER'S funeral.)*

CELIE
*(Shares a bench with HARPO, TWO BROTHERS, SISTER. She at one end,
HARPO at the other.)*

HARPO
*(Looking about. Spots SOFIA. She is holding fine fat baby, who is very active. She
sits between her sister ODESSA and JACK. All three seem proud of the baby.
SOFIA especially. She meets HARPO'S gaze serenely. Even with pity. In his cow-
ardice, he is missing the very miracle of life.)*

SQUEAK
(Sitting with her MOTHER and SISTERS. Glances at HARPO.)

MISTER

*(Sits near the door with his legs crossed, toying with his unlit pipe. Skeptical, bored.
Eager to be out.)*

PREACHER

(Tan, balding, plump. Blue suit and tie.)

> I say a sinful woman, it say in the
> Good Book, is an abomination before
> God.

(Beat.)

> But for every sin, ladies, I say the
> Devil gonna make you pay.

LADIES

*(Holding fans that advertise funeral homes and Christ. Some sneak glances at
CELIE, some look at SOFIA.)*

> Amen, Amen.

*(All the LADIES fan a little harder. A few who can't squeeze out an Amen cough
discreetly into hanskers.)*

PREACHER

> Take a young woman most of us know . . .

LADIES

(Looking uncomfortable.)

PREACHER

> She run wild in the road while she was
> still little more than a child. Mama
> couldn't do nothing with her. Papa
> couldn't do nothing neither. A *wild* child.

(He is working up a rhythm.)

CONGREGATION

> Amen!

PREACHER

> She had to have . . . that man.

CONGREGATION

> Preach!

PREACHER

(Mournfully.)

Two little children born out of
wedlock . . .

CELIE

(Tenses. Thinks PREACHER is talking about her.)

PREACHER

. . . and she refuse to raise 'em.
Said, Here Mama, Here, Papa, you all
have to raise my children—and you
know children is God's most precious
gift to anyone—I just got to keep
running after that man.

LADIES

(Sucking teeth. Striking self-righteous attitudes, though most were probably pregnant
before they married, as birth control doesn't for the most part exist.)

Ugh, ugh, ugh.

PREACHER

Now the man already had a wife . . .

LADIES

Preach!

PREACHER

. . . but she stole him away from her.
And the wife had four little children
too. But that didn't stop her. Um,
didn't even slow her down. She wanted
that woman's husband, and she took
him. . . . And you know just how weak
some men is . . .

LADIES

Amen. That's the truth. Yessir.

PREACHER

. . . The spirit and image of Adam, every
last one, when it come to a good-
looking 'oman. And this woman I'm

talkin 'bout was—I say *was*, a good-
lookin' woman.

LADIES
Ummm ...

PREACHER
Naw. She don't look so good no more.
'Cause you see, the Devil whispered in
the man's wife's ear and she started
to run in the road just like her husband
and his woman. But she tried to do it
with the wrong man—and he kilt her.
Shot her dead right in the yard of this
church.

CONGREGATION
(*Some people actually turn to look at MISTER. All know this tale is about him and
his wife and SHUG AVERY.*)
Ummm. Hummm ... sure did, Lord.

CELIE
(*Surprised. Looks back at him too.*)

MISTER
(*No change except to shift his legs and recross them.*)

PREACHER
Naw. She don't look so good now.
'Cause she got all that evil on her
conscience. Done give away her own
children. Done made another woman's
children motherless. . . . And then she have the
nerve to try to sing.

CONGREGATION
(*Totally against blues, jazz, ragtime and anything else you can dance to.*)
Preach!

PREACHER
Now ain't that just what the Bible
is talkin' about! A woman do all kind
of sin. Smokin' and drinkin' in public

over respectable men's wives. Dancin'
all time of night. Layin' up with
other women's mens. Takin' bread out of
little children's mouths. Then, what
they do? They have the gall to git up
in public and sing about it . . .

CONGREGATION
Ugh, ugh, ugh.

PREACHER
But she don't sing so good now, neither.
'Cause God don't like ugly. And he ain't
stuck on pretty. And don't nothing seem
more ugly in his sight than a good-lookin'
pretty woman gone bad.
(He is preaching SHUG AVERY'S funeral, and she isn't even dead.)

MISTER
(Clenches jaws. Angry.)

PREACHER
She thought she could run over this
world. But God put a few rocks in her
way. Up North where she went she
thought she'd have it easy. Washing
and ironing white folks' clothes down
here with the rest of y'all wasn't good
enough for her. She wanted to stand up
half-nekked in the jookjoints and sing.
At first she thought she had caught a
bad cold. But then it turnt into
pnewmonia. Maybe done turnt into gallopin'
consumption by now . . . 'cause
God *don't* like ugly, and a sinful woman
is an abomination before God . . .

CELIE
(Looks back where MISTER was sitting. He is gone.)

SOFIA
(Baby is crying. She lifts up her blouse to nurse. Camera tight on nursing baby.)

EXT. DAY   FRONT PORCH—ODESSA'S AND JACK'S
BABY
(Still being nursed.)

PREACHER
*(Same PREACHER. He is standing facing the yard and HARPO and SOFIA.
ODESSA, JACK and CELIE stand to one side.)*
> . . . but an obedient wife is as a
> treasure in the eyes of the Lord.
> I now pronounce you man and wife.
> You may kiss the bride.

*(HARPO leans over the nursing baby and kisses SOFIA somewhat timidly, but with
pride, too, on the lips. SOFIA, never one to restrain her feelings, and stimulated as
well by the baby's sucking, swoons completely into the kiss, causing BABY to stick out
a leg in protest.)*

ODESSA, JACK, CELIE AND PREACHER
(Exchange looks as time ticks by.)

PREACHER
*(Coughs. Then, surprisingly, grins broadly. Everyone laughs or chuckles good-
naturedly. Including HARPO and SOFIA, who have come up for air.
CELIE doesn't realize it yet but already she is infected with SOFIA'S womanish manner. It makes her feel proud of herself as a woman for the first time. Pride, envy,
amazement mingle in her look. SOFIA and HARPO'S wedding is the first happy oc-
casion in the film and the wedding is something of a rebellion against MISTER, who is
conspicuously absent.)*

INT. NIGHT   CELIE AND MISTER'S BEDROOM
CELIE
*(Sitting in a chair by the bed reading her Bible. Which, on closer inspection, reveals
the picture of SHUG AVERY. CELIE'S fingers and eyes caress the picture, and
looking into the photo as if into a mirror, she then touches her own face and hair.
Then, with a new sense of ease in her movements, she puts the Bible down and
crosses to the chifforobe. She looks over her shoulder once, and lifts out a stack of
quilted squares. As she spreads the pieces on the bed we begin to see that she is quilting
the story of her life. Each square represents a scene from the past. She strokes NET-
TIE'S "farewell purple sun" and looks out into space longingly. Then she begins her
work. Cutting and sewing and laying out. There is a sense of total absorption in what
she is doing. And a sadness. And a peace. As she works, she gradually sinks to her
knees beside the bed—cutting out shapes, pinning, sewing.)*

EXT. DAY

CELIE

(Sweeping the yard with a brush broom, a broom made of a lot of small branches tied together. For the house she would use a straw broom made from straw "wrung" from the fields. Again, ease in her movements. Self-absorption. Peace. MISTER'S absence is a liberation. So that the sound of wagon wheels is particularly jarring. She moves quickly to the top of the steps and peers off down the road. She sees the wagon, with a canopy of blankets over it.)

EXT. DAY

MISTER

(Close-up of MISTER in the wagon seat, holding the reins loosely.)

CELIE

(Confused. Moves toward broom left lying in the yard. Then moves toward kitchen door. Then, almost coquettishly [a new look entirely for her and unexpected], runs her hands up to her hair, where they encounter her dusty head rag, which she yanks off, only to feel the unmistakable bumpiness of an unkempt, botched hairstyle. Her braids are frizzy, coming loose, and a fright. She looks down at her dress. A disaster. Farther down at her shoes. Big toes busting out. In a final act of desperation she sniffs her armpits—reels back from the scent. She resolves to clamp her arms close to her sides, stand in one spot and try to blend into the wall.)

MISTER, HARPO, SOFIA, BABY

(Down in the yard looking into back of wagon.)

MISTER

(Takes in the new situation with HARPO and SOFIA but is too tired to speak on it.)
Help me get her in the house.

HARPO

Who she is?

MISTER

The woman should have been your
mammy but wasn't.

HARPO

Shug Avery?
(HARPO and MISTER reach up into the wagon as two black and elegant hands reach out.)

Shug Avery
(A very sick-looking woman so wasted from illness that her stylish clothes seem about to slip off her. Her face is caked with powder and her lips are gruesomely red. Her eyebrows are plucked and all in all she looks half dead.)

Mister, Harpo, Shug
(Passing CELIE, arms clamped to her sides, still near the railing. Her eyes show great joy. The rest of her seems servile and absurd.)

Mister
(Looks at CELIE in disgust, and sighs.)

Shug Avery
(Looks over at CELIE, then back at MISTER. Sneers.)
> What the hell is it?

INT. NIGHT

Celie
(An untouched tray—with flower—is on the dresser. CELIE is giving SHUG a bath. The most thrilling thing she ever did in her life. She scrubs her back, touches SHUG'S body gently, reverently. SHUG frowns. She looks like an ill-humored cadaver, and is impatient with CELIE. When CELIE puts her satin nightgown over her head slowly and admiringly, she snatches it down out of CELIE'S hands, hatefully.)

Shug
(With disdain.)
> I guess you never even seen satin
> before.

Celie
(Still mesmerized by it, as by SHUG'S bedroom slippers, clothes, perfumes, every-thing. Humbly.)
> No ma'am.

Shug
(Has a cruel brainstorm. Reaches under her gown and pulls off her satin drawers, which she flings at CELIE.)
> Here.

Celie
(Missing the cruelty entirely.)
> Thank you!
(Rapturously. Burying her face in them.)

SHUG
(Groans at such denseness.)

INT. NIGHT   SHUG'S BEDROOM
(Clock indicates it's 2 A.M.)

SHUG
(Sleeping fitfully.)

ALBERT (MISTER)
(Sitting quietly, wide awake in a corner of the room. Holding unlit pipe. Looking at SHUG and silently weeping.)

EXT. DAY   ALBERT AND CELIE'S FRONT PORCH

ALBERT
(Sitting on porch, smoking pipe.)

ALBERT'S FATHER
(Sitting. Leaning forward on his cane.)
> I see you just couldn't rest til
> you got her in your house.   .   . .

ALBERT
(Between humility and resignation.)
> No sir. I reckon I couldn't.

CELIE
(Bringing glasses of water from kitchen, stops before reaching outside door to listen.)

ALBERT'S FATHER
> I never could see what you saw in
> her anyhow. She black as tar, she
> nappy-headed, she got legs like
> baseball bats.

CELIE
(Spits into one of the glasses of water.)

ALBERT'S FATHER
> Why, I hear she ain't even clean.
> Layin' round with so many different
> mens she got that nasty 'oman
> disease.

ALBERT

That's a lie.

CELIE

(Sticks her finger in the glass of water with the spit. Twirls it around. Wipes her fingers on her dress.)

ALBERT'S FATHER

And all her mama's children got
different daddies. That whole family
is just too trifling, niggerish and
confuse.

ALBERT

Well, both of SHUG AVERY'S children
got the same daddy. I vouch for
that. *(Pause.)*
You just ain't got
it in you to understand. I love
SHUG AVERY and always will. I should
have married her when I had the
chance.

ALBERT'S FATHER

You would have done it without any of
my houses *(Looking down at HARPO and
SOFIA'S house)* or my land.

CELIE

(Comes out on the porch. Gives one glass of water to ALBERT. The one containing spit to ALBERT'S FATHER. Watches innocently as he drinks.)

ALBERT'S FATHER

(Looking up at her.)

Ah! That sure hits the spot.
(Hands her the glass.)

I have to give it to you, Miss CELIE
not many womens would let they
husband's whore lay up in they house.

ALBERT

(Terse.)

Hand PA his hat, CELIE.

CELIE

(Hands hat to ALBERT'S FATHER. She and ALBERT exchange their first empathetic glance.)

INT. NIGHT   SHUG'S BEDROOM

CELIE AND SHUG

(They are in SHUG'S bed. CELIE sitting behind SHUG combing and braiding her hair, which is dry and discolored from over-use of lye. On a stool beside the bed is a lavishly full tray of food. SHUG looks cross. Then begins to relax and lean back between CELIE'S knees. Idly SHUG reaches pickily over the tray and brings up a large piece of home-cured ham, which she holds up to her nose as if it is a flower, sniffing. Slowly she takes a bite of it, then munches it hungrily.)

CELIE

(Holds her breath, watching this. Beams as SHUG munches. Continues corn-rowing SHUG'S hair.)

SHUG

(Starts to hum the theme of The Color Purple.)

EXT. DAY

HARPO AND ALBERT

(On ALBERT'S porch, looking down toward HARPO and SOFIA'S house. SOFIA is dressed in overalls, a head rag and heavy shoes. Shingling the roof. The sound of her hammering is loud. It is background to this conversation.)

HARPO

The only fault I find with her is, she
won't mind. I tell her to do one thing,
she do another. Always back talk. No
matter what I ast her to do, she do
what she please.

(There is actually some pride, even bragging, in this complaint.)

MISTER/ALBERT

(Blowing smoke.)

You beat her ass yet?

HARPO

(Looking down at his hands.)

Naw suh.

MISTER/ALBERT
Well how you 'spect her to mind?
Women is like childrens, you have
to let 'em know who got the upper
hand.

INT. NIGHT   HARPO AND SOFIA'S HOUSE
(HARPO and SOFIA are fighting. They fight exactly as two men would fight. And it
is clear that SOFIA is the stronger of the two. Sounds of crashing, breaking, tearing.
The oldest boy, three, watches in astonishment while hovering protectively over twin
babies in a crib.)

INT. DAY   CELIE AND ALBERT'S KITCHEN
CELIE
(CELIE is washing dishes.)

HARPO
What you think I ought to do to
her to make her mind?

CELIE
Beat her.

EXT. DAY   CELIE AND ALBERT'S KITCHEN
(HARPO, CELIE, MISTER/ALBERT, SHUG seated around kitchen table eating.
A noonday meal: fried chicken, peas with okra and ham, greens, corn bread, butter-
milk and lemonade. Pie [on the stove]. A subdued atmosphere. Only the sighing of
the cooling woodstove and the ticking of the grandfather clock and its chimes are
heard.)
CELIE AND ALBERT AND SHUG
(Cast sidelong glances at HARPO.)

HARPO
(His face is a mess. Cuts and bruises everywhere. One eye blackened and completely
closed. He is stuffing himself seriously, almost violently.)

CELIE
(Beat.)
You can eat here every day till
SOFIA and the children come back.

HARPO
(Chewing furiously.)
She ain't comin' back.

MISTER/ALBERT
Good riddance!

HARPO
(*Gets up abruptly, snatches a piece of pie off the stove, jams it into his mouth. Leaves.*)

SHUG
Some womens won't let *nobody*
beat on 'em for nothin'.

CELIE
(*Looks down at her plate.*)

EXT. DAY　　　PATH TO ALBERT AND CELIE'S HOUSE
SOFIA
(*Her arms laden with odds and ends of items CELIE has given her. Which she dumps on the porch at CELIE'S feet.*)

CELIE
(*Quilting at a quilting frame hanging from the rafters of the porch. Surprised. Scared. Noticing a bruise on SOFIA'S face.*)

SOFIA
Here your curtains. Here your
smoothing iron. Here that pan you
lent me.

CELIE
(*Afraid to open her mouth.*)

SOFIA
You told HARPO to beat me.

CELIE
(*Weakly. Getting up.*)
Naw.

SOFIA
Don't lie.

CELIE
I'm so shame of myself.

SOFIA
All my life I had to fight.
A girl child ain't safe in a
world of men. But I always
look to another woman for help.

CELIE
(Looking like she could be bought for two cents.)

SOFIA
(Taking pity.)

What you do when you git mad?

CELIE
I don't never git mad. Sometime
MISTER git on me pretty bad. I
have to call on Old Maker to git
through. But this life soon be
over, heaven last always.

SOFIA
You ought to bash MISTER'S head
open, anytime he bother you.
Think 'bout heaven later.

(They laugh.)

SOFIA
(Tearing the curtains into strips.)

Let's just add these curtains to
your next quilt.

EXT. DAY   HARPO AND SOFIA'S HOUSE
(The sound of hammering. A pile of rubbish is burning in the yard.)

INT. DAY

HARPO AND SWAIN
(Are banging the last nails into a bar that is now where HARPO and SOFIA's bedroom was.)

EXT. DAY

HARPO
(Tacking up a sign on the side of the house. It reads: HARPO'S PLACE.)

INT. NIGHT   HARPO'S PLACE
(*A real regular down-home jook joint. People—some dressed in Sunday-go-to-meeting clothes, some in field clothes—at small tables playing cards, talking, drinking, smoking. But all this activity is frozen temporarily because of . . .*)

SHUG AVERY
(*Dressed in red and looking almost well, singing "A Good Man Is Hard to Find." This is her first night and she's a little unsure of herself. SWAIN, an extremely soulful looking and playing brother, accompanies her on guitar. The audience could go either way. Love her or hate her. This is the original Apollo crowd before they moved North, and their standards are even more exacting.*)

CELIE AND MISTER/ALBERT
(*Seated at small table near the minuscule "stage." Both gaze at SHUG with adoration.*)

SHUG
(*Looks over at them. Locks glances with ALBERT and we see the embers are still smoldering.*)

CELIE
(*Noticing this. Is painfully aware of her own unglamorous appearance. And of the fact that SHUG isn't supposed to look at her with passion because she's a woman. Confused and sad, she drops her head and tries to hide her tears with her hand.*)

SHUG
(*Looks from ALBERT to CELIE.*)
                    This next song I'm gonna sing is called
                    "Miss Celie's Song." 'Cause she help
                    scratch it out of my head when I was
                    sick.

CELIE
(*Brings her head up. Her face radiant.*)

SHUG
(*Starts to sing the song we first heard her hum while CELIE was doing her hair.*)

AUDIENCE
(*Loves the song. Loves what she said about MISS CELIE helping her. Can't miss CELIE looking like she just received the moon. Everybody claps and whistles and stomps.*)

MISTER/ALBERT
(Looks at CELIE. For the first time notices the intensity of her feelings for SHUG.)

INT. NIGHT   SHUG'S BEDROOM

(SHUG and ALBERT making love. Noisily.)

INT. NIGHT   CELIE'S BEDROOM
(Lying in her bed alone. Wide awake. Slowly pulls the quilt over her head.)

INT. NIGHT   HARPO'S
(The joint is jumping. CELIE, SHUG, ALBERT share a table. HARPO and SQUEAK serve drinks and barbeque behind the counter. SWAIN picks his box. Mellow, sensual, blues guitar.)

SOFIA
(Looking great and sizzling hot, dancing with a muscular, good-looking man. Having a ball.)

HARPO
(Watches her.)

SQUEAK
(Watches HARPO.)

HARPO
(Going up to SOFIA and "PRIZEFIGHTER" with a newly learned swagger, unable to resist flirting with his wife.)

> A good-lookin' fox like you ought
> to stay at home.

SOFIA
(Sizing him up.)

> This is my home. Though I do
> think it go better as a jookjoint.

HARPO
Where your children at?

SOFIA
My children at home. Where
yours?

HARPO
(With some bluster, to PRIZEFIGHTER.)
>Mind if I dance with my wife?

PRIZEFIGHTER
(Relinquishing SOFIA.)
>My job not to fight SOFIA'S
>battles. My job just to love
>her and take her where she want
>to go.

HARPO AND SOFIA
(Slow drag out across the floor.)

SQUEAK
(Attempting to cut in. HARPO swings SOFIA the other way. SQUEAK persists. SOFIA and HARPO stop dancing.)

HARPO
(Exasperated, but full of stuff, too.)
>Can't a man dance with his own
>wife?

SQUEAK
>Not if he my man, he can't.
(To SOFIA.)
>You better leave my man alone.

SOFIA
(Disengaging herself from HARPO.)
>Hey, fine with me.

HARPO
(Holds her back.)
>Wait a minute. This your house.
>You don't have to go nowhere.

SQUEAK
(To SOFIA.)
>This *was* your house. You walked
>out on your house. Now your man
>*and* your house belongs to me.

SOFIA
Fine with me.
(Tries to leave. HARPO still holds her arm.)

HARPO
Wait a minute, SQUEAK—

SQUEAK
(Slaps SOFIA.)

SOFIA
(Draws back her fist and knocks two of SQUEAK'S teeth out. SQUEAK drops to the floor, examining her teeth and sobbing.)

HARPO
(Stoops to cradle SQUEAK in his arms. Puts his handkerchief to her cut lip. But his eyes follow SOFIA—and admiration for her is not lacking—as she and the PRIZE-FIGHTER go out the door. And we hear a car motor start.)

INT. EVENING   CELIE'S BEDROOM
(SHUG is looking at herself in the mirror. She is dressed in a gold-colored dress, very revealing, for another night at HARPO'S. She is well. She takes up a bottle of CELIE'S cheap perfume, sniffs. Makes a face.)
I bet you never even seen it.

CELIE
(Looking more presentable than usual because she is wearing some of SHUG'S clothes. Perhaps the blouse or jacket SHUG wore the first day. Her hair is also different. It has been straightened and is in a pompadour. We get the feeling she's wearing her satin drawers.
Her look says No, she never did.)

SHUG
I bet you never seen ALBERT down
there neither.

CELIE
(Frowning.)
I felt him.

SHUG
(Handing mirror to CELIE.)
Go look at yourself.

CELIE

(Takes mirror but doesn't move.)

SHUG

What! Too shame-face to look at your
own self in the lookin' glass!

CELIE

(Coyly.)

You come with me.

SHUG

(Laughs.)

CELIE AND SHUG

*(Enter SHUG'S room. SHUG bolts the door and leans against it. There is a playful,
girlish mood between the women.)*

SHUG

Okay. Nobody coming. Coast clear.

CELIE

*(On her back, under the covers, as she slides off her panties and slides the mirror be-
tween her legs.
Grimaces.)*

SHUG

(Looks at her. Laughs.)

CELIE

(Grimace turns to sudden smile. Almost wonder.)
Um.

SHUG

It's a heap prettier than you thought,
ain't it?

CELIE

(Surprisingly confident.)
It's mine.

EXT. DAY

CELIE AND SHUG

(In the barn shucking corn. CELIE is an expert and corn piles up in her bucket. SHUG is clumsy and slow, concerned about her nails.)

SHUG

You sure you don't mind if ALBERT
sleep with me?

CELIE

I don't care who ALBERT sleep
with.

EXT. NIGHT   PORCH

ALBERT AND SHUG

(Making love against the steps in the shadow of the porch. Not quite far enough away from CELIE'S window.)

CELIE

(In her bed. Hears their sighs and moans. Pulls covers over her head. Then, slowly reaches between her legs to comfort herself.)

EXT. DAY   PORCH

SHUG AND CELIE AND ALBERT

(Shug is dressed for travel. Looks wonderful. Her suitcases at her feet. CELIE and ALBERT look pitiful. SHUG trying to be cheery. CELIE looks a thousand times better than she did when SHUG arrived. She is even wearing some of SHUG'S nail polish.)

SHUG

(Tucks a plait behind CELIE'S ear.)
You look so sweet with your hair
this way.

CELIE

(Watching ALBERT'S back as he goes down into the yard where HARPO and SWAIN wait in a car whose back door is open. Tears are in her eyes. Softly. As ALBERT puts a suitcase in the car.)
He beat me when you not here.

SHUG

Who do? ALBERT?

CELIE

(Turns away, as ALBERT approaches. Puts her hand to her mouth.)

SHUG

(Taking CELIE into her arms. Looking over her shoulder at ALBERT. Speaking, really, to ALBERT.)

> I wish you had told me this before.
> Well. He done beat you for the
> last time, if he ever 'spect to
> lay eyes again on me.

(Looks at ALBERT with contempt.)

ALBERT

(Shoots CELIE a venomous look. Then looks at the floor.)

> Well, I just don't love nobody but
> you, baby.

SHUG

> That ain't no reason to mistreat
> CELIE.

ALBERT

(Desperate.)

> When you comin' back?

SHUG

> When you can give CELIE the same
> consideration you give me.

(She picks up her make-up case and goes down to the car. Gets in. The car moves off. She waves.)

CELIE AND ALBERT

(Both wiping away tears.)

ALBERT

(Hauls off and hits CELIE so hard he sends her sprawling.)

INT. NIGHT   CELIE'S BEDROOM

(Putting down her Bible. Taking out her quilt pieces. Getting on her knees beside the bed. Smoothing out, then somberly cutting up one of SHUG'S dresses.)

EXT. DAY   A SMALL SOUTHERN PLANTATION TOWN OF TWO
STREETS
SOFIA, THE PRIZEFIGHTER, AND SOFIA'S FOUR CHILDREN
(*Tall eight-year-old boy. Twins, girl and boy, six; and toddler, little boy. All well dressed, shining. Getting out of new, nice-looking car. They stand waiting beside the sidewalk until white people pass. This is a town where black and white people don't use the sidewalk at the same time.*)

MAYOR AND MIZ MILLIE (MAYOR'S WIFE)
(*Strolling arm in arm. Black people—old, young, sharecropping families, schoolteachers, laborers, everyone—moving off sidewalk into gutter as they pass. They pass SOFIA, CHILDREN, and PRIZEFIGHTER. MIZ MILLIE stops. Turns around smartly. Dragging MAYOR. MIZ MILLIE stares at SOFIA [who looks so much better than she does]. Checks out PRIZEFIGHTER, SOFIA'S dress, wristwatch, the car, the children.*)

> You all so clean. And so many
> children.

(*Begins to rummage in her purse. Brings out four pennies, which she holds out to SOFIA'S children. They stare at her.*)

> Cute as little buttons though.

SOFIA
(*Annoyed.*)

MIZ MILLIE
(*Reaches down to touch a head. Thinks better of it. Admires and fingers a starched white shirt collar instead.*)

SOFIA
(*Extremely annoyed.*)

MAYOR
(*Indulgent.*)

> Now, Miz MILLIE. Always going
> on over colored.

MIZ MILLIE
(*To SOFIA.*)

> Would you like to work for me.
> Be my maid?

SOFIA

> Hell, no.

MIZ MILLIE

(Shocked.)

MAYOR

(Pushing MIZ MILLIE behind him.)
            What you say to MIZ MILLIE, girl?

SOFIA

            I say, Hell, no.

MAYOR

(Slaps her.)

SOFIA

(Hits him with her fist. All her children start to kick and bite him. MIZ MILLIE screams. White proprietors look out store windows. Grab their guns. Race to surround the fracas and to pull SOFIA and HER CHILDREN off MAYOR. The PRIZEFIGHTER gathers up the children as the men beat and kick SOFIA to the ground, as MIZ MILLIE and MAYOR look on. One storekeeper, wearing apron, keeps gun on PRIZEFIGHTER and CHILDREN.)

EXT. DAY   THE TOWN JAIL
(Tiny, dusty, desolate.)

SOFIA

(Looking out the window through the bars of her cell. Aged. Hair unkempt, graying. Bad color. Scarred face. Sadness.
Music: distilled blues.)

INT. DAY   PRISON LAUNDRY

SOFIA

(Washing an enormous pile of convict uniforms, the kind with stripes. A stack of other dirty clothes, bedding—blankets, etc., included—reaches well above her head.)

INT. DAY

SOFIA

(In solitary. A tiny cell that is like a box. She can only stand or lean. A piece of bread is slid underneath the door and a rat beats her to it. She is nude.)

EXT. DAY   MAYOR'S HOUSE
(Large, Southern-style, nouveau Big House. White. Columns. Large green rocking chairs on porch/verandah.)

INT. DAY   MAYOR'S HOUSE

MIZ MILLIE AND SOFIA

(*Wide foyer, separating obviously spacious front rooms. MIZ MILLIE is looking at newel post at bottom of winding staircase, which SOFIA is dusting.*)

MIZ MILLIE

We never should have let your
people talk us into letting you
out of prison as a contract
laborer. You don't make no
kind of maid. As many times as
I tell you not to let finger
prints stay on this post,
every time I look—fingerprints.
How I can put up with twelve
years of sloppy work and your
ugly face too is more than I can
imagine.

SOFIA

(*Dressed as a maid in black dress, white apron and cap, continues to dust the newel post. A little white girl—MISS ELEANOR JANE—runs to help her, using the bottom of her skirt. The child looks up at SOFIA for approval. SOFIA looks at her blankly, seeming to ignore her. Mentally she has placed one of her own children there beside her, helping her dust.*)

INT. DAY   SOFIA'S HOUSE

CHILD

(*SOFIA'S oldest boy. He dusts. Looks up at SOFIA with longing. They are dusting an old table.*)

INT. NIGHT   SOFIA'S ROOM

SOFIA

(*After the opulence of the rest of the Big House, her room is like a closet. And is one. It contains a single old and lumpy bed. A bare lightbulb dangling from the ceiling. Her few clothes, mainly maid's uniforms, hang on nails. Some pictures of her children are stuck in the mirror frame above the bureau. She sits in a chair beside the radio, which is on very low. Almost inaudible. Her worn, run-over shoes are beside her. More than anything else, they express her condition. Her feet are calloused and flat. She is piecing a quilt. Wearily, she rubs her eyes.*
Music.)

EXT. DAY   MANY YEARS LATER
CELIE, SHUG, ALBERT AND GRADY
(CELIE and SHUG are walking behind ALBERT and GRADY, who are dragging a large Christmas tree. ALBERT also carries the axe. CELIE and SHUG are warmly dressed and SHUG wears a pair of soft, loose-fitting pants.)

SHUG
(Struts and skips.)

These are the best Christmas present
I ever had. What made you think to
make me pants?

CELIE

Anybody git around much as you do,
need to be able to move they legs.

SHUG

You still plowing in a dress?
(They pass SHUG and GRADY'S car in the yard. New, stylish, expensive. A Packard.)

CELIE AND SHUG
(Decorating the tree in the front room. SHUG adding expensive, glittering tree decorations and presents from slick big-city shopping bags.)

CELIE
(Marveling at each decoration. Mostly animals. Silver turtles and elephants predominate.)

Look like you got yourself a pretty
nice husband.

SHUG
(Significantly.)

And he can *drive*, too.

CELIE
What is it like up there in Memphis?

SHUG
Crazy. But I never had such a
good time in my life.

CELIE
You looks good.

SHUG
Why, thank you ma'am.

(Beat.)

You and ALBERT get along any better?

CELIE

(Resigned.)

Us try. But us don't seem to git
nowhere much.

SHUG
You ever come?

CELIE
Come where?

SHUG
You know, in your treasure box.

CELIE

(Alarmed and scandalized.)

SHUG

(Laughs.)

From a boy that used to could drive
me crazy, ALBERT sound like a man
that could drive you to sleep.

INT. NIGHT   SHUG AND GRADY'S BEDROOM
CELIE AND SHUG

(In bed, talking.)

SHUG
What your sister NETTIE look like?

CELIE

(Longingly.)

Oh. Everything about her shined.
Face, figure, heart and soul, too.
Just like a light.

SHUG
How you know she dead?

> CELIE
> All these years. If NETTIE
> wasn't dead, she'd have wrote.

> SHUG
> She wouldn't be where they use
> real funny-looking stamps? When
> I use to sleep with ALBERT sometimes
> he'd have a letter stamp just as
> funny in his coat.

> CELIE
> Naw. ALBERT mean. But he not that
> mean.

> SHUG

(Wondering.)

EXT. DAY

> SHUG AND ALBERT
(*Arm in arm, walking from the mailbox. SHUG is really grinning and tomming and laying it on thick. ALBERT is flattered. ALBERT holds the day's mail in his hands. SHUG reaches for his hand playfully. He extracts one letter and places it in his coat pocket.*)

> CELIE AND GRADY
(*Seated on porch steps watching ALBERT and SHUG.
[POV] SHUG and ALBERT seem to be getting involved again. Their faces show rejection and suffering. GRADY lights up a reefer, draws on it hard.*)

INT. NIGHT   CELIE AND ALBERT'S BEDROOM
> SHUG
(*SHUG'S hand stealthily reaching into ALBERT'S jacket pocket—which hangs on a chair by the bed, with him asleep in the bed. Comes out empty. Hesitates. Tries the other pocket. Nothing.*)

INT. NIGHT   SHUG'S ROOM
> CELIE AND SHUG
(*SHUG is dressed in a luxurious robe and slippers, tissuing off her make-up. CELIE lies on the bed watching her. With her whole soul.*)
> You look just like some kind of
> wild rose.

SHUG
(Smiles, but is obviously thinking of something else.)
                    Where ALBERT put stuff he don't
                    want nobody to see?

INT. NIGHT   CELIE AND ALBERT'S BEDROOM
                    CELIE AND SHUG
(Kneeling beside ALBERT'S trunk. SHUG turns the key in the lock, lifts the lid.
Pornographic postcards. Some of SHUG'S underwear. Sticks of peppermint candy.
Tins of tobacco. She sinks back on her heels in disappointment.)

CELIE
(Notices a cut-out handle in middle of trunk. Lifts it. There is a bottom layer to the
trunk and it is filled, stuffed, with letters.)

SHUG
(Takes out one letter, which has palm tree and Queen Victoria stamps, and hands it
to CELIE. Watches her.)

CELIE
(Holds the letter. Glances at NETTIE'S handwriting. The years-long stack of letters.
Tears come to her eyes and a flush to her face. She sags against the trunk as against a
coffin.)

SHUG
(Briskly taking all the letters out and taking off her robe, she wraps the letters in it.
Then she reaches down and gently takes CELIE'S hand.)
                    Come on.

INT. NIGHT   CELIE AND ALBERT'S KITCHEN
                    CELIE AND SHUG
(Steam letters open over the kettle.)

INT. NIGHT   CELIE AND ALBERT'S BEDROOM
                    CELIE AND SHUG
(Replacing empty envelopes in trunk.)

INT. NIGHT   SHUG AND GRADY'S BEDROOM
                    CELIE AND SHUG
(CELIE lies in bed in a state of shock. SHUG is sitting beside the bed in a chair,
holding the letters.)

CELIE
Just read me a little bit, tonight.
Just to know she alive. My old
heart . . .
(She places her hand over her heart. Tears.)

SHUG

(Reading.)
"When I left, ALBERT followed me on
his horse . . ."
(On the screen, over NETTIE'S words, we see a mule, HARPO, and CELIE, backs to camera, heading toward the field. MISTER/ALBERT watching from the porch. Then we see ALBERT saddling his horse. Then galloping. Then coming up behind NETTIE, slowly, as she walks purposefully along.
He is down beside her, talking. Touching her. She is frightened.)
"When I said no, he tried to drag
me off into the bushes . . ."
(MISTER and NETTIE struggle. NETTIE finally gets in a good thudding kick to MISTER'S groin, sending him to his knees and cutting the struggle short. At the unexpected anguish on his face, she reaches down, instinctively, to help him.)
"But the good Lord was with me and
I hurt him real bad."
(MISTER/ALBERT sneeringly refusing her hand. Shouting at her.)
"He said for what I had done, you
would never see or hear from me
again."

CELIE

(Her face tense, listening.)

SHUG

(Continuing. Another letter.)
"Picture how surprised I was when a
little girl opened the door and she
had your eyes set in your face!"
(NETTIE with bags at her feet, at the door of a small house that stands beside a church. A little girl, six-ish, looks up at her. The resemblance to CELIE is striking.)

INT. SUPPER TIME   THE PARSONAGE DINING ROOM
(NETTIE, SAMUEL, CORRINE, OLIVIA and ADAM at the table, eating. SAMUEL wears his clerical suit and collar, CORRINE is wearing a high-necked white blouse with bow, and long, dark skirt. The children are also dressed soberly, in clothing of the period—the twenties. Though the meal scene is central, open trunks, clothes, boxes, books, etc., are scattered about, indicating imminent transition.)

SHUG

(Reading.)

> "They have both of your children,
> CELIE. Their names are SAMUEL and
> CORRINE. Your children's names are
> OLIVIA and ADAM. They are
> missionaries and want to take me
> with them to Africa!

CELIE

(Puzzled.)

Mission—What?

EXT. DAY   OCEAN   SHIP, THE MALAGA.

INT. DAY   NETTIE

(In a cramped third class cabin at a tiny desk piled high with books about Africa. On the page she is studying there is a large picture of enslaved Africans packed spoon-fashion in a slave ship, like sardines. There is a knock on the door, and OLIVIA and ADAM burst in. NETTIE puts the book down, and hugs them.)

SHUG

(Reading the words that accompany this scene.)

> "Missionaries are people who help
> the poor in places like Africa . . .
> where, for one reason or another,
> folks have fallen on very hard
> times . . ."

NETTIE

(As she hugs CHILDREN the book she put down reveals a different page. On this page there is a picture of a very patrician African man of late middle age, beautifully dressed in a kente cloth robe. His bearing is still that of an important personage; however, around his neck is a spiked collar made of iron designed to make escape impossible.)

SHUG

(Reading another letter. NETTIE'S VOICE.)

> "We have been here now five years . . .
> and still no word from you . . ."

EXT. DAY   THE OLINKA VILLAGE, WEST AFRICA

NETTIE

(A more mature NETTIE under a thatched-roofed, open-sided structure, a school, standing in front of 20 or so AFRICAN YOUNGSTERS, teaching.)

"Your children are growing like
weeds . . ."
(Close-up of two children among the others, ADAM and OLIVIA.)
"Our village is beautiful but
very hot . . ."
(NETTIE, perspiring, getting up out of her mosquito-netting–shrouded bed, dragging
her small writing table out into the moonlight to write. Long shot of village. Peaceful,
serene, lovely, under a full moon.)

SHUG

(Reading. But NETTIE'S VOICE.)
"We buried CORRINE today. She died
of African fever, but also of a
broken heart. She thought, because
the children look so much like me,
they must be my children. And that
SAMUEL is their father!"
(OLINKA BURIAL. Mourners wear white. Faces painted white. CORRINE'S
body wrapped in bark cloth, carried on a beautifully carved board.)
"SAMUEL told me about the man who
gave him your children. He knew him
when he was a boy. Celie, the man
who outraged you and gave away your
children, the man we knew as PA is
not our real father. Our father
was lynched by white folks when we
were babies . . ."

CELIE

(Astonished.)
Oh.
(Clutches her heart.)

INT. NIGHT   SHUG AND GRADY'S BEDROOM
CELIE AND SHUG
(In bed. CELIE on her back, hugs the letters to her chest. Crying.)
Nobody ever love me, but NETTIE.

SHUG

(Leans over slowly and slowly begins to kiss away her tears.)
I love you, MISS CELIE.
(Kisses her mouth.)

CELIE

(Returns the kiss.)

        Um.

(Surprise. Joy. Innocence in this um. It is also part weariness. Part sob.)

INT. NIGHT   SHUG AND GRADY'S BEDROOM

CELIE AND SHUG

(Sound asleep in each other's arms. Noise of car driving up outside. Doors slamming. Drunken staggering and laughter in kitchen.)

INT. NIGHT   KITCHEN

ALBERT AND GRADY

(Drunk but hungry. Rummaging in the safe and stove for food. Find chicken and pie.)

ALBERT

      Sh ...

(As he eats.)

GRADY

(Suddenly turns green. Staggers out.)

INT. NIGHT   CELIE AND ALBERT'S BEDROOM

ALBERT

(Falls into bed. Next to CELIE. Who appears to be fast asleep.)

INT. NIGHT   AN HOUR OR SO LATER

ALBERT

(Snoring.)

CELIE

(Leaning over him. ALBERT'S straight razor in her hand and pressed against his throat.)

INT. DAY   MAYOR'S HOUSE—LIVING ROOM

MAYOR

(Reclining in big chair, reading the paper.)

MIZ MILLIE

(On settee, fidgety. Looking out of window at a brand-new coupe.)

MAYOR

(Looks up at MIZ MILLIE.)
> How're you enjoyin' her, MIZ
> MILLIE?

MIZ MILLIE

(Flounces off the settee in a huff.)

EXT. DAY   INTERIOR OF CAR IN MAYOR'S YARD
SOFIA AND MIZ MILLIE

SOFIA

(SOFIA is seated next to MIZ MILLIE, showing her how to start the car.)

MIZ MILLIE

(Listening to SOFIA but impatient with her too. Annoyed that SOFIA knows how to do something only whites, in her opinion, should be able to do.)

SOFIA

(Moves closer. Demonstrates the gearshift and concomitant depression of accelerator. The car sputters. Starts. Lurches forward.)

EXT. DAY   MIZ MILLIE'S FIFTH DRIVING LESSON
(MIZ MILLIE gets in the car with some assurance. Hesitates before opening the front car door for SOFIA. They go off down the road.)

EXT. DAY   MIZ MILLIE
(Is in the car, revving the engine. She looks pleased as punch with herself, but it is also obvious she has no place to go. She sits, revving the engine, and her eye falls on SOFIA, who is sweeping the walk.)
> SOFIA, it's been a while since you
> saw your family, hasn't it?

SOFIA

(Looking up.)
> Yes ma'am. It's been five years.

MIZ MILLIE
> Get in.

SOFIA
> Ma'am?

MIZ MILLIE
Get in. I'm gonna take you home
to see your children. You can
stay all day.

SOFIA
(Throwing down the broom. She comes to the side of the car and tries to open the front door. It is locked.)

MIZ MILLIE
(Laughs.)
This is the South.

SOFIA
(Gets into the backseat.)

MIZ MILLIE
(Zooms off down the road. Oblivious. Pleased with her good deed.)

EXT. DAY   JACK AND ODESSA'S YARD
MIZ MILLIE
(Pulls into the yard.)

JACK, ODESSA, SOFIA'S CHILDREN
(Emerge from house. There is a moment of hesitation. Then SOFIA is nearly smothered in hugs. MIZ MILLIE is forgotten as SOFIA is swept into the house.)

MIZ MILLIE
(Looks as if she feels left out. Then attempts to back the car out but doesn't know how to reverse it.)

INT. DAY   JACK AND ODESSA'S HOUSE
SOFIA AND FAMILY
(Excited reunion gradually dying as they become aware of the noise MIZ MILLIE is making trying to leave. Finally it is clear she is damaging the engine. SOFIA looks at her children wearily and longingly, and then she and JACK lead the way back outside.)

EXT. DAY   JACK AND ODESSA'S YARD
SOFIA
(Leans her head in the window and tries to show MIZ MILLIE how to reverse. But with so many colored people watching her, MIZ MILLIE is incapable of catching on. The engine dies.)

EXT. DAY   ON THE ROAD IN JACK'S TRUCK
(*SOFIA is seated between JACK and MIZ MILLIE. MIZ MILLIE'S car is being towed, behind.*)

EXT. DAY   ODESSA AND JACK'S YARD
(*ODESSA and SOFIA'S CHILDREN stand looking in the direction SOFIA went.*)

EXT. DAY   INTERIOR OF SHUG'S CAR
CELIE
(*Puzzled. Looking up at a large, beautiful house surrounded by flowers, and an aura of prosperity and peace. The sound of singing birds.*)
> This ain't it. Us must have
> took the wrong turn. This some
> white person's house.

SHUG
(*Glancing in the rearview mirror as another car, shiny, as nice as hers, pulls up behind them. She watches as a man and a very young woman dressed entirely in pink get out.*)
> That him?

CELIE
> You can tell by that little child he with.

EXT. DAY   FRONT PORCH
(*PA/ALPHONSO is seated in a large, fanback wooden chair. DAISY, chewing gum, is seated on arm of chair. She has her arm around his shoulder. ALPHONSO, smug.*)

DAISY
> He told me how he brought up two
> little girls that wasn't even his.
> I never really believe it until
> now.

SHUG
> Naw. He never told them 'bout
> they real daddy.
(*On the screen, as she says this, we see CELIE'S REAL FATHER firing a rifle from a window inside his house. There is desperation and determination in his look.*)

ALPHONSO
(*To CELIE.*)
> Your daddy never understood
> white folks . . .

(On the screen we see a huge, howling mob composed of Ku Klux Klansmen. They have torches and guns and they are firing into CELIE'S REAL FATHER'S house.)

> ... always had the fool notion that
> colored ways is best.

(CELIE'S REAL FATHER being dragged from his porch, fighting, kicking, butting with his head. Close-up of the Klansmen's gaudy regalia and a few far from spotless bedsheets. His hands are tied behind him and he is bloody from the blows delivered by rocks and gun stocks. Whenever he can, however, he stands tall. The men tie him to the rear of one of their horses by running the rope under his arms and around his chest. When the horse is struck, he is yanked to the ground and dragged off. CELIE'S MOTHER, at window of house, screaming, devastated. Two small children huddle fearfully in a corner. CELIE AND NETTIE.)

> But hell—

(Gesturing at his prosperity.)

> —when in Rome ...

CELIE

(Wanting to kill him.)

> Where my daddy buried at?

ALPHONSO

> Next to your mammy.

CELIE

> Got any marker?

ALPHONSO

(Idly fondling DAISY'S arm.)

> Lynched people don't git no
> marker.

EXT. DAY   OVERGROWN CEMETERY

CELIE AND SHUG

(Searching. Not finding. Weeds, bushes abound. CELIE suffering. SHUG puts her arms around her.)

SHUG

> Us each other's peoples now.

INT. DAY   FAMILY DINNER   JACK AND ODESSA'S HOUSE

(CELIE, ALBERT, ODESSA, JACK, SOFIA, HARPO, SQUEAK, THEIR DAUGHTER, SUZIE Q., also known as JOLENTHA, and SOFIA'S large children are finishing a super Southern meal. Everything from chitlins to sweet potato pie.)

SHUG
(*Pushing back her plate and lighting a cigarette.*)
Now is come the time to tell y'all.

HARPO
(*Looking around for the coffee.*)
Tell us what?

SHUG
Us leaving.
(*Beat.*)

ALBERT
(*Looks stricken.*)

CELIE
(*Face glued to her plate.*)

SQUEAK
(*Fiddles with the lace on JOLENTHA'S dress.*)

SOFIA
(*Looks awkward and out of place. The mark of her imprisonment still upon her.*)

SHUG
CELIE is coming with us.

ALBERT
Over my dead body.

SHUG
You satisfied that's what you
want?

ALBERT
(*To CELIE.*)

I thought you was finally
happy. What's wrong now?

CELIE
You a low-down dog is what's
wrong. It's time to leave you
and enter into The Creation.

And your dead body just the
welcome mat I need.

ALBERT

(Shocked.)

Say which?
(Everybody at the table is shocked.)

CELIE

You took my sister NETTIE away
from me and she was the only
somebody love me in the world.

ALBERT

(Sputtering.)

But But But . . .
(He looks from CELIE to SHUG and realizes SHUG knows the whole story.)

CELIE

But NETTIE and my children be home
soon. And when they is, all us
together gon whup your ass.

ALBERT

NETTIE and your children! You
talkin' crazy!

CELIE

(Proudly.)

I got children. Being brought up
in Africa. Good schools, lots
of fresh air and exercise.
Turning out a heap better than
the fools of yours you didn't
even try to raise.

HARPO

(Stung.)

Hold on.

CELIE

Oh, hold on hell. If you hadn't
tried to rule over SOFIA, the

white folks never would have
caught her.

HARPO

That's a lie.

SOFIA

A little truth in it.

CELIE

(Letting it all hang out.)

You was all rotten children. You
made my life a hell on earth. And
your daddy here ain't dead horse's
shit.

ALBERT

(Reaches across table to slap CELIE.)

CELIE

(Jabs her knife into his hand.)

ALBERT

(Sits down abruptly, holding his bleeding hand.)

You bitch. What will people say,
you running off to Memphis like
you don't have a house to look
after?

SHUG

ALBERT, try to think like you got
some sense. Why any woman give a
shit what people think is a mystery
to me.

GRADY

Well. A woman can't git a man
if peoples talk.

SHUG

*(Looks at CELIE. They start to giggle. Then laugh. Then SQUEAK laughs. Then
SOFIA. Even the children laugh.)*

Ain't they *somethin'*?

CELIE, SQUEAK, SOFIA
(A chorus of um-hums. Slaps on the table, etc.)

HARPO
(To SQUEAK.)
Shut up, SQUEAK. It's bad luck
for a woman to laugh at a man.

SQUEAK/MARY AGNES
(Tries to press her face straight.)

HARPO
(Glares at SOFIA.)

SOFIA
(Makes no effort to stop laughing.)
I already had my bad luck. I
had enough to keep me laughing
the rest of my life.

ALBERT
(Looking at CELIE.)
You not gittin' a penny of my
money.

CELIE
Did I ever ast you for money?
I never ast you for nothin', not
even for your sorry hand in
marriage.

SQUEAK
(Timidly, but flinging herself into the breach.)
I'm goin' too.

HARPO
What?!

SQUEAK
I want to sing.

HARPO
Sing! You got as much call to
sing as a rusty door hinge.

SQUEAK

(Lifting JOLENTHA into her lap.)
I ain't sung in public since
JOLENTHA was born.

HARPO

You ain't had to sing in public
since JOLENTHA was born. Everything
you need I done provided for.

SQUEAK

I need to sing.

HARPO

Listen, SQUEAK, you can't go to
Memphis, and that's all there is
to it.

SQUEAK

MARY AGNES.

HARPO

SQUEAK, MARY AGNES. What
difference it make?

SQUEAK

It make a lot. When I was
MARY AGNES I could sing in
public.

(Knock on door.)

ODESSA AND JACK

(Look at each other.)

JACK

Come in.

ELEANOR JANE, GROWN-UP DAUGHTER OF
MAYOR AND MIZ MILLIE

(Distraught. Sticks the upper part of her very thin body into the room. Sees they are at dinner.)
Oh, excuse me.
(Looks around for SOFIA.)

SOFIA, can I talk to you for a
minute?

EXT.   PORCH

ELEANOR JANE
(Begins explaining something to SOFIA. Starts to cry. SOFIA listens wearily.)

INT.   DINNER TABLE
(Subdued atmosphere. No one speaks.)

SOFIA'S CHILDREN
(Looks of anger, of being abandoned, of being second place.)

EXT. DAY   FOREST AND FIELDS

ALBERT
(Walking. He looks at the world around him as if seeing it for the first time. The result of bereavement and loneliness. He stops to touch a leaf. He pauses to watch harvester ants collecting food. He notices the intricacy of a flower petal. He notices colors. There is something in his face that not only questions this new feeling and awareness but is actually a little frightened by it. Luckily it's an involuntary process.)

ALBERT
(Arrives at the nearly completed new house of HARPO and SOFIA. Knocks.)

INT. DAY   HARPO AND SOFIA'S HOUSE

SOFIA
(Opens the door.)

In Africa, Miss Celie say they feed
'em yams but she don't like yams.

ALBERT
I brought her some peanuts. I
know she like them.

INT. DAY   JOLENTHA'S ROOM
(JOLENTHA is lying in bed, pale and sick. A victim of sickle-cell anemia. She looks up when ALBERT and SOFIA come in.)

ALBERT
(In a gentle, hearty voice that isn't his.)

Here. I brung you somethin'.

JOLENTHA

(Takes the bag, listlessly.)
> Thank you.

INT. DAY   HARPO AND SOFIA'S KITCHEN

SOFIA

(Pouring coffee.)
> Of course she miss her mama
> too. That would make anybody
> sick.

INT. DAY   ALBERT'S (AND CELIE'S) BEDROOM

ALBERT

(Drinking. Whiskey bottle on bedside table. He is emptying the dresser drawers of CELIE'S miserably few possessions—a broken comb, ratty brush, an old tarnished lipstick, a fake pearl necklace, with the string broken. The "pearls" scatter and bounce on the floor. He sweeps the top of the dresser with his hand. Cheap bottles, most of them empty [Evening in Paris, etc.], crash to the floor. Magazine cut-outs flutter onto the pile. He then turns his attention to the chifforobe where he pulls out an even more miserable bunch of clothes. Rags, dresses of improbable old-fashioned styles. A pair of button-up shoes that belonged to CELIE'S mother or to his dead first wife.

He then approaches a large bottom drawer. Hesitates. Then opens it slowly. On top of her quilt, CELIE has left her Bible. He picks it up. It falls open to an old picture of SHUG AVERY inscribed: "To Albert, the man I love, SHUG AVERY." He puts it aside and takes up, as if to fling it on the rubbish heap, CELIE'S quilt, but it falls open and the first word he reads on it is "help." There are only two other words written on it. "Dear God" appears in the very first square and there is a tiny black figure praying to a large white one with a halo around his head. Curious, he spreads the quilt out and begins to "read" the squares. There is the sickness and death of CELIE'S mother; the rape of CELIE by her stepfather; there is CELIE holding her babies; CELIE'S children being stolen from her. There is the beating of CELIE by ALBERT. CELIE carrying two buckets of water. Scrubbing. CELIE and NETTIE parting. SOFIA and HARPO marrying. Fighting. ALBERT speaking abusively to CELIE. The vicious face CELIE has given him is a surprise to ALBERT, for whom her feelings have never been real, or mattered: His hair seems to be burning. Flames are coming out of his mouth.

There is a square in which CELIE is holding the photo of SHUG AVERY. There is a square in which CELIE and SHUG AVERY kiss . . .

It is a life that ALBERT has not expected, and the art that depicts it, in CELIE'S humble quilt, acts on him forcefully. Stricken, he throws it on the rubbish pile after all. But as it falls, he notices it is unfinished. The blank ending intrigues him. He slumps to the floor beside the foot of the bed, sobering, contemplating it.)

EXT. DAY   ALBERT'S HOUSE

JOLENTHA

(She is carrying a covered plate of food. She knocks on ALBERT'S door. Listens. Enters.)

INT. DAY   ALBERT'S HOUSE

JOLENTHA

(She is a skinny nine years old. Saddened by the departure of her mother, MARY AGNES, and periodically zapped by sickle-cell seizures which will ultimately prove fatal. Now living with her father, HARPO, and SOFIA, whom she calls BIG MAMA. Hearing a noise, she goes to the doorway of ALBERT'S room. He is still sitting on the floor, studying CELIE'S quilt. She comes in and looks at it too. But from a distance.)

> BIG MAMA sent you somethin'
> to eat.

ALBERT

(Looks up at her and sees the bereft, fragile womanchild that he might have seen in CELIE, if he had let himself. It is the moment that heralds the reconstruction of his earliest self.)

INT. NIGHT   ALBERT'S BEDROOM

(Albert on the floor, under the quilt, dreaming, untouched plate beside him. CELIE'S voice: "You made my life a hell on earth." His own face as she saw it rises up before him. His hair ablaze. Flames coming from his mouth. On closer inspection, his face is disintegrating. Frightened, he wakes up.)

EXT. DAY   THE PATH TO ALBERT'S (AND CELIE'S) HOUSE

ALBERT AND JOLENTHA

(Walking from the mailbox. ALBERT hands her a letter.)

INT. NIGHT   ALBERT'S KITCHEN TABLE

ALBERT AND JOLENTHA

(JOLENTHA is putting NETTIE'S letter in envelope, addressing and stamping it. ALBERT attempting to cook flapjacks, sneaking in minute slivers of yam.)

INT. DAY   ALBERT'S BARN

ALBERT AND JOLENTHA

(Shucking corn. Their faces, as in previous scenes, are solemn. We should feel it is their solemnity and grief over being abandoned that draws them together. And that ALBERT is finally learning about women, from a child.)

EXT. DAY   SHUG'S HOUSE

(A large, two-story pink house with white columns surrounded by numerous statues

*of people and animals; a lovely lawn and an enormous fountain are especially notice-
able.)*

CELIE

*(CELIE, dressed in blouse and slacks and looking so good we hardly recognize her,
comes to the porch, takes a letter from the box, goes back inside.)*

INT. DAY   UPSTAIRS AT SHUG'S

*(An enormous room with a bandstand at one end occupied by a band: five or six mu-
sicians playing guitar, piano, trombone, saxophone, clarinet. Dressed in casual
clothes. Relaxed. Sleeves rolled up. Hair processed [some of them]. One especially
cute young one is playing a flute that he can't quite get to blend in. SHUG is singing.
Standing in front of a mike that is not turned on. She is comfortably dressed in a
blouse and pair of CELIE'S pants.)*

MARY AGNES

*(Is off to one side behind her own mike, mimicking SHUG. She and the flute player
are having identical problems. Her voice, like the flute, is too light, too neutral. Too
insubstantial. In fact, it sounds distressingly white. As she sings along with SHUG—
who, like Bessie Smith, doesn't even need a mike—her face gets redder and redder and
she seems more and more discouraged.)*

GRADY

*(Is the audience, looking first from MARY AGNES to SHUG and trying to gaze
with equal adoration at both. He is smoking an enormous reefer.)*

CELIE

*(Enters the room, waves the letter at SHUG and sits down next to GRADY in a
chair from which she first takes up her sewing: another pair of pants.)*

SHUG AND BAND

*(Playing and singing, a bluesy late thirties–early forties tune. SHUG stops singing.
Band stops playing. SHUG turns around. Looks at young flutist. Glances at MARY
AGNES. Back at flutist, who looks worried.)*

> Let's face it, sugar plum, the
> flute just ain't a colored
> instrument.

CELIE

(Sewing and SHUG forgotten, is reading NETTIE'S letter.)

> "All this season the road builders
> have been building a road that
> stretches from here to the coast . . ."

*(We see road builders leveling gigantic trees in a luxuriant primeval forest. They are
African men, some with tribal scarification marks, dressed mainly in tattered shorts.
A European man is overseer and leans against a truck. He is armed. The*

AFRICANS *are singing but their eyes are turned inward. AFRICAN WOMEN approach them periodically with water.)*

>   "Nearer and nearer came the road,
>   and some days almost every boy in
>   my class went out to see it . . ."

(Children running to watch road builders.)

>   "And now there are white men about
>   looking into our wells, tasting
>   our water and eating our food, but
>   saying nothing of why they are
>   here . . ."

(Two white men: One is a surveyor who is industriously surveying the village using a tripod. The other is sitting under a tree writing figures in a ledger. A gracious AFRICAN WOMAN very respectfully offers him a plate of food. He accepts it but neither smiles at nor thanks her. The WOMAN stands a moment looking at what he is writing, but can make no sense of it.)

EXT. DAY   SHUG'S HOUSE
SHUG

(SHUG is sitting on back steps picking over a large bunch of collards. Peas, tomatoes and okra are in little baskets around her. She is absorbed in preparing this fresh produce for dinner. Suddenly she hears the sound of a flute trying to sound bluesy but sounding jazzy instead. She listens. Frowns. Another effort. Another. The sound is coming from a back window.
SHUG sets down her greens, and goes inside.)

INT. DAY   DOWNSTAIRS HALLWAY OF SHUG'S HOUSE—DOOR TO HALL TOILET
(SHUG stops to listen outside door. More flute blues turning to jazz.)

INT. DAY   TOILET
(GERMAINE is sitting on the commode with his pants down, everything forgotten but his flute, which he is playing seriously. Groaning each time a light flightiness creeps into what should be a heavy-duty blues mood. There is an innate playfulness in his spirit that inevitably shows up in his music. It is beautiful, but because it isn't "blues" he is distressed.)

INT. DAY   SHUG'S KITCHEN
(SHUG and GERMAINE are preparing dinner. While she is busy at the stove, he chops onions and peppers. They are listening to soft jazz on the radio.)
SHUG

(Glances at him, noticing he is as absorbed preparing food as he is when making music. She's impressed. And inclined to flirt: he's so young, what harm can it do?)

>   You're cute.

GERMAINE

(Blushes . . . but comes back fairly strong.)
>>I don't let nobody call me cute but my mama.

(He stares intently at her.)

SHUG
>Oh-oh.

(She is flustered.)

GERMAINE

(Enjoying it.)
>My goodness.

EXT. DAY   DOWNTOWN MEMPHIS
(SHUG and CELIE emerge from a fashionable dry goods store, arms piled high with packages. GRADY sits in the car at the curb. They get in. He takes a drag on a medium-sized reefer and screeches off.)

INT. NIGHT   CELIE'S ROOM
(Everything is pale yellow. Curtains, bedspread, rug. There is a large vanity mirror that reflects CELIE herself dressed in yellow so that she looks like the dark center of a large, pale, brown-eyed Susan.
SHUG reclines on the bed watching CELIE'S delight as she tries on her new clothes.)

CELIE
>I never was the first one in my
>own clothes till now.

SHUG
>You deserve to be the first in more
>than clothes.

(Beat.)

>God knows you the first with me.

CELIE
>GRADY gon' wring our necks.

SHUG
>We have to git him off of
>MARY AGNES' first.

CELIE
(Grins. Looks at herself in the mirror.)

SHUG

    If MARY AGNES was a reefer she'd be
    smoked up by now.

INT. NIGHT   SHUG'S BEDROOM
(SHUG and CELIE are sleeping in SHUG's big round satin-covered bed. The phone
rings. CELIE fumblingly picks it up.)

CELIE

(Sleepily.)

    Say what?
    Who died?
    ALPHONSO?
    Belongst to me and NETTIE?
    Naw. Well, anything coming
    from him I don't want it.

SHUG

(Waking up. Listening. Nudges CELIE under the covers with her foot.)

CELIE

(Placing her hand over the mouthpiece.)
    ALPHONSO dead.

SHUG

    Who?

CELIE

    My stepdaddy. My real daddy left
    the house and all the land and a
    store—to me and NETTIE. He just
    didn't think to tell us 'bout it.

SHUG

    Well, I be damned, woman, you rich.

EXT. DAY   CEMETERY
(CELIE and SHUG stand looking at the immense tombstone that rises dramatically
over all the others. CELIE reads aloud:)
    ALPHONSO JOHNSON
    Loving Husband and Father . . .
    Outstanding businessman and
        Farmer
    Kind to the poor and Helpless . . .
    Look at all these flowers . . .

SHUG
(Yawning and stretching herself.
Beat.)

The son of a bitch still dead.

EXT. DAY   ALPHONSO'S HOUSE
(Clearly copied from a prosperous white person's house. Immense, super-Victorian, three stories, a showy anachronism. Turrets, porticoes, a modified Queen Anne. The only concession to his personal taste is that it is painted red, with white trim.)

INT. DAY   BACK PARLOR
DAISY
(Standing in front of the ornately tiled fireplace. Pregnant. A bit nervous but not particularly sad.)

That old house that your daddy
left was tore down so ALPHONSO
could build this one. He got
a white architect come all the
way from Atlanta. But this still
the house that go with the place,
right on.

(Shot of room stripped bare.)

Of course I did take the
furnishings 'cause ALPHONSO
bought them special for me.

INT.   FRONT PARLOR
CELIE
(Running her hand over the top of a bookcase.)
I can't believe it. Me and
NETTIE have us a house.
(Suddenly she begins running all through the house, and up the stairs. Opening doors and windows. SHUG following behind her smiling.)

INT. DAY   THE ATTIC
SHUG
(Takes some cedar sticks from her handbag and lights them. She hands one to CELIE and keeps the other.)

We're gonna smoke out all the evil
and make this house safe for good.

CELIE
Amen.
(They make their way down the stairs, pausing at every door, every nook and cranny of the house, letting the cleansing smoke permeate all.)

EXT. DAY   FRONT YARD
SHUG
(Is about to start her car. CELIE is outside. Her foot on the running board.)
I sure hate to leave you here by
yourself, baby girl.

CELIE
With all this fallin' in my lap,
don't look like I'm by myself.

SHUG
That's the truth. God know where
you live.
Still, I wouldn't go off like this
if I didn't have a gig to play.
You know I loves to be with you in
the good times just like the bad.

CELIE
I know it. You just go on. I'll
be home before you have a chance
to miss me good.
(She leans inside the car and embraces SHUG'S head.)
I love you.

SHUG
MISS CELIE, you sure know how to
send a woman off proud.
(SHUG drives off. Waves as she leaves the driveway. CELIE stands in front of her enormous new house.)

INT. NIGHT   NIGHT CLUB   MEMPHIS
(Lights are low, ambiance mellow. SHUG and GERMAINE are dancing close and sexily. MARY AGNES is singing—in all her glory. The squeaky "whiteness" of her voice somehow transformed into a vibrant new sound, more akin to Billie Holiday's than to Bessie Smith's or SHUG'S. The people in the audience like it. MARY AGNES, dressed glamorously, is enjoying her triumph, as GRADY, reefer ever present, looks on possessively.)

INT. DAY   CELIE'S HOUSE   FRONT PARLOR
(Now furnished. Comfortable. CELIE dressed for travel, stands a moment looking it over. Pictures of SHUG, an old picture of NETTIE, are on the mantel. Then she picks up her suitcase and opens the door.)

EXT. DAY   CELIE'S HOUSE   FRONT DOOR
(*CELIE locks the door. When she turns and walks down the steps, we see she has painted the house pale yellow. It looks—with its blooming bushes and shrubs—almost too pretty to leave. Nevertheless, she gets into her own car and drives off.*)

INT. AFTERNOON   SHUG'S BEDROOM
(*Clothing is strewn about: a man and a woman's. SHUG is lying in bed fast asleep. GERMAINE, beside her, is sitting up wide awake and playing a deeply melodic and peaceful number on his flute.*)

INT. NIGHT   CHINESE RESTAURANT
                    CELIE
(*Reaching for her fortune cookie.*)
                    I loves fortune cookies, they
                    so *cute*.
(*Reads hers.*)
                    Because you are who you are, the
                    future looks happy and bright.
(*Beams at SHUG.*)
                    I sure am glad to be back.

                    SHUG
(*Looking embarrassed. Reaches for her own fortune cookie and knocks over her water glass. As she mops up the water CELIE looks at her closely.*)

                    CELIE
                    What yours say?

                    SHUG
(*Not looking at hers.*)
                    It say I got the hots for a boy of nineteen.

                    CELIE
(*Looks at her quizzically. Then takes SHUG'S slip of paper and reads it aloud.*)
                    It say "A burnt finger remember
                    the fire."

                    SHUG
                    I'm trying to tell you.

                    CELIE
                    Trying to tell me what?

SHUG
Remember how I always said the
flute ain't colored?

CELIE
(*More puzzled still.*)

SHUG
Well, just my luck it's *real*
colored . . .

CELIE
You not making a bit of sense.

SHUG
I been sleepin' with GERMAINE.

CELIE
(*Unable to believe her ears. A great weight descends upon her.*)

SHUG
Well, you know. He young. He
so cute and sweet. He make me
think of my own children sometime,
to tell the truth. He love to
dance and make me laugh. Always
so full of fun, it was hard to
say no.

CELIE
Stop, you killin' me.

SHUG
Oh, MISS CELIE, I'm sorry! I just
been dyin' to tell somebody 'bout
this boy—an' you the somebody I
usually tell.

CELIE
Well, if words could kill, I'd be
in the ambulance.

INT. NIGHT   CELIE'S BEDROOM—SHUG'S HOUSE
(CELIE is brushing her short, unstraightened hair and gazing at herself in the mirror.)

SHUG
(Enters the room. Walks over to CELIE and kneels at her feet.)

He just a baby. How long can
it last?

CELIE

He a man.

SHUG

I know he is, and I know how you
feels about men. But baby
darlin', some mens can be a lots
of fun.

CELIE

Spare me.

SHUG

(Thoughtfully.)

'Course a woman'd have to be a fool
to take any of 'em seriously.
Just let me have my last fling,
CELIE. I'm too weak a woman to turn
it down. I promise I'll make it up
to you.
Just give me six months, CELIE, and
I'll try to make our life together
like it was.

CELIE

(In pain.)

SHUG

Do you love me, CELIE?

CELIE

I love you. But I can't stay
here.

SHUG

But you my friend. Don't leave
me, please. This boy is probably
going to hurt me worse than I'm
hurtin' you.

*(The sound of a car pulling up outside; a door slamming. Footsteps. The doorbell.
SHUG listens, squeezes CELIE'S arms, wipes her eyes, rises, checks herself in the
mirror—and leaves the room.)*

CELIE

*(Remains at the vanity as SHUG left her. Listens as front door closes, as footsteps go
to car, car doors slam, car starts. Drives off.)*

EXT. DAY   THE SOUTHWEST DESERT

*(Car is speeding along a dirt road in the spectacular Southwest desert. Cacti, moun-
tains. Endless sky.
SHUG and GERMAINE are in the car. GERMAINE driving.)*

SHUG

(Fondling GERMAINE'S neck, his hair.)
I ain't seen either one of my kids
since they was babies. This one
out here with the Indians is the
only one want to see me now.

GERMAINE

*(Turning into a desolate settlement on what we now see is an Indian reservation.
GERMAINE stops at a tiny adobe house. Ragged and hungry-looking Indian children
surround the car. A man, SHUG'S SON, comes out to greet them. Followed by his
wife and two children.)*

SHUG'S SON

(Shakes hands with them.)
You all come in.

INT. EVENING   DINING ROOM/KITCHEN

(The family is eating.)

SHUG'S SON

I always wondered what my mama looked
like. Oh, I used to see your picture
stuck up all along the road on trees
and on the sides of barns. But you
look different from what I thought.

SHUG

Look like MA and PA did a real good
job of raising you. How you like
living with Indians?

SON

I always felt like an Indian myself.

SHUG

Your grandmama's mama was Indian; but
the white folks told so many lies on
her peoples she was shame to admit it.
But the reason you feel it is 'cause
it's in you.

SON

(To GERMAINE.)

You a musician? What instrument do
you play?

GERMAINE

(Looks at SHUG.)

Flute.

SHUG

(Looks back at him and fluffs the back of her hair.)

EXT. DAY   DESERT

a) (Car speeding along through Monument Valley.)
b) (Car stopped. On a large, imposing rock SHUG and GERMAINE
   are finishing a picnic.)
c) (SHUG is stretched out with her chin in her hand gazing at the
   scenery. GERMAINE takes out his flute. Looks at her profile
   against all this and begins to play.)

INT. DAY   CHURCH
*(JOLENTHA'S funeral. A small white casket, half of it open, the other half covered
with flowers, is in front of the altar. JOLENTHA, flowers in her hair, is inside. A
slow line of mourners pass by. MARY AGNES and GRADY, looking very much a
couple, as MARY AGNES breaks down over the coffin and GRADY comforts her.
SOFIA and HARPO. And finally ALBERT, who hovers over the coffin too grief-
stricken to speak, which he tries to do. He pats JOLENTHA'S shoulder instead.*

On his way back to his seat he spots CELIE. She raises her fan and looks out the window.)

EXT. DUSK   CELIE'S FRONT PORCH
(CELIE is sitting on the steps of her house watching the sun go down.)

EXT. DUSK   WEST AFRICA: THE OLINKA VILLAGE
(The sun is also going down on the ruins of the Olinka village, wrecked by the road builders. It is deserted. There is a nearly inaudible whimper as of a small baby. There are bloated bodies of people and animals. Vultures sit on piles of rubbish and wheel about overhead.)

EXT. DUSK   CELIE'S FRONT PORCH
ALBERT
I brung you somethin'.
(He opens the package and shakes out CELIE'S quilt.)

CELIE
(Takes hold of it and studies it. Looks at the squares representing her and SHUG. Sighs.)
Thank you.
(Folds the quilt and places it beside her.)

ALBERT
(As if she doesn't know.)
You didn't finish it.

CELIE
I stop believin'.

ALBERT
You look real good since you went
up North.

CELIE
SHUG took good care of me.

ALBERT
How you make your livin' up there?

CELIE
(Gesturing at her pants.)
Sellin' pants.

ALBERT
I notice just about everybody 'round
here wearin' pants you made.

CELIE
Yeah. I sell 'em in my store.
But I really first start making 'em
when I was livin' in your house and
had to do somethin' with my hands
to keep from killin' you.

ALBERT
I'm real sorry 'bout NETTIE, CELIE.

CELIE
The letters stop coming, but I don't
believe she dead. I still feel her
as much as ever.

ALBERT
Well, nice talkin' to you, MISS CELIE.
I'll say good evenin'.
(He takes a beautiful small white shell from his pocket and places it on the railing.)

CELIE
Good evenin', ALBERT. Thank you.
(She remains on the steps. Gazing at the shell. It is shot through, and delicately edged, in purple.)

INT. DAY   DRY GOODS STORE

a) (A young white man waits on a young white couple, up front, both
   of whom are trying on and buying CELIE'S pants.)
b) (HARPO and SOFIA are waiting on a colored couple, in back,
   the mirror image of the white couple, doing exactly the same
   thing.)
c) (All four leave the store, wearing their new pants, looking comfortable and pleased with themselves—although, this being the South,
   they pretend not to notice each other.)

EXT. DAY   STREET OUTSIDE THE STORE
(A sign says "CELIE & NETTIE'S, folkspants a specialty.")

EXT. DAY   CELIE'S PORCH
(ALBERT is on hands and knees cutting out a new shirt pattern he's designed him-self. He is the picture of the artist as enthusiastic beginner. CELIE is steadily sewing and smoking. There is now a row of shells on the railing.)

EXT. DAY   CELIE'S PORCH
(Lots of shells.)

ALBERT
(Sewing, but thinking of something else.)
> CELIE, you don't like me 'cause I'm
> a man?

CELIE
(Looking at him earnestly.)
> Take off they clothes, and mens look
> like frogs to me. No matter how you
> kiss 'em, frogs is what they stay.

ALBERT
Us still man and wife, you know.

CELIE
Us never was.

ALBERT
I hate to see you by yourself.

CELIE
You here, ain't you?

ALBERT
Amen.

EXT. DAY   CELIE'S PORCH
(CELIE and ALBERT sewing.)

ALBERT
> What so special 'bout your pants,
> anyhow?

CELIE
> Anybody can wear 'em.

ALBERT

Men and women not suppose to wear
the same thing. Men suppose to
wear the pants.

CELIE

You ought to tell that to the mens
in Africa.

ALBERT

Say what?

CELIE

Folks in Africa be tryin' to beat
the heat. That's hard to do,
wearin' pants.

EXT. DAY   CELIE'S PORCH

CELIE

NETTIE say folks over in Africa
think white people black people's
children.

ALBERT

(Deep in his sewing. Looking at the rainbow of colored thread he's got.)
They do?

CELIE

Yeah, they say Adam wasn't the first
man, neither, just the first man that
was white. They name my boy ADAM
something else the minute he arrive.
Sound like OMATANGU. It mean the
first man that figured out that's what
he was. . . . They say nobody so crazy
they think they can say who was the
first man. 'Specially since the first
man was bound to be a woman.

ALBERT

(Laughs.)

Them Africans sure must have a heap
of time just to sit and think.

CELIE

NETTIE say they real good at thinkin'.
But they think so much in terms of
thousands of years they have a hard
time sometime gittin' themself through
one.

EXT. DAY   A NEW AFRICAN "HOMELAND," i.e. RESERVATION
(The OLINKA—women, children, men—and SAMUEL, NETTIE, ADAM and
OLIVIA are behind a fence that imprisons them on a stretch of dusty, barren land.
Guards, two white men with rifles and hip pistols and half a dozen black men with
truncheons. The PEOPLE are protesting vigorously and pressing against the fence,
NETTIE among them. The fence starts to give and in the panic the truncheons come
down indiscriminately. NETTIE is knocked, bleeding and unconscious, to the
ground.)

EXT. DUSK   CELIE'S PORCH
CELIE
(Holding SHUG and NETTIE'S photos in her lap. CELIE is sitting on the steps
watching the sunset.)

EXT. DAY   CELIE'S GARDEN
CELIE
(CELIE is hoeing among her plants, a wide straw hat protecting her head from the
sun. She does not see ALBERT until she stands straight and sways her back to rest it
from the hoe.)
            What's the matter?

ALBERT
(Holds out a telegram.)

CELIE
(Puts the hoe down. Takes the telegram.
We see: ". . . NETTIE JOHNSON . . . THE SHIP ARCADIA . . . SUNK BY
GERMAN MINES . . .")

CELIE
(Drops to the ground. ALBERT reads the telegram. Drops down beside her and takes
her in his arms.)

INT. NIGHT   CELIE'S BEDROOM—SECOND FLOOR
(CELIE is crying in her sleep. She wakes, gets up. Gets out her quilt. Begins to try to
design the final square. This does not bring relief. In a kind of trance, she goes to the
window, opens it, and throws the quilt out. It falls to the ground.)

EXT. NIGHT

ALBERT

(Sitting quietly on the porch below, unknown to CELIE, nodding, his unlit pipe in his hand. He is awakened by the sound of the quilt landing. He walks over and picks it up. Looks up at CELIE'S window.)

INT. DAY   CELIE'S HOUSE

CELIE

a) (Walks, sleepwalks, through her large beautiful house. Its emptiness mocking her.)
b) (In the yard looking at her flowers. They are beginning to wilt from lack of water. So what? She makes no move to save them.)
c) (On the porch she picks up a shell. It falls and breaks. Next to it she notices a rudely carved purple frog. She picks it up, nearly smiles. Sighs, instead.)
d) (In the front parlor lying on the sofa. Vacant.)
e) (Walking away from the house.)
f) (Lying face down in the furrow of a freshly plowed field.)
g) (In the cemetery. Walking among the graves.)
h) (Standing on the porch looking off down the road as she used to do when she was MISTER'S wife. But without expectation or hope.)

EXT. DAY   ROAD

CELIE'S POV (FROM STEPS)

(A car is coming.)

EXT. DAY   CELIE'S DRIVE

(The car stops. SHUG emerges.)

CELIE

(Doesn't change her expression. Arms at her side as if tied.)

SHUG

(Climbs the steps and embraces her.)

> I missed you more than I missed my
> own mama.

EXT. DAY   CELIE'S PORCH

(CELIE, ALBERT, SHUG sit in rocking chairs. SHUG is fanning herself, every once in a while. Totally back, at home, and relaxed. ALBERT is sewing on his shirt and CELIE is sewing on something entirely new—neither quilt nor pants—having reached, somehow, another level in her creativity.)

ALBERT
(Looking off down the road.)
Somebody comin'.

SHUG
Fast too.

CELIE
Probably HARPO.

ALBERT
Naw. Probably SOFIA. You know
she the one drive like a maniac.

EXT. DAY   DRIVE IN FRONT OF CELIE'S HOUSE
*(A large car stuffed with people and bundles, boxes and bags, stops and the people
and their possessions are slowly disgorged. SAMUEL, NETTIE, ADAM, TASHI
and OLIVIA stand still for a few moments looking about them. They look at the yard
and the fields. SHUG and ALBERT and CELIE'S cars. They then look up at the
house and begin a slow, stately ascent.)*

EXT. DAY   CELIE'S FRONT PORCH
CELIE
(Ashen.)

ALBERT
It's NETTIE.

CELIE
Naw.
(She tries to stand up. Almost falls.)

ALBERT
(Reaches over to help her up.)

SHUG
(Takes hold of her firmly, pulls her up and supports her on her feet.)

NETTIE
*(Her family falls behind her as she places her foot on the step. The sound of her foot-
step is like a heartbeat.)*

CELIE
(Feels it as a heartbeat.)

NETTIE
(A middle-aged woman, with a face that has seen horrible things and is still good and beautiful, walks up onto the porch and begins to lose her strength. She sways.)

CELIE
(NETTIE'S apparent weakness springs her into action. She totters toward her.)

CELIE
Nettie.

NETTIE
Celie.

CELIE AND NETTIE
(Trying to embrace without thinking to open their arms causes them to bump into each other with some force; they sink to their knees, their arms slowly coming into use. They hug. And kiss. And hug.)

NETTIE
(Finally looking up.)

These are our children, ADAM and OLIVIA. This is TASHI, our daughter-in-law. And this is my husband and your new brother, SAMUEL.

CELIE
(Looking up.)

And these my peoples, SHUG and ALBERT.

CELIE AND NETTIE
(Standing but not letting go of each other's waists. They begin to hug each other's peoples. Solemnly. Thoroughly. One by one.)

EXT. DAY   CELIE'S YARD   FOURTH OF JULY
(Half a hog is being barbequed under the trees. A table loaded with all kinds of food. Lemonade is everywhere. So are children and dogs.)
HARPO
(At table under trees shaving ice for the lemonade, which is in a large silver-colored milk can.)

CHILD
(To HARPO.)

Why us always have to have Fourth of July in July. It's so hot.

HARPO
Here. Suck on a piece of ice.
(Gives the child a sliver.)

GRADY
(Asleep under a tree.)

MARY AGNES AND SOFIA
(Cutting up potatoes for potato salad.)

MARY AGNES
(Looking towards GRADY.)
Us just friends. After while, being
with him, I couldn't think . . . smokin'
so much reefer.
How you and HARPO?

SOFIA
Well, it just a struggle, in general,
don't you think? But us doin'
alright.

ALBERT AND SHUG
(Are sitting in rocking chairs out under the trees, drinking lemonade.)

OLIVIA, ADAM AND TASHI
(Are walking through CELIE'S flower garden dressed in OLINKA robes as brilliant
as the garden.)

CELIE AND NETTIE
(On a bench under a grape arbor.)

CELIE
(Is holding a bundle.)

NETTIE
(Touching her face.)
I wrote to you because when I
didn't I felt like I was choking
on my own heart.
(Beat.)
I know you didn't get my letters
until it was almost too late

to do any good . . . but did you
ever write to me?

CELIE
I wrote to you all the time.
(She hands NETTIE the bundle.)
Here your letter.

NETTIE
(Opens the bundle. Takes out the quilt. "Reads" the squares. Gets to the last one, now completed. It is a large rising purple sun with yellow/orange rays, filling the square, filling Life. Coming up.)

ALICE WALKER AND QUINCY JONES ON THE SET OF
The Color Purple.

CONFLUENCE

AND

FLOW

> *Most womens can do a heap more to plea-*
> *sure themselves than a man can. If you*
> *don't believe me, ask one that don't give a*
> *damn what men think. Shug didn't give a*
> *damn. Many a time I heard her say—*
> *cause she was talking to me—I got more*
> *cock in my finger than you got in your*
> *pants.*

—ALBERT TALKING ABOUT SHUG*

After "auditioning" Steven Spielberg (his word) for the role of director, I set out to interview Quincy Jones. It was a long, thorough
interview during which I was moved by his sincerity, honesty, and
general largeheartedness. Unfortunately I did not record his responses, only my questions, some of which follow.

> Being around you seems to make people happier in an
> alert, receptive and playful way. This often happens
> with famous people and isn't usually lasting. With
> you, it doesn't seem your fame people respond to, but
> your personality. Have you ever remarked on your
> impact on people to yourself? Why do you think they
> respond to you as they do?

---

*A comment that appears neither in the novel nor the film, proving that characters
sometimes continue talking long after "the work" is done.

Who named you Q. Delightt (two ts) Jones? Do you think it was prophetic?

You make friends easily and appear to have many who love you. What is the meaning of friendship in your life? As a new friend over the past year, I've been amazed at your thoughtfulness, the ways you've tried to affirm our friendship, tried to let me know you are there. Are you this way with all your friends?

Noël Pointer's rendition of "Many Rains Ago" stirs something in me that is very deep and is reached by that music alone. I still can't believe you wrote this music. Did you, really? I just can't believe the intensity of my love for this music would lead me to its creator. (Because of course this music from the Roots Suite is why I wanted to work with you on Purple.) But—what were your feelings when you wrote it? Of whom, of what, were you thinking? But it's obvious, in the music itself, isn't it? What I felt was the incredible tenderness and longing between African-Americans as they remembered they have loved each other for centuries, through all kinds of barbarity and distance and time.

To me it is a music of healing. At first, every time I heard it I would cry. With grief and loss and longing. Then gradually I began to feel what was still left between us, as black people. Black women and men. So now when I play it I'm healed by the confidence that a lot of love is left.

Very often I hear and like your music without realizing it is yours. Does this happen to you a lot? Why is this? Do you often find such ignorance in the general listening audience?

Before I heard "Sister" I had moments of real concern that the song you came up with would be wonderful but dreadful. "Sister" seemed such a gift, so right. How did it happen?

You are rich, handsome, and famous! Is this very much better than being well enough off, handsome, and fairly well known? What are the perils of money that you've found? The perils of being good-looking? The perils of fame?

Peggy [Lipton, Jones' former wife] and you have said that after the operation to save your life from aneurysms in the brain you became a different person. What do you mean? Did you have an out-of-body experience before or after or during the operation? How did it change your view of death? Of life? Of work?

When things don't work out the way you've planned you often say: There's a train leaving every ten minutes. When did you learn this attitude?

To a comparatively slow-moving, country-loving person like me, your life seems quite fast paced, and in fact I've heard you say you have New York energy. Was there ever a time when you took to the hills and just let the natural world work on you for a while? Does the idea not attract you? Are you like Langston [Hughes], always longing for pavement?

Why was it so important that Steven direct *The Color Purple*? Why do you feel so strongly that he's the only one to do it? Since many people could do it, it would just be done very differently. And also, interestingly, he's the only one who has asked. If a woman directed it, for instance, I could imagine quite a beautiful film but made with fewer amenities, less mobility and cooperation "in the business" and less money.

I am impressed that you wanted to be involved as producer and with the music in this film because I've found many black men are threatened and offended by the story and by me personally. Why weren't you?

How does it feel to have so many daughters [six]? What has the experience taught you?

March 1984

Dear Quincy,

I hardly know what else to say about Shug Avery.
It is like trying to explain a poem. If you could,
you wouldn't have written the poem. However, one
thing occurred to me finally, and it is that size
is irrelevant, essentially; though when I think
of Shug she looks a lot like Bernice Reagon. Diana Ross could be Shug if she really wanted to. I
saw and loved her in *Lady Sings the Blues* and what
I loved was her love of Billie that was manifested
so clearly in her hard work. She would be a different Shug and it would be hard to see someone so
slight standing up to so much, but, slight folks
have done so.

Shug is a free person. This is her rarity. She
has decided to give herself and her love where
she pleases—she has understood that society,
not having been arranged for her benefit, is not
owed any of her loyalty. But this doesn't mean
she was born with this attitude or that she isn't
vulnerable. She is in fact, like the rest of us,
shaped by her experience. Her time of greatest
vulnerability would have been as a teenager,
dealing with a cold, critical mother and then
with Albert, a passionate but sexually irresponsible and cowardly lover. This period of
vulnerability continued into her sojourn in the
North (working as a domestic and then singing)
and culminated in her complete physical and emotional breakdown.

When Shug is brought home by Albert to be
nursed by Celie she is prepared for death. This
liberates her. Snatched out of the jaws of physical death by Celie, Shug's spirit changes entirely. She becomes free. In a sense it is her
lack of attachment (to things, men, money) that
causes them to become plentifully available to
her. Death is a lack of attachment. But Shug
lives, with this same lack, because she loves—

though, again, without attachment. It is only after running off with Germaine that she begins to feel her attachment to Celie and it is a surprise to her. She is free of everything except the ability and need to love.

I mentioned Diana Ross because I know you have been considering her (and to my mind she'd make a much better Squeak) but there are other women who would be absolutely right in terms of having, in a sense, "lived the role." Too bad Esther Phillips is dead. But Tina Turner isn't. I know *The Color Purple* must make her think of Ike. Or it could be someone unknown.

I hope this is useful, and that you still have the notes I sent you on all the characters some months ago. I have a copy if you need it.

Robert and I spent an idyllic four days at Wild Trees. We had a traditional Thanksgiving dinner of red beans and rice (with Louisiana sausage!) and turnip greens from the garden. And he cooked his classic Deep South & Dish sweet potato pie. Then we spent most of the day planting daffodils, my astrological flower—which, to my joy, I read in *Western Gardening* gophers don't eat! So I planted dozens of bulbs in gopher holes.

Rebecca spent the holidays in Georgia visiting relatives.

Now I've nursed the fire to life and will soon drive to Boonville in search of peach trees. The deer ate the one I had.

love,

alice

Apr. 26, 1985

Some notes on *The Color Purple* film for Quincy, Menno, and Steven from Alice:

To Quincy: As you know, in the book Celie doesn't sing. In the film, she does. As I read the script, she begins to hum as she's fixing breakfast, with a lot of love, for Shug. Shug overhears, likes it, embellishes and improvises on it, and returns it to Celie as a gift. It is their child, really, something they've created together; saved from being exploitive of Celie by Shug's public return of it to her. Now what would Celie hum? I think, since church music is all she would be really comfortable with and most of what she's heard, she'd hum church music. She'd hum the moan I sent you. Shug would take that moan, which is religious (because religiously, spiritually is also how Celie loves Shug, like God), and turn it into a secular song, a blues. And this is, in fact, the truth of the music.

Now, in the novel, since Shug creates "Miss Celie's Song," the song is about some man doin' her wrong, again. But Celie's reason for singing is different from Shug's. Since men don't really exist for her except as obstacles, she needn't sing about them. She hums because she's in love, she's filled with the Spirit: it's all come together for Celie— So what, I can hear you asking, would she sing? Well that's as far as I've thought. What do you think she'd sing?

To Menno and Steven: After a week of thinking about Menno's script, which remains so alive, there are only a couple of things in addition to my margin notes (and the language in places that Menno and I can straigthen out) I wish you would consider. It is really important to me that we get God out of the church and back into nature (which is still a kind of small way of thinking about it); but I suggest that Shug has a touch-

stone rock, a boulder, outside the church that she
has felt supported by since childhood. She could
touch it on the way in to see her father the first
time, hug it on the way out. At the end, she could
lead her father and the people there. I would hate
the last scene with Shug to be inside a church,
when you just know her rock of ages is of longer
and surer duration. Possible?

As much as I like Albert on his horse, to end
with him on his horse seems too John Wayne-ish,
and makes it seem he's more responsible and in
control of the happiness he's observing than he
is. It sets him apart, when by now he really
isn't, and in doing so, sets him above. The
feeling of the people is *circle*, not hierarchy.
A more moving scene for me is of the little
aged hands; though, you know, they're not *that*
old. Still, it would be great to have people
leave the theatre doing patty-cake with each
other. But basically, this is a reunited family, and no one would be off on his horse at
this thrilling time. Except John Wayne. And
need I say, us ain't he?

Love

Alice

December 9th, 1985

Dear Madelaine and Quincy,

How are you both? I know Quincy is in New
York, and New York is an answer in itself. Here
are the liner notes. It is Monday, the 9th, and
I still have not received what must be the de-
finitive sound track tape. However, my notes
cover most of the songs and . . . I hope you like
them. If not, I will keep them for my journal.

    Quincy, I've been listening to you sing! I
didn't know about this! What's Goin' on?

Much love, some jitters,

Alice

THE COLOR PURPLE
Liner Notes
by Alice Walker

"DIRTY DOZENS"

The first day on *The Color Purple* set I was very nervous, anticipating a
jookjoint that looked like a McDonald's and a cast that resembled I knew not
what. It was a great delight to see Margaret Avery, as Shug, in a gleaming red
dress and "hat like Indian chiefs" standing before a crowd of enthusiastic
"woofers" singing "Dirty Dozens." I could hardly believe it. The atmosphere—
of sweat, sex, moonshine guzzling and moochie dancing—was so real I felt
much too young to be there. But of course I stayed, as she sang along with the
incredibly *accurate* voice of Tata Vega, who is responsible for the raunchy, cul-
turally authentic vocals.

    Later at a recording studio I met Tata Vega, a small, round, friendly woman
who seemed capable of singing anything and whom someone in the studio referred to as "the woman of a thousand voices." "All of them sweet," I thought,
as she uncomplainingly went over what seemed to me perfectly sung lines again
and again and again in an effort to get them "just right."

    There is a kind of miracle contained in "Dirty Dozens." It is this: Legend has
it that in order to train ourselves not to be provoked (and therefore beaten or
killed) by our pathological overseers and masters during our enslavement in
America, we devised word "games" that contained extremely derogatory and
untrue information about ourselves and our relatives, particularly our fathers
and mothers. These we made into songs so that we could become inured to the
most gross insults any white person might make. It is true that the white person
frequently leaves us alone now and some of us are still calling each other
names, but that is not the point I am making here. No, the point here, and the

miracle, as well, is that as Shug sings what was once a terrible song, we are inclined not to feel depressed, or oppressed, but to smile at each other and to dance. So what if "Papa is our cousin" and "funny" besides, or "Mama do the lawdy-lawd"? They were fully creative and alive in their response to a system that sought to cripple them and so, through their inventiveness, are we.

"MISS CELIE'S BLUES"
"SISTER"

I will never forget the moment the phone rang and Quincy Jones announced on the other end that they (he, Rod Temperton, and Lionel Richie) "had it." Meaning the theme song, the all-important song Shug sings to Celie in the jookjoint. The song in which Shug's love for Celie is first expressed. "Oh no," I thought. "I'm not ready."

"How did you get it?" I asked, stalling.

"Oh, we just stayed up all night—and got it," said Quincy. "Want to hear it?"

"Do I have a choice?" I wondered.

"Here it is!" he said, laughing.

And over the phone came this wonderful, mellow, slightly crooked, slightly strutting tune. Then Quincy read the lyrics, and then put Rod and then Lionel on. They were warm, enthusiastic, happy—and exhausted. Lionel complaining that Quincy had got him up before dawn. It wasn't until a few days later—after Tata Vega recorded the lyrics and Quincy express-mailed me a cassette—that I understood fully why they all felt so pleased.

"Sister" is a beautiful song. So beautiful I was annoyed at first that brothers wrote it! What do they know about it? I'm so used to asking.

The humming that opens "Sister" is so—womanist. With its roots in the African eternity before we came here, in the slave coffle, in the white woman's kitchen, the white man's fields, the church, the jook. It is the essence of the pain and the transcendence. Then the opening lines

> "Sister, you've been on my mind
> Sister, we're two of a kind
> Sister, I'm keeping my eyes on you"

caused me to just stand there in my kitchen next to my box and shake my head (hands on hips, of course) and say "damn."

It is a song that all the people on the set—actors, crew, everybody—immediately loved as well, and it was a great joy to stroll about the studio lot and hear people of all kinds and colors singing and humming this song. In a part of the movie that was edited out of the finished version, there is a scene where Shug and Albert are about to make love (against her best intelligence) and Celie, knowing this, and listening on the other side of the bedroom wall, begins to hum "Sister." Shug hears her, "remembers her name," and leaves Albert high and dry.

I love to think of "Sister"—particularly the humming—becoming a modern code that we can use to signal each other to help us avoid unnecessary pain and danger. "MmmmMmm, MmmmMmm" could become the women's national anthem.

"DON'T MAKE ME NO NEVERMIND"
"Don't Make Me No Nevermind," which I always thought was called "It Was Late at Midnight"—because I used to hear it as a small child, when the rest of the lyrics meant nothing to me—is a classic "dawg" song. This man just wants to get "done." *Irregardless.* And yet the rawness of his insufficiently (one feels) examined feelings moves us. His unconstrained sexual expressiveness makes us laugh. If the singer were not, finally, such a great artist (marrying sincerity to content and style) this song would make us uncomfortable, as if we were privy to what should be a very private declaration of need. What is genuine, however, though not necessarily mirroring our own experience, nonetheless arouses appreciation; the pain, the lust, the confusion *and the humanity* are all naked in this song. Of its kind it is a gem. It is the real thing. When I listen to it I am reminded that one of the things I love most about black men is their outrageousness.

"KALIMBA (HIGH LIFE) WITH RAIN"
I remember one day on the set in North Carolina sitting next to Quincy (in our high—director's—chairs) watching his fingers as he tapped out a tune only he could hear, along the side of his chair. The next day he brought "Kalimba (High Life) with Rain." In the sticky heat of the Southern countryside (it was, in fact, July 4th) he passed cassette player and headset around so that I, friends from San Francisco who were visiting, and my sister, up from Georgia, could hear this melodic melding of nature (rain) and human beings (kalimba players) that celebrates, in a quiet but spirited way, the very origins of music, and the way the universe is, in all things, our first teacher.

"J. B. KING"
This song was created by black men in the South to help them cope with the brutality and boredom they endured while working on the road gangs and plantations of the white colonialists. Though the lyrics were generally unintelligible to the white overseer, the black men—who were not permitted to carry on conversations with each other ("You're here to work, not talk")—constantly changed the words of the songs so that they could relate news and give and receive personal messages. There is much bitterness concealed in the neutrally stated line "My old mistress promised me when Jesus died he set me free." Notice how clearly this man's face comes into focus even if you've never seen it. It is the "world face" of the enslaved indigenous male.

"HEAVEN BELONGS TO YOU"

Listening to the fervent "Heaven Belongs to You" I am reminded of the heaven I tried to envision as a child who heard much about that magical place at home and in church. It was always described as something "up yonder" or "over there." Something only death could bring. Many of our ancestors—especially those who were enslaved, with few if any joys on this plane—must have found comfort in this thought. Yet many of them, even in slavery, must have discovered that heaven is within. That when you "live right, talk right, and *pray right*," this "heaven," i.e., your own clearness of spirit, your own peace, "belongs to you." It is not, then, inconceivable that many of the ancestors—partly *because* of the adversity of their lives under a system that ground their physical bodies into the dust—realized depths of spirituality that those who enslaved them could only hopelessly envy.

"OH DEATH BE EASY" AND "OLD SHIP OF ZION"

You hear some of the ancestors' serenity in "Oh Death Be Easy" and "Old Ship of Zion." The ancestors *are* the old ship of Zion, and they have carried us *safely* to where we are today. (Not *perfectly*, *safely*.) They did this against every conceivable obstacle—humming their hums, moaning their moans and never losing sight of the indispensable foundation for human life that is the soul. "The soul *must* be preserved, whatever else is lost" would be a good motto for the ancestors, which explains why, in America, black people have sometimes lost so much. And yet, occasionally—if we're really lucky, and if we're open to it— we'll hear a phrase, a "yea, yea, yea," from a sister whose day is spent scrubbing floors on Wall Street and whose nights are often spent on her knees and we will wonder who, in America, is really rich. To whom "heaven" really belongs.

"KATU TOKA CORRINE"

"Katu Toka Corrine," written by Caiphus Semenya and sung by the movingly beautiful Letta Mbulu, is one of the most achingly haunting songs I've ever heard. A good-bye chant to the dead missionary and sister, Corrine, in *The Color Purple*, it manages to encompass the feeling of loss itself, so that, hearing it, the soul tends to ramble down the centuries to mourn many Corrines (or Samuels) and to join in this expression (so sincerely felt and expressed!) of love and farewell.

"MISS CELIE'S BLUES"

The sassy version of "Miss Celie's Blues," 1943, isn't as immediately appealing as the 1922 version. Dresses are shorter (Celie's in pants), hair straighter, hearts a bit more frivolous. World War II has had a liberating effect on American women, even black ones. But what we finally do hear in this version of the song—before Shug cuts it off and heads for the church—is *fun*. And women's right to have it. And to have it, if they like, with each other.

"MAYBE GOD'S TRYING TO TELL YOU SOMETHING"

In "Maybe God's Trying to Tell You Something" we come, in many ways, to the crux of the matter where religion is concerned. For we must ask who or what is this "God" who is trying to "tell us something." And who is the "Jesus" we are being advised to listen to? Is he someone or something completely outside ourselves? Or are "God" and "Jesus" essentially code names for the voice that speaks within us and finds its echo in the mysteriousness of the perceived and imperceivable universe? For someone brought up in the church as I was, and found it obstructionist rather than helpful in finding "God," labels of any kind attached to the inner voice and the outer spirit are distracting. And loaded with racist, classist, sexist, ideological baggage. For instance, the word "Lord" is so man-derived, so oppressively classist, that its effect is to stifle the urge to worship, rather than stimulate it.

But once again the magic of music strikes. For whatever the inner voice is called—God, Jesus, Lord, or Goddess—the voices in this song direct us to a feeling recognition of the inner voice itself, refusing to let us get stuck outside ourselves, struggling over and fussing with names.

Not only are we the world, we are the universe, the cosmos. There is no separation between us whatsoever. Therefore we have only to truly *listen* to hear ourselves speak.

"BURUNDI YODEL"

I don't know what these young girls are saying, but I feel good listening to it. I can hear my sisters and myself singing this song long ago in Africa, perhaps during a ring game. It makes me feel pleasantly old, ancient even, as if I've been born and died many times and they were singing when I came and singing when I went, and will be singing, too, when I return again.

"BODY AND SOUL"

I remember many discussions about music with Quincy Jones, who loves the music and the folk with equal passion. He asked me once what kind of jazz I particularly enjoyed. On names and songs and musicians my mind went blank. But "I love that bluesy, blowsy saxophone music that makes you want to bite somebody," I offered. He laughed and said "Coleman Hawkins."

It is gratifying to hear this music "glowing" underneath a scene in *The Color Purple* in which Celie is making her way in the world, Albert has lost his, and Harpo and Sofia have found theirs. Here freedom, loss, sadness and peace are shown to be entirely compatible and necessary notes in the same song.

THE FILMING OF THE COLOR PURPLE,
NOTEBOOK ENTRIES,* 1985–86

My ——— soul for-saken
Un-til ——— you come
My ——— head bowed low
in shame ———
But now ——— you ——— here
Don't go no ——— where ———
I b'lieve my life
be turnin' 'round.

This song begins in Celie's hum to Shug; Shug jazzes it up, names it "Miss Celie's Blues" but sings it to Albert (where its meaning still applies). *Then*, at the end, Albert "sings" this song to Celie (via jukebox). It applies to all three of them, and makes a circle of their love.

Journal Entry
May 1984
London

I am giving readings at the Lewisham Theatre, the Poetry Centre of London and The Africa Center. We are also trying to sell our first Wild Trees Press book to English publishers. Mid-week there is an urgent call from Steven, which takes two days to answer, given the transatlantic difference in time and the nasty hoarding of the single lobby telephone by our hostile receptionist. "Alice," he says, "how is it that Nettie knows Albert's name?" "Everyone knows his name," I reply. "Even Celie. She doesn't write it on her letters out of fear." "That's what I thought," he says. "But we were wishing you were here because some folks felt differently. Anyhow, we shot it that way."

•　　•　　•

*From a note to Quincy Jones re: the song that eventually became "Sister."

Two "Memorable Moments in Moviemaking":

The day, well into shooting in North Carolina, when Whoopi told me she'd never read the script.

The day Steven referred to *Gone with the Wind* as "the greatest movie ever made" and said his favorite character was Prissy.

June 5, 1985
Anxiety dream — night before filming began
Dreamed I was at a large hall filled with enthusiastic, mostly white, people who were waiting for me to speak. I was being introduced by a beaming white man who looked like the liberal version of Eatonton's (my hometown in Georgia, pop. 4,800) mayor — sans crew cut. I was getting more and more nervous and couldn't decide what to read when he finished, as he piled on more and more platitudes. Also felt I might be menstruating, bleeding through my pad. So while he introduced me, so lengthily, I left the crowded hall and went looking for a place to add reinforcement.

The only place I found was the small, cluttered, airless, closet-like room of a very black man, an African, sitting busily working (typing) at his desk. I ducked in, apologized for disturbing him, told him I thought I might be leaking and asked if I could add some tissue to my pad in his office. He said, "Sure." From somewhere I got orange-colored tissue and stuffed it into my panties. Lumpy but effective. I thanked him and picked up my books (which I'd put down on entering) and started back to the hall, still worried about what I would read. Looking at my books I saw several were missing, and that the African man had replaced them with some of his own, and they were battered, dusty and unread. They also had rather lugubrious titles. Knowing my audience was getting impatient, I hurried back and asked for my books. He was just sitting down from putting something on a high shelf in the closet. He said he hadn't seen my books. I looked about. No books. Frustrated, I left. This time when I looked down all my books were gone, replaced by his books. I put them down beside the corridor wall and walked on, heart sinking, down to the street and on to the hall. People were coming back out in small groups. One woman said: They're still waiting for you, because they remember how well you spoke when you were here before. But her expression showed disgust. I felt terrible. I had no books. Nothing to read. I was uncharacteristically terrified (usually before a reading I'm fairly calm). The thought flashed through my mind to ask someone in the audience to supply a book—another thought was just to tell them what had happened. In short, trust them. But this impulse died and instead I fell down the steps leading to the lecture hall, my heart beating wildly, terrified—but also feeling theatrical.

I woke up. Meditated. Decided that in real life if I have no book to read or if my story is stolen from me I'll just present myself. I'll share my fears and experience with my audience and trust them to help me/us out.

It helped to sing Marley's words:

"Guide and protect I and I, oh Jah Jah."

Now—on to Burbank and the filming of the jookjoint, which I secretly fear will look like a McDonald's.

After return from Burbank (and such an authentic jookjoint I felt much too young to be there):

I dreamed I was in a large house in a sizeable kitchen, like a cafeteria, and there were people, mostly black men, sitting about at tables. I was at the stove fixing a small blue bowl of food for myself. There appeared at the window a youngish black man (30s) dressed like a hobo but with great humor and spirit in his eyes. He motioned that he'd appreciate some food. I said, "Of course." I put my bowl down on the window. It was greens with wedge-cut tomatoes on top. Then I started washing a plate for him. He asked if he could have my bowl of food. I said "No, that's mine," and started to fill his plate. Some men, lounging by the

*window, looked like they didn't want the brother there. So I called out to
him loudly and asked if he liked greens. He said he did. I felt happy fork-
ing up the greens and sliding over the dish, also of hush puppies. I loved
feeding this man.*

June 1984
Monday
On the set in Burbank

Unlike last week, which was sweltering, today is cooling off to an
alarming degree. I want to go home. I'm feeling tired—and I've in-
vited the actors to dinner in a Chinese restaurant near the hotel.
Oprah Winfrey, Whoopi (and her mother), Rae Dawn Chong,
Margaret Avery, and Akosua Busia—or, in other words, and the
way I feel about them already: Sofia, Celie (and her lost mother),
Squeak, Shug and Nettie. They are wildly perfect in their roles and
I love them all at once. If only I'd brought my coat.

The experience on a set is strange; even the sunshine is make-
believe. And I don't understand the ways of film. Talking to Rod
Temperton made me realize this. He said "When you see the
'dailies' you don't see anything. Everything is constructed in the
editing." This pressed my cynical button. Why waste my tears—as
I did the other day—on the dailies if they're not necessarily what's
going to be seen? But then, my less tired self says: Whatever is constructed will be constructed *from* the dailies. So cheer up.

It would have been different if I'd invited Robert and he'd come.
He'd put his long warm arms around me now. He'd make the waiting time (of which there is lots) easier. For the first time I miss him.
I think of how he worked to make the time at home pleasant. Doing the wash and taking me to the hot tub. The wonderful massage.

Wild Trees
June 17, 1985

As I was coming down the hill from the studio just now it occurred to me that Sofia in the movie will work in Harpo's, not in Celie's, store. Also Harpo has been made into a "man" in the heavy-duty sense of owning something and lording over it. I don't mind this; it's just that Celie's industry is not made anything of. I think as the script stands now there's one scene of her and some women sewing on the porch. This change is obviously because men are in charge and they cannot apparently break the stereotype that the man provides and the woman is subsidiary. This is very different from the first version of the script, which followed the book more closely. The emphasis on the jookjoint reflects another way the music has been expanded.

I went back down on Monday. And asked Robert to come down on Tuesday. He was good enough to bring warm things for me and Rebecca and also some suggestions for the script I had given Menno and which he'd forgot to take.

When I'm on the set I'm so into communicating support to the actors and enjoying the characters coming to life that I'm sure a lot of things (changes in meaning, etc.) slip right by me. And I notice that the few things I suggested, other than language, have not appeared in this new script, which in my opinion falls apart ridiculously near the end where there are odds and ends of characters long cut but suddenly appearing.

I'm impressed by Steven's dedication to getting just the scene he wants—no matter how many times it must be shot. In the heat, the heavy oil-based smoke (for "atmosphere"), he seems perfectly relaxed and happy. Rebecca called to tell me Steven and Amy's baby was born while Celie was in labor. Another in the long line of oddities, synchronicities: the unexpected and near-miraculous telepathic rapport between Quincy and me—after all my fears of him as "the African man"; my sense that Steven was the "right" one to direct the movie almost as soon as I saw him (his eyes reveal that he has seen a good bit of the light); Oprah = Harpo, Margaret Avery,

Shug Avery; going to see Whoopi's show at just the right moment to suggest her for the role of Celie, etc. etc.

I feel the assistance of the universe on this movie; I am reassured by this when I see the changes wrought to the script.

So—Robert is in the city. Nancy Morejon (a poet from Cuba) was here for two days. We talked about Cuban movies, which I love; not just the finished product, but the process. She was incredulous when I told her there were actors and technicians on our film who didn't even know the story they were filming. In Cuba, there would have been long sessions of study and debate by everyone involved. Everyone would have to know the history of the period covered in the film and they would be encouraged to air opinions about its interpretation. On our film everything is done hurriedly, and if anyone asks a question there is a definite increase in the level of tension on the set. Actors are required to "trust" the director as if they are only paintbrushes with which he paints his canvas. This is the way films are made, for the most part, in America. I think it has to be damaging, ultimately, to everyone involved. And the films are so often terrible.

San Francisco
June 24, 1985
Another anxiety dream: There was rioting, perhaps on a campus, with lots of noise and gaseous (yellowish) bombs going off to dispel the crowds, mainly students. I was with someone, a man, I think, and we ducked into a crowded subway car to be safe. The car was filled with Third World people. Lots of women and children, Latin looking or Asian. I was looking out the window at the rioting when I blacked out. When I woke, my companion was gone. I too left the car, as the rioting appeared to be over. At some point as I moved along I became aware that the clothes I was wearing did not belong to me. Only my old raspberry tee shirt and underwear belonged to me. The rest (black lace-up oxfords, too large; a blue work shirt, very stiff; and odd, washed-out

jeans) belonged to someone else. Also credit cards and driver's license were missing. However, in my little woven leather purse I still had $150. I had been mugged (?), robbed of my possessions while I slept and was now wearing ill-fitting replacements. I hadn't the faintest idea how to find my stuff. But I told what had happened to me to several people including Quincy. I was very disturbed. He and the others listened but seemed unable to help. Later in the dream I was in a large museum-like room full of boxes and crates. I seemed to be trying to live there. Or perhaps I was there temporarily looking for my stuff. I hope so, since I hate museums and think of them as art zoos.

August 16, 1985
On location in North Carolina
The 58th day of shooting

Robert and I arrived here in #157 at the Holiday Inn in Monroe two nights ago. It is our third visit to the Southern set. The air conditioner is noisy, so is the highway, so are the cars in the parking lot, coming and going. It is hot and muggy. Food terrible. The good news is that the film is going well. That is to say the performances have been excellent and both the acting and directing has often seemed to me inspired: everyone—actors, technicians, extras, stray townspeople and relatives of local extras, Steven—seems to be reading the book. I sign innumerable copies and get to hold almost as many babies, including tiny Max Spielberg, whom I seem to already know from some age before. Also Desreta Jackson's (young Celie's) little sister Cassie, an extra in the movie who starts crying at the parting scene between Celie and Nettie and can't stop. I cuddle her until she goes to sleep, and when the scene changes we are lifted chair and all by Robert and "Harpo" (Willard Pugh) to the new location. Rebecca (a production assistant) is convinced that Steven doesn't listen to me—and we talk *very* little (I feel there is mutual good feeling and respect, but also a mutual uneasiness)—and I agree with her. He doesn't listen to anyone. But suddenly, days later, you notice he's changed the thing that bothered you or he's managed to put your idea somewhere in the scene—with Menno's help, of course. It might not look exactly like your suggestion anymore but there's still enough of it to recognize. The end of the movie—which we saw last night—is really the cinematic expression of the alternate title of my script, "Watch for Me in the Sunset." Menno and Quincy tell me Steven is afraid of me, which I don't understand at all—except, perhaps if I were filming *his* book I'd be afraid I wasn't doing it right. Fear is such a crippling emotion; it effectively destroys freedom of expression between people. Every exchange between us is strained.

Whoopi is *incredible* as Celie; and Margaret, whom nobody seems to really like for the role, is wonderful, I think, as *a* Shug. And is, in many ways, the most vulnerable and brave of the actors, since she is aware that there are those who thought Tina Turner more appropriate. Not me. Margaret has an immense sweetness (which is, after all, how Shug got her name) and an innate, frustrated dignity. And she tries so hard and unfailingly to do the scenes right. I like the vulnerability that's in her eyes. She has beautiful eyes; it's what you notice first and last. And in the scenes where nothing else could hold you, her eyes do. They're real eyes that show experience as plainly as her face does—not marbles that show nothing no matter what they've seen.

Anyway, after dailies she came up and kissed me and wanted to talk about a movie premiere benefit in L.A. for a black community organization called Kwanza.

My daughter amazes me with her beauty and competence. Everyone congratulates me. It is the purest joy to hear her loud, ringing voice piercing the set (over hill and pond): "Rolling!" "That's a cut!" "Hold that vehicle!" etc. And to see her striding in her yellow Reeboks, dreadlocks flying, with bullhorn (which she rarely needs to use—her natural voice is louder, I tease her) and walkie-talkie on her hip. I like her tallness, her directness, her characteristic cheerful and no-shit attitude. I know she would not like to get along without me, but she could. She is already herself.

Not only is Danny Glover a great actor, he's a healer. Watching him play Mister (based on my extremely misogynistic grandfather, whom I nonetheless adored—which infuriated me) completely reconciled me to my love for him. My grandfather taught me one of the best things I know: you don't have to be perfect to be loved. I watch Danny portraying my grandfather at his worst times and I understand anew that the creation of art is truly a prayer for the souls of those we love, the "good word" before the throne of God. If I love you, Grandfather, surely that means the Universe does too.

San Francisco
September 7, 1985; 6:45 A.M.
Deep insomnia. Pre-period, I suppose. But an interesting dream, before I woke up. I was more or less driving a large black plastic (in the sense of very flexible, like a cartoon) car very fast on a somewhat crowded free-way—the car was full of people, all kinds and colors, and I was zipping in and out of traffic like a pro, and as if I could actually see where I was going, which I could not. Fortunately I realized what the chances were of not having an accident and careened off to the side of the road where I knew I would either switch drivers or conjure up a smaller, less plastic and speedy car.

Perhaps this reflects my feelings about the film, now that it's done—the shooting, that is. My recent, and last, trip to the set, Africa, U.S.A., was very strange. I hadn't planned to go at all. In fact, I'd just bought and planted hordes of petunias, a kind of flowering sage and three wonderful purple butterfly bushes to celebrate being home for good after North Carolina. Then—because I had an appointment—I went down to the city. At some point Quincy's secretary, Madeline, called to tell me I would be receiving some of the music for the film shortly. Since I am to write the liner notes. While we were talking Quincy arrived in his office and came to the phone and we started talking about the African music, and I realized I should be there when it was played, especially since he has hired the best kalimba player in the world to play. Then I remembered Steven had asked that I be present when Akosua (Nettie) did her voice-overs: they call this process "looping," for some reason. And there was also my daughter down there, working hard and no doubt needing a hug.

So off I went.

Of all the scenes I've seen shot I'm least happy with the African ones. The location of the village is wrong, the scarification ceremony is wrong (not to mention how every person's scar has a different design, whereas if they're from the same tribe the scar would be the same) and there's no way you could have a rubber plantation on this dry, barren land. So anyway I arrived on the set and almost immediately got into an intense, sad conversation with an expatriate Liberian physician who is one of the extras. (One good thing is there are *lots* of Africans in this movie—in fact, when Nettie returns to Celie, Carl Anderson [Samuel] is the only non-African in the bunch. Susan [Tashi] is from Kenya, Akosua [Nettie] is from Ghana, Adam and Olivia are from Zambia.) Anyway, this man, beautifully dressed in rather Nigerian-looking robes, sat beside me on the hot dry grass and told me, among other things, that Firestone Rubber owns 168,000 acres of rubber plantations in Liberia, for which they paid a penny an acre, in perpetuity.

He talked about the lack of health care among the workers. The high incidence of blindness because of the fumes given off when ammonia is added to the latex to change its character. He talked of having devised an eyewash solution and of teaching the workers how to use it. He was very sad. He spoke without emotion and almost as if drugged, as he told me about the coup in Liberia in which five of his friends, cabinet ministers, were killed.

I asked about the African-American settlers who'd "returned" to Africa after the Civil War. He said there was little distinctive trace of them. That though they had been mostly, how do you say, "high yellow," they were by now quite dark. It was an amusing thought: the people who "returned" to Africa for the most part had never been.

I hung out a lot with the mothers and the children, my natural allies. I'm so impressed by the motherlove and pride. They come and stand for hours as their children go through scenes. (On the Southern set, fathers and sometimes grandfathers came too.) I was especially moved by everyone's response to the sudden cold weather, for which no one was dressed—this being sunny, hot "Africa" and all. Between takes the mothers, shivering themselves, rushed up and laid their own light sweaters and jackets across their children's shoulders. Whenever they could, they'd point out their children to me and tell me how happy they were that their children were in the movie. One little boy, the most cold-looking and most stoic, came up to tell me quite seriously, that he'd read the book and thought it very good. He looked about six. In fact, I worried that the children would have negative thoughts plus nightmares from the scarification ceremony scene. But just as I was at my most worried one of the "African Elders" in a lovely Sierra Leonian robe and Cameroonian hat came up and gave me a book called *The Peoples of Kenya.* I opened it almost instantly to a page describing female "circumcision," i.e., sexual torture and mutilation. The author, Joy Adamson, tells of having witnessed such a mutilation ("circumcision") done by a group of women to a small 12 year old girl. The child was held down by several women, on the ground, in the cold, while the "surgeon" rubbed her genitals with dried chicken dung, "washed" her dull knife in "greenish, filthy" water, and proceeded to cut off the child's clitoris, after which the child was forced to jump up and down three times to see how much or whether she'd bleed. If not, the "surgeon" got a goat, as payment for her "services." If so, only eggs. Ms. Adamson kept her eye on the child, last seen slumped exhausted and stunned on the ground, and on the severed clitoris. This she noticed was placed between the toes of another woman whose task it was to kick it away, out into the bush.

I flipped back to the front of the book, hoping this event had taken place centuries ago. Alas, the book was published in 1968. The rationale for cliteridectomy: no man would marry a woman whose clitoris was intact. A woman without sex drive is, I suppose, thought to be more docile—more of the stuff of which wives are made. I turn page after page; every woman's face—violated and hurt—breaks my heart.

I thought of the Kenyan exiles I met in London and about the atrocities committed by so many African leaders against their people. These atrocities have their foundation, I believe, in the "cultural" and "traditional" atrocities inflicted on women and children, and particularly on children who are women.

When the movie opens, will black critics be open to the centuries of pain borne by our children, or will they be more concerned that acknowledgment of how we have caused our children to suffer necessarily means a re-visioning of how we perceive ourselves? Reflected in the children's tears will they notice, not that the children are crying, but only that their own image is "distorted"?

I want to grab and imprison these women who are abusing this child; I don't care how black they are, whose "culture" it is, or what anyone else thinks about it whatsoever. I also want to hold them, collectively and individually, and weep with them over the little hurt child within themselves. The betrayed child in all of us. How much of ourselves we forget, when we forget our pain.

San Francisco
December 6, 1985
I'm being besieged by reporters—*L.A. Times, N.Y. Times, The Chronicle*, etc.—who want to interview me about the film, which I have by now seen. I've managed to cancel or avoid most of them. Now the publicist at Pocket Books wants a statement to hand out. One basic way I feel about the film—after one viewing—is terrible. It looks slick, sanitized and apolitical to me. Some of the words coming out of Shug and Celie's mouths are ludicrous. The film looks like a cartoon. There are anachronisms: Would Shug's father be driving a horse and buggy in the '30s? for instance. In short, on

first viewing, I noticed only the flaws. Plus, I went into mourning for the characters who appeared to much better advantage in dailies than in the finished movie. How frustrating for the actors! In the movie they seem miniaturized, when not actually chopped to bits. Samuel almost doesn't appear (gone, that wonderful scene of he and Corrine with the baby!). Harpo lacks fullness—the fullness I *saw* in dailies. Oprah is *wonderful* as Sofia—but too aged after her jail scene, regardless of how hard a time she had. And who straightened her hair? The big house, once you see the columns—which I lobbied against—is just that. Everyone is too well dressed—which is ironic, since my initial struggle with the set and costume designers was to prove that these particular black landowners did not dress in rags and could afford wallpaper. And the distortion, at times, of the folk speech!

These are all my negative thoughts. I sat there tense as a bow and my head has been aching ever since.

The things I like: not the *Oliver Twist* or the carved heart in the tree, which are so cutesy and tired as to be alienating, but the parting scene between Celie and Nettie, and the scene where Nettie defends herself against Mister. Nettie, in fact, is quite wonderful, and looks so much like my grandmother (when young) it makes me wonder. The kissing scene between Celie and Shug. The whole section where Shug and Celie find the letters and begin to read them. Especially the scene where Celie smells the dried flower petal. Shug in the jookjoint, first song. Second song sounds strained and too small for Shug's body, so the effect is a distancing from the emotions of Celie and Shug. The scenes in the church are all fine, although the last one is hokey and I resent the imposition of Shug's father between her and "God." The music is wonderful. Although Nettie in Africa is teaching reading and writing, not music.

The ending is moving. But I wanted Mister up on the porch too! And a hug in our culture has always seemed more soulful than a kiss.

The BBC was just here for two days. The director, a white male named Nigel (after I had agreed to a documentary because of a black woman named Samira, who I thought would direct), told the story of two reclusive artists he'd filmed and how horrified they were at the results. They said, when they saw what he'd done: "Well, I suppose it turned out as well as it could have done." That is how I feel. But I feel disappointed too that it didn't turn out better.

But it didn't turn out better because . . . ? I *saw* how hard everyone worked. How earnestly they tried to do it right. I helped as much as I could. All this week I've wanted to weep. I fear I have failed the ancestors. But no. I did my best and the ancestors themselves are far from perfect. We try everything in an effort to express ourselves. They did this. *I* do this. I do so hope it's true that there are no mistakes, only lessons. This one could be big.

Wild Trees
Mendocino County
Jan. 22, 1986

This notebook certainly reveals the chaos of the last year. This one will be somewhat calmer and orderly, I trust. A lot has happened; in my stars and elsewhere. Just before Christmas I went shopping for presents at Woman Crafts West, a store owned by a beautiful, gray-haired, young-faced black sister named Pell. I bought lots of lovely women-made things, and then, just before leaving the store, I caught sight of the real reason I was shopping there. On a shelf, down low, behind the glass, there was something I knew instantly I had to have—a magic wand! It is over a foot long with a handle made of black walnut and with almost a two-inch crystal on the end. I bought it with great joy and recognition. Then I felt ready to see the film a second time at the premiere in New York, for which Robert looked (and was) spectacular! Dressed in a tux that only a laid-back Mendocino philosopher and lover would wear, with a cummerbund *and* headband and a silk fish as his bow tie. Well. I was myself resplendent in a black silk dress covered with sequins and gold leaves. A sister named Deborah Matthews, who does it for love and a living, dressed me. It was wonderful. I felt very Shuggish and quite protected by the wand.

There were all kinds of people there: everyone from the movie, my sister Ruth and cousin Betty, a *lot* of black women writers— yeah! Toni Morrison and Toni Cade Bambara, Sonia Sanchez; there were Ruby Dee and Ossie Davis and Bill Cosby and Camille—and best of absolute all, my friend Carole Darden from Sarah Lawrence, who once cracked her family's safe to save my life. Looking lovely, smelling sweet. Big smiles. I was so happy she was with us and that we could send her home in the limo. Which again tickled me. They are like prehistoric cars and in New York you truly feel you are lumbering along on the road to extinction.

I *loved* the film. So did Ruth, who had also had deep reservations about it. I was finally able to see *it*, and to let go of the scenes that were *not* there. It is far more conventional than the novel, especially in terms of religion vs. spirituality and Shug and Celie's relationship, and even Celie and Mister's relationship and Harpo and Sofia's too, but I still felt a lot of the soul of the people—and that was lovely. It is just the opposite of reading a book—I mean, seeing a movie with lots of people (I saw it the first time with just Robert and our friend Belvie, in an otherwise empty theatre), which helped tremendously. Reading a book is a solitary pleasure. You don't want someone guffawing in your ear. But watching a movie is better with lots of people—unless of course it's a dreadful, embarrassing film. Which I'm happy to say "Purple" is not. Thank the Universe.

I think my magic wand helped and afterward Gloria [Steinem] and Mort [Zuckerman] came up and we hugged and she was very happy for me. I felt so much for her. For of everyone she's been the most supportive, a real champion of me and "Purple." She said, knowing how worried I'd been: "You don't have to worry anymore. It's beautiful." Quincy had been saying this all along, of course, but somehow it wasn't *quite* the same. Yet I do trust both of them because of what I feel is a deep, abiding, *innate* decency. And both of them are models of love.

Robert, Rebecca, Carole and I got to sit with the Reading Is Fundamental folks (for whom the screening was a benefit), which was a bit of a struggle. Long involved questions over the table that I declined to answer. My greatest joy was that I sincerely loved the film. It had bothered me greatly that I would have to say publicly that I thought it was terrible. I had lost sleep trying to think of new and painless ways of phrasing it on the *Good Morning America* show—which, incidentally, I'd never seen. It went well, I thought, next day, and I talked about Mama and how excited she was thinking of the premiere in Eatonton in a month, and how, bedridden though she is, she wants to come see the movie in a gown and slippers with heels.

WHAT IS
THROWN
OUT OF
THE RIVER

Journal Entries
January 26, 1984

The new year has begun. Today is sunny, bright. Gorgeous in the best SF style. I've had many happy days already, but several not so happy ones. I still feel betrayed by David Bradley's article in the *Times* ("Novelist Alice Walker: Telling the Black Woman's Story," *The New York Times Magazine* cover story, January 8, 1984). For such a well-done piece I hope he was paid 30 pieces of gold. I thought I was over any real pain regarding my eye, but apparently not. Just when I felt comfortable discussing its blindness, he writes in the *Times* that it is artificial. And implies that this (and the way it happened: my brother shooting me with a pellet gun when we were children) accounts for my "distorted" vision, vis-à-vis black men. I see falsely because I have a false eye. The rest of the piece is as dishonest. None of the discussion of my "politics," which was the Trojan horse that got him inside my door for the interview. Of my essays he made hash. Of *Meridian*. His curious response to the fact that I often like old men is to get "very, very angry." He seems to think this means I dislike younger ones. Old men sometimes have a sweetness that goes right to my heart. Why should this bother anyone?

He casually accuses me of trying to suppress the work of another black woman writer. No name, no circumstance, no nothing. Just the bald assertion. He also claims we'd met before and even had lunch. I have zero memory of this. He says I flirt.

But I've received many wonderful letters of condolence (for the article) and support. Everyone, except for one or two people I don't trust anyway, seems to have seen through it. Mary Helen [Washington] says someone said they put the wrong picture on the cover. It should have been Bradley, since the piece was about him.

January 26, 1984

So. Down from that. (Bradley's article; the reduction of my work to the level of an unresolved grievance; the dehumanization of having my disability erroneously described and not honored for its gifts: one of which has been that I more readily see the suffering of others.) And my mother's third or fourth stroke. She rambles hurtfully at times about O.C.'s lesbianism. (O.C. is the highly competent, loving and skilled niece I hired to look after her at home; someone my mother always loved.) Ruth says she called her a "hermaphrodite" and said she shouldn't be around "normal" people. This is as amusing as it is sad: if she is around some of my family she isn't around "normal" people. What with the wife-beaters and child-molesters, the gun-toters, and, lately, the drug-afflicted. And do "normal" people exist? What would be normal to my mother, now that she's fallen into the clutches of the Jehovah's Witnesses? It is O.C. who fights tirelessly against the tide of grease that has traditionally covered much of what my mother, and family, eat, leading to arteries, in her case, that were like candle wax.

January 26, 1994 (Ten years later.)
Paying Attention to What Is Thrown Out of the River:
Often It's Heart

One of the most painful things for me to accept has been my
mother's fundamentalist Christian prejudice against many of the
people and things I love. She was devoutly religious all her life, and
assumed, I think, that she learned her best qualities from the Bible
and from church. I disagree with that assumption. I believe she,
like people everywhere, was born good, and that Nature, which she
loved, supported this goodness; I believe her religions (she was a
Methodist most of her life; then a Jehovah's Witness) indoctri-
nated her negatively, where her lack of knowledge about other
people, other ways, was concerned. This is the shadow side of her I
can face even now only by calling on the most loving but determined spiritual force. I am enchanted always by her magnificence,
her largeness of spirit: I find it hard to add to this reality, tack on, as
it were, the areas in which she was small.

I wanted to sit down with my mother when I heard about the
hurtful comments she had made, so unworthy of her, and take her
once work-callused, now illness-smoothed hands in mine. I wanted
to say to her: Mama, I love lesbians. Lesbians are some of the best
people I have ever known. You also like them. I wanted to remind
her that when she came to visit me in California, the goat keeping,
garden tending friends of mine with whom she immediately felt
comfortable, and whom she raved about for months, were lesbian.
Muriel Rukeyser, the woman who helped start me in my writing career, is now thought to have been bisexual, though she never felt free
to tell me so. Langston Hughes, to whom Muriel sent me, and who
published my first short story and fathered my spirit my first years
away from home, is now thought to have been gay. Certainly James
Baldwin, who brothered me, was. Many of the women I have loved,
and who have loved me, are lesbian. Mama, I wanted to say, though
I have been in relationships with men since I was sixteen, and this is
how you've known me, the part of me that I most respect is woman-
loving. Or as I prefer to call it, "womanist." How could this not be so,

since you are the person I've most respected and loved in life? If she had been well, I would have spoken to her in just this way; and if I were speaking to her in person, not over the phone, which she was unable to hold to her ear. I did not want her to miss the love between women in *The Color Purple*. And so I lobbied for a kiss. I refused to believe intolerance for anyone was my mother's true nature. (In the movie almost all the women kiss each other, making the kiss between Celie and Shug less significant.)

Reading this entry after her death, missing her and loving her as much as ever, I was reminded of her words on meeting the Jewish law student who would become my husband. Screwing up her face in a concentrated mental attempt to locate some familiar place from whence he might have come, and expressing her compassion at the same time that she discovered that place, she said, even smiling a little: "You're one of the ones that killed Christ," and took his hand. To my mother my husband came directly from the Bible. It is an understatement to say I hardly knew where to begin, explaining to her what she'd done.

Left to herself, my mother might have said something equally cutting to this young white man who had the nerve to court her black daughter, for she was born under the sign of Sagittarius and was rarely known to hold, or even to temper, her tongue. She was forced to be respectful all her life to white men she despised (except for the few times she simply exploded in rage and could not stop herself). But she had also, as a good Christian, struggled to forgive white men their many sins, the consequences of which she suffered daily, and this effectively silenced her. She had never met a Jew before. Her reference to my future husband's Jewishness, so harmful, so hurtful, so uninformed it cast a shadow over her relationship with him, was from the Bible-interpreting minister of her church. Over the years of our marriage, my husband's practice of his personal religion, kindness, won my mother's loyalty; she considered him one of the most loving and honorable people she'd ever known. "A little like Jesus," she would say. To which I'd respond: "Same tribe."

My mother had not only never met a Jew, she had never seen a white man "pay attention" to black children. That my husband related naturally and lovingly to black children never ceased to astonish her. He was as much a marvel and mystery to her, because of this behavior, as my computer remains to me, doing the magical things it does with such apparent ease. I loved watching this beautiful woman blossom beyond her expectations and prejudices about all white men and Jews. Years later, however, growth would be required on another front. In my absence, another interpreter of "God's Word" would show her a demon where a niece she loved had been.

Nor was my mother alone in being led astray by religion. My husband's mother, on hearing her son had married a black woman, screamed often and for many days, and wept bitterly. She removed all the clothing she'd bought for him out of his dormitory room at N.Y.U. Law School, and would, I think, have removed the education from his head, which she'd also paid for, if she had been able to. She then informed his brothers and other members of the family that they were not to speak to him, or even of him. Then, though she never went to synagogue, she chose to enact one of the cruelest rituals of her religion: she sat *shiva* for her living son. Which marked him as deceased.

My husband and I, caught between two doctrines of hatred from the women who gave birth to us, never doubted our duty was to love. The months dragged on, after our departure to and settlement in Mississippi. His mother began to understand that nothing stood between her son and the deranged racists she watched daily on television in New York. The horribly battered bodies of two young Jewish men, and that of their black friend (Andrew Goodman, Michael Schwerner and James Cheney), had been recently found not so many hours away from where we lived. She began to think killing her son figuratively was a bad idea, since there were so many people in the world, and especially in Mississippi, who would happily do it literally. She came South, in obvious pain, to embrace her son and to attempt to tolerate me.

These two grandmothers, who sometimes complained they couldn't understand each other's accents, were both present just after the birth of their granddaughter, Rebecca, when we brought her home from the hospital. They kept in touch long after my former husband and I were divorced, and sent messages and cards back and forth until my mother died. My mother-in-law never noticed Nature except to find something wrong with it. It both amused and amazed me that my Nature-enthralled mother still found her likeable, or in her word, "cute."

Everything I've ever learned of love I have taken home; the place where, when I was growing up, love seemed so rarely and obliquely expressed. That was the spirit in which I planned to get the movie of *The Color Purple* to Eatonton, Georgia. Ever since I was a child, I had been aware of the high rate of domestic violence in our town, among our people; wives shot or stabbed to death, children sometimes abused and beaten. Miserable men who seemed unable not to ruin their lives; who seemed born with the prison door stretched wide before them. Men who had been taught from the Bible that women are the cause of all evil in the world, and were not, simply as female human beings, to be trusted and certainly not to be honored, respected, loved, or held in reverence as the center of human life. The Bible had been the only reading matter black people were permitted during our long enslavement; for 300 years they were not even allowed to read it for themselves. This was indoctrination at its most relentless; naive to think it would not leave a deadly, self-despising mark. One might be expected to love one's neighbor as one's self—such a beautiful sentiment—but never one's wife, one's mother, one's mate. We needed to see how we looked, I thought, behaving as if still under the spell of a religion that made it nearly impossible to love the female body that was our source.

I also wanted to give my family and friends an opportunity to see women-loving women—lesbian, heterosexual, bi-sexual, "two-spirited"—womanist women in a recognizable context. I wanted them, I suppose, to see me. I had forgotten about this journal entry

[Jan. 26, 1984] until I began extracting entries for this book. A deliberate forgetfulness, obviously. At first I threw it out of the river, for did it not suggest that another reason my mother might not have cared to read *The Color Purple*, or have it read to her—beyond the first five pages, where the language Celie uses to describe her rape she said offended her—was because she was homophobic? And, since I love women and men, and have been sexual with both, would that not mean my mother's fear of and rejection of me? How could I bear the stress of her disapproval? How had I borne it all along?

I've often felt that to my family, I have sometimes been a curious, even miraculous, stranger. Forging ahead, insisting this is wonderful, that is ok, love is the main thing, freedom is great, while they have waited for me to trip over my optimism and fall on my face in disillusionment. This could still happen, of course. But it will have to happen as a consequence of my being who I truly am. For that great gift, that I am me: with this spirit, this hair, this skin, this fluid, whole sexuality, this vision and this heart, I dare not apologize. I am too grateful. One of the last things my mother said coherently to me before she died, while looking at me as if seeing me for the first time (also a possibility), was "You('re) a little mess, ain't you." Meaning someone selfish enough to fully express her being. We looked deep into each other's eyes. I said "Yes." It was a long moment and the only moment in which I felt my mother understood who she'd brought into the world and that she and I were well matched. That I wished to share that being with her, and that this Being that I am loves her completely, I hope that is the message she fully understood.

I not only stretched my mother physically before I was born and during my birth, I was born to stretch her spiritually. To show her ever more of the magic and playfulness and exuberant variety of Creation. Men and their religions have tended to make love for anything and anybody other than themselves and their Gods an objectionable thing, a shame. But that is not the message of Nature, the Universe, the Earth or of the unindoctrinated Human

Heart, where everything is profusion, chaos, multiplicity, but also creativity, containment and care. Love. Wildness. And to me, Wildness means following the growth of love. Like a plant that reaches through stone toward the sun.

When I traveled to Africa to help make the film *Warrior Marks*, I spoke to many mothers who mutilated their daughters genitally because they were taught, originally by men, and then by other women, that genital mutilation is desired by their male God. The mutilation, most frequently performed without warning or anesthetic, causes lifelong injury to women and threatens the health and well-being of any offspring they might bear. It is clearly a patriarchal attempt to rob women of their autonomy, to make them weak and pleasureless vessels through which longed-for male children will pass. Without exception, the women were kept ignorant of the fact that this particular injury to female children is not a requirement mentioned in their holy book, whether the Bible or the Koran.

I thought of my mother and her prejudices while I listened to these mothers who always, quite poignantly, expressed caring for their children. I felt then, as I do now, that we daughters must not forsake our mothers, who have been led—by men holding books that justify despicable behavior toward women and Nature—into the very evils Nature and common sense would have them avoid. And we mothers must stand by our daughters, and protect them from harm, using what wits we have left after five millennia of patriarchal destruction, domination and control.

In any event, I think mothers and daughters are meant to give birth to each other, over and over; that is why our challenges to each other are so fierce; that is why, when love and trust have not been too badly blemished or destroyed, the teaching and learning one from the other is so indelible and bittersweet. We daughters must risk losing the only love we instinctively feel we can't live without in order to be who we are, and I am convinced this sends a message to our mothers to break their own chains, though they may be anchored in prehistory and attached to their own great grandmothers' hearts.

RAPIDS

ALICE WALKER ON THE SET OF *The Color Purple*.

Journal Entry
June 1984
Robert called to say there's a group that wants to ban *The Color Purple*. Banning *The Color Purple* would be like banning the color blue—you'd miss it. Whereas—why don't they ban nuclear power?

THE STRANGE AND WONDER-FUL STORY OF THE MAKING OF "THE COLOR PURPLE"

Can one reclusive spirit who wrote a great American novel, one big-time Hollywood director, one obscure Dutch screenwriter, a celebrated musical wizard, and a black performance artist named Whoopi Goldberg make a big-budget movie the film event of the year?

Alice Walker was apprehensive—and with good reason. It is not often that a novel of emotion like *The Color Purple* can be successfully translated to the screen.

When an offer for the film rights came from producers Peter Guber and Jon Peters, Walker had no way of evaluating it herself, being a reclusive and thoughtful novelist, a gardener, and not a soulmate of popular culture.

In fact, she didn't even know who Guber and Peters were (they produced "Flashdance" and "Missing"). She thought Guber spelled his name Goober, like the peanuts. But she asked around among her friends—Ruby Dee and Ossie Davis, Maya Angelou, Toni Cade Bambara, Gloria Steinem—and assured herself at least that the money they offered was not peanuts.

When Guber came to see her, he turned out "not to be a Hollywood mogul type" as she had expected, "not balding, fat, cigar-chomping." No, he was very slim, she said, and young, carrying a backpack as he wandered around her San Francisco neighborhood, looking for her door. He pitched the film project to her for an hour or so. He mentioned director Steven Spielberg (who directed "Close Encounters of the Third Kind" and "E.T.," among other blockbusters).

Walker did not know who Spielberg was. She was not really interested until Guber mentioned Quincy Jones.

Quincy Jones is a genius of popular music and a prolific composer of Hollywood movie sound tracks. He has scored more than 30 films from "The Pawnbroker" to "The Wiz," as well as the television miniseries "Roots." He produced "We Are the World," featuring 45 of the biggest names in rock music, a benefit for African famine relief. He produced Michael Jackson's all-time best-selling album "Thriller."

Quincy Jones had broken the black musical artist through the top of fame and fortune into big money, the biggest. "And he has a social conscience," Walker said. "That was very important to me."

Jones had already made his arrangement with Guber. "Guber came to me about writing the music," Jones explained, "and I asked him to just let me have the whole project. Let me produce it and go as far as I can until I make a wrong move and then somebody can pull me back." Guber agreed. When he went to San Francisco to sell Alice Walker the idea of making her book into a movie, he was really offering her Quincy Jones as line producer, guardian angel, guarantor of her art, ideals, and political concerns.

Once Walker knew that Jones was involved, she took Guber's offer very seriously and called a meeting of her own personal advisory committee: Barbara Christian, a literary critic and a professor at Berkeley; Daphne Muse, a writer and social activist; Faith Mitchell, a medical anthropologist; Belvie Rooks, a filmmaker; Rebecca Walker Leventhal, Walker's 16-year-old daughter ("probably the most savvy of us all," according to her mom); and Robert Allen, Walker's partner in life, and associate in her small publishing house, Wild Trees Press, as well as a political writer and, at that time, a professor at Mills College in Oakland. ("Robert was the only man," says Walker, "but he was ample.")

For most of the afternoon, everybody said: " 'Don't do it.' Mainly because of what our experience has been with Hollywood," explained Walker, "and with white people trying to do black work. . . . All you have to do is go to the average movie where you have one black person surrounded by a million white people, and you see how artificial the black character becomes. I did not want that."

On the other hand, all the people at the meeting knew of Quincy Jones and admired him, *trusted* him. "If we always refuse," Barbara Christian offered, "how will we ever know? What will we change if we don't take a risk?"

Here was a novel about 35 years in the life of Celie, a rural Southern black woman undone by tragedy as a young girl, who grows through anger and passion and loneliness and faith to find her life's victory in the payoff of love. Walker had won a Pulitzer prize and an American Book Award for this book. And still millions of people whom she wanted to reach could not read Celie's story. "So much of my constituency just doesn't read," she said, "people in other countries, in Africa, who can't read English. I knew that people in my own hometown [Eatonton, Georgia] might not read the book. But I knew they would see the film. . . . I wanted it to be there, to appear in the villages."

Alice Walker acknowledges that she is a risk-taker at heart. She went to see Quincy Jones.

He asked her what her biggest fears were.

"I don't want them to embarrass us," she said.

He told her not to worry, that he would be on her side.

Jones brought director Steven Spielberg to see her, in a limousine so enormous that it would not fit in her driveway. Walker laughs thinking about that, even now, two years later. "What impressed me about that meeting was Steven's absolute grasp of the essentials of the book, the feeling, the spirit. He loved Sofia [the strong-willed wife of Celie's stepson, Harpo]; he loved her fighting spirit and her strength. Right away he saw everything visually. He said: wouldn't it be great if you had Shug singing beautifully in one room and Squeak trying to mimic her in another room, right next door . . . things like that . . . I liked that . . ."

Walker saw that Spielberg had a picture in his mind of Shug Avery, the lusty blues singer who is loved by Celie's husband, Mister, and also by Celie, and how the spirit of her personality and her music would fire the smaller talents of Squeak, the girlfriend of Celie's stepson. She saw that these women and their breaking hearts and soaring spirits did not feel strange to Spielberg.

"Well, maybe if he can do Martians, he can do us," she wisecracked to Rebecca. By then Walker knew about "E.T."

"In ancient times, people believed that you thought with your heart," Walker said. "They didn't really know about the brain. In more modern times, people say you think with your brain. Only there are a few of us who still actually think with our hearts, and after talking to Steven, I had a lot of confidence that he was one."

She had her terms written into the contract: at least one half the population of the film offscreen would be "women or blacks or Third World people." She got the financial terms arranged so that they reflected the advice of her movie-wise friends. Quincy Jones assured her that she would be consulted about the movie all the way.

"Most people just buy the book and shove the author under the rug," he said. "Not this time. At every moment, Alice was considered the last word."

With these assurances, Alice Walker agreed to let them make their picture. However, she was having anxiety dreams.

Spielberg and Jones asked Walker to write the screenplay. She had never done one before. "I went up to the country and spent about three months working on it," Walker said. "But Steven had no idea how tired I was." Having won the Pulitzer, she had just lived through a year of interviews and notoriety, her privacy and her precious quiet times all yielded to the public. "I had told Robert and Rebecca that after the novel and the Pulitzer, I would be theirs, because I had put them through a lot; they were always being interrupted, intruded upon. And then there I was going up to the country again to work on the screenplay. . . . Rebecca started having a lot of physical ailments that I understood to be signals that she really needed attention, really wanted me home even though she was her usual supportive and plucky self, trying to give me the space I needed. But I could tell . . .

"So I finished a draft and sent it down to Steven. I added things like descriptions of the houses, the rooms, the clothes, the shoes, the parasols—things you wouldn't necessarily get from the book that they could use in the real screenplay. And I gave it up."

It turned out not to be so easy to find someone besides Alice Walker who could adapt Alice Walker. The writers Spielberg saw kept saying it couldn't be done. *The Color Purple* is written in the form of a series of letters to God and back and forth between Celie in the American South and her sister Nettie, a missionary in Africa. This exchange did not immediately suggest the way it could be made visual.

Menno Meyjes (pronounced Minnow May-yes) did not agree. A Dutchman by birth, he had been in this country since 1972. He had the foreigner's freedom with English, and it was his screenplay about the Children's Crusade—called "Lionheart," scheduled for production later this year—that made Spielberg notice him.

"They'd seen just about everybody," Meyjes said, "and thought they might as well see me too. The more I read *The Color Purple*, the more I realized that it could *very easily* be made into a film.

"First of all, it had what all great works of art have—simplicity. Outside of the somewhat unusual structure—the letters—it is a simple story; almost all one location; one person's life; one person's point of view; one woman's evolution."

But wouldn't he have to adapt the story by making Celie's narrative the *voice-over* for scenes on camera?

"Of course!" he said. "Voice-over works for me. It worked for me in Terry Malick's film, 'Days of Heaven.' And it worked in 'Badlands,' too."

But Meyjes was apprehensive, and with good reason. "Not only am I foreigner, I'm also white, I'm a man. . . ."

Walker had been introduced to one possible woman writer—Melissa Mathison, author of "E.T." "But the chemistry was not right there," she recalls. "Her being a woman and me being a woman didn't do it." When she met Meyjes, however, she found they "resonated" well.

What was especially important to Walker was: "Even though he's not American, he comes from a part of Holland that has its own folk speech that is looked down upon by people who speak standard Dutch . . . and he had a real feel for what folk speech is and how it's not substandard, just different. I didn't have the feeling that Menno was a stranger."

Walker had been concerned that the script and the visual design would not take into account that though the characters speak in a certain way, they are not all poor: Mister owns land, and Celie's family gets on in business and commerce. A white writer might be deceived by the speech into making the wrong judgment about economic class.

"I locked myself up in my hotel room," Meyjes said, "with the novel on my lap and the typewriter on the desk and a pencil. I realized that if I didn't write the script very fast, all those things I was worried about would daunt me, I would end up lying next to my typewriter like a dead puppy."

As the drafts proceeded, Meyjes would come to the set of "The Goonies" (one of Spielberg's ongoing projects at the time) and work with him on "The Color Purple," "underlining stuff in red, maybe forty-five minutes. We called it Bible Class." Then Meyjes would sit in the office next to Spielberg's at Amblin Entertainment and turn out 10 to 12 pages a day. In the evening they both would go over what he had written.

"There would be times when I would really be feeling the strain, and then Quincy would call me up and say, 'Hey, how're you doing?' It would just lift my spirits," Meyjes said. "Quincy was an angel on this movie, everywhere at once, his influence is all pervasive. He couldn't be heavy-handed if he tried."

As the film went into production last summer in Los Angeles, North Carolina, later in Africa, a phenomenon almost never witnessed in Hollywood projects occurred. The writer of the book and the writer of the screenplay, usually exiles from the production, usually strangers to each other, were on the set, working together, all the time. "There was a party," Meyjes said, "and I wandered over to Alice's room. I said, 'Alice, I need some lines for Sofia.' Three minutes later, I had a legal pad filled with Alice's suggestions, and I sort of ambled back to the party.

"The next day Steven put it in. It's in the movie."

Jones was making good on his promises. With Kathleen Kennedy and Frank Marshall of Spielberg's organization handling the nuts and bolts; with Jones himself in command on every single decision; with Lucy Fisher at Warner Brothers and Guber and Peters doling out freedom and money and confidence, what did Alice Walker have to worry about?

Plenty. She had an anxiety dream that the set for the juke joint would look like a McDonald's. But when she got to the set, she found that the juke joint looked just right.

She worried about the power of the music—for the score Quincy Jones was writing encompassed African music, church music, jazz, and blues. Lionel Richie and Rod Temperton (who has written several of Michael Jackson's hits) were helping, as well as gospel singer Andrae Crouch; Tata Vega was dubbing the vocals of Shug Avery; blues artist Sonny Terry and big-band musician Eugene "Snookie" Young were scheduled to be heard on the track; Caiphus Semenya and Letta Mbulu were performing the African music. The richness of the score could sweep the story away. But Walker knew Spielberg and Jones by now—she knew that they "would not let such a thing happen, that they'd fight it out between them." And besides, she knew that Jones would not forget that his score—like the score of "Amadeus"—was the soul of the *character*, not the other way around.

"Celie *is* the blues," Jones told her. She trusted him.

When Reuben Cannon, the casting director (one of the few blacks in that business), presented the actors to her, they looked to her exactly like the characters in her book.

Inside the toiling movie, there was a kind of ensemble peace. But in the wide disgruntled world outside, somebody was asking, "Why couldn't they find a woman to direct, a woman to write? This is a woman's story, dammit!" And, "Why do they have to put a lesbian love affair in a black movie? It'll hurt the image of our people!" and "Who gave this white Jew with a background in kiddie flicks the right to mess with our story?! Why didn't Sidney Poitier direct this movie?!"

"These people bitch and moan that you never see a black face in the movies," growled Whoopi Goldberg, who plays Celie, "and as soon as there's a movie with a black cast that is not singin' and dancin', they bitch and moan about it. This is not a movie only about sexual relationships. [The film will probably have a PG-13 rating.] It happened that a woman awakened another woman to a new life. Then people are pissed because Spielberg directed it, which is to me very ridiculous. It's like saying if you're not a junkie, you can't tell anyone that heroin screws up your body. It's like my handicapped lady [a character in Whoopi's one-woman show on Broadway and on HBO this year] . . . I don't have to be handicapped to know how

people treat handicapped people, I can see it! I can feel it! I am open to it!

"I say to people, cool the fuck out, and see what this man does with the movie."

On the day Walker won the Pulitzer for *The Color Purple*, Whoopi Goldberg—then performing in small clubs in the San Francisco area—had bought the book. She was a performance artist. She had invented characters black and white, male and female: a junkie discovering Anne Frank, a Valley Girl getting an abortion, a disabled woman accepting love. Whoopi Goldberg wrote to Alice and said please let me play Celie.

Alice wrote back to this then fringy and unknown actor and said, "I know your work, of course; you're wonderful." And when Quincy asked Alice who should play Celie, she said Whoopi Goldberg.

For the role of Shug Avery, Whoopi Goldberg favored Tina Turner. "If I'm going to kiss a woman, let it be Tina," she told Gloria Steinem in New York. And Meyjes says he was swept away by the idea of Turner playing Shug. Walker simply says, "Steven and Quincy were trying hard to get the people together, they wanted to cast someone whom Whoopi felt she would like to work with, so they offered it to Tina."

Turner turned it down.

Too close to home, she said. The deep South, the bad old days, too close to home.

Beating around in the fringes where so many good black actors work, casting director Cannon got lots of ideas for Shug. Margaret Avery, who eventually got the part, says she was not one of them, but she begged him for a chance to read. The day before her screen test, she ran down Hollywood Boulevard looking for something Shug-ish to wear. "I found this red ostrich feather in a little porno place," she said. "I just prayed, let's hope this feather has been nowhere but on this rack."

There was talk of Lola Falana, Patti LaBelle. Guber made sounds about wanting to cast Diana Ross as Shug, which gave Alice Walker another anxiety attack.

But Spielberg gave Margaret Avery the role.

Quincy Jones was in Chicago and turned on the TV in his hotel room and saw a popular Chicago talk show whose host was a voluptuous rollicking woman named Oprah Winfrey. She became Sofia, Harpo's wife, whose fighting spirit Celie envies, but finally admires.

Danny Glover came on board to play Mister.

In the novel, Mister is a heavy, mean and cold to Celie, humanized only by his love for Shug and for his son Harpo, who has a lot of woman-trouble. Danny Glover played a heavy once before—in Peter Weir's "Witness" starring Harrison Ford. Glover had first made his mark on the screen as the fatherly Moze in Robert Benton's "Places in the Heart," and as a sharpshooting but good-guy-type outlaw in Lawrence Kasdan's "Silverado."

Glover is as gentle as a great kind bear, not at all slick—sweetness and maybe the fear of God in his expressive eyes. The odds were that when they cast him, Quincy Jones and Steven Spielberg were playing a bit of their own tune on the character of Mister.

"Sure, Danny is a bastard as Mister," Jones said. "Drama is conflict. Not everything is nicey-nicey here. But maybe the men in the movie are a little more sympathetic than in the book."

Alice Walker had come through the movie, every step of the way, and she saw what was happening. "Danny is so wonderful in this," she said. "He was in almost every scene, in almost every shot, and sometimes I would worry that it was going to become his story—Mister's story, not Celie's. I think it's true that a feminist woman director would have made different choices in terms of how much of the woman's story there would be. If I had directed it, for instance, I would have placed much more emphasis on what happened between Shug and Celie after they went to Memphis together, whereas in this movie, there's no Memphis. What you have is Celie coming back changed. I think Susan Seidelman ["Desperately Seeking Susan"] or Lynne Littman ["Testament"] or Barbra Streisand ["Yentl"] or you or me or Gloria Steinem would have been much more interested in showing the development of Celie under Shug's loving attention in Memphis, and we would also have had fun showing this humongous house with the statues and all the 'women's culture.' But Steven, I think, was more interested in showing the transformation of Mister to Albert, as well as Celie's changes . . . I think you really understand Albert better in the movie than in the book. I may be totally surprised at how I feel when I see the film, but so far, I don't think it bothers me very much. When I realized how many ideas Steven has and how quickly he works, I understood that he would necessarily bring a lot of himself to how he manipulates the scenes.

"We may miss our favorite part," concludes Walker, "but what is there will be its own gift, and I hope people will be able to accept that in the spirit that it's given."

The reclusive novelist with anxiety dreams had been transformed into an artistic collaborator.

Quincy Jones had been on the gig longer than anybody. For him "The Color Purple" was a breakthrough to film producing. Just as he had done with Michael Jackson, he was bringing the black experience through the top to visibility and celebration, applying the hottest and most successful director in the business, applying a $14 million budget.

"I don't know how to punt," he said. "I have to go for the ultimate. I have never seen a black dramatic film made with total quality from top to bottom that could stand up against any major picture. I wanted a great director, who had all the sensibilities in every aspect to make this a great film. . . . Who could handle the million decisions that

it takes with skill and confidence? with the strong personal insight and directing skill? White, black, man, woman: these are the wrong considerations. They once asked Stravinsky whether he was thinking about the Acropolis when he wrote 'Apollo.' He said, 'I was thinking about violins.' "

By September, the film had gone for editing to Michael Kahn (an Oscar-winner for "Raiders of the Lost Ark"), and Jones worked on the score. Alice Walker relaxed. Danny Glover went to Europe to promote "Silverado." Menno Meyjes went to New York to work with Malcolm McLaren on a production for the Public Theater.

Whoopi Goldberg acknowledged that in her career she had been "born with a silver spoon in my mouth," having been brought to Broadway for the first time by Mike Nichols and to the screen for the first time by Steven Spielberg. But Whoopi Goldberg mentioned the critics a lot because she has been stung in her time by scathing reviews. "I can always go back to hundred-seat theaters," she said.

Some had said that Whoopi Goldberg had compromised her blackness with her pan-cultural name and had flown to success on the magic carpet of liberal guilt. But in her anxiety about how this movie would be received, she stuck steadfastly to her being as an actress and her belief in the universality of Walker's story.

" 'The Color Purple' is not a movie about race," she said. "What happens to Celie is happening to women all over the world, of all races and backgrounds, that is the fact. This is a story about the trials of the human spirit."

As is his habit, the director kept his movie pretty much a secret. It was said in the industry that he is a control freak, and also that he had embarked on this particular journey in order finally to get himself an Academy Award.

But within the proud and upright partnership at the core of the film, no one forgot for a minute that Spielberg's fame rests on his uncanny ability to imagine that encounters between strangers could turn out to be filled with fun and love and self-discovery.

SUSAN DWORKIN
MS. DECEMBER 1985

THE MAKING OF 'THE COLOR PURPLE'

An exclusive report from the set with Alice Walker, Steven Spielberg, Whoopi Goldberg, Danny Glover and Quincy Jones.

For the past two years, Elena Featherston has been filming a documentary on the life and work of Alice Walker. A longtime admirer of Walker's writing, Featherston contacted the author in 1983 to ask for permission and cooperation in the making of *Alice Walker: Visions of the Spirit*. Three months later, Walker's novel *The Color Purple* won an American Book Award and a Pulitzer Prize for fiction. The novel has since sold more than a million copies—and it soon will reach an even larger audience.

This month, the movie based on Alice Walker's extraordinary novel will open at theatres across the country. Directed by Steven Spielberg and produced jointly by Spielberg, Quincy Jones, Kathleen Kennedy and Frank Marshall, the movie was filmed in North Carolina. Besides Alice Walker, who served as a consultant to the production, many Bay Area folks brought their talents to *The Color Purple* set, including Whoopi Goldberg, Danny Glover and Leonard Jackson, who have major roles in the film, as well as costume designer Aggie Rodgers.

At the invitation of Alice Walker, Featherston spent three weeks on location with the *Color Purple* crew. It was a rare glimpse behind the scenes into the filming of what may be the most important release of the season. Here's her report.—*Editor*

When Alice Walker was first approached about selling the film rights to *The Color Purple*, she had profound misgivings. After all, Hollywood is notoriously insensitive to the concerns of women and people of color. Organizations such as the NAACP have threatened boycotts to protest the movie industry's negative depiction of blacks and its perpetuation of tired, old racial stereotypes, and black actors have decried the dearth of meaningful roles available to them. Could Celie, Nettie, Shug, Squeak, Sofia and the other remarkable black female characters who inhabit Walker's complex novel be entrusted to the white—and, yes, predominantly male—Hollywood establishment?

Set in the rural South, *The Color Purple* spans four decades in the lives of Celie and Nettie, two black sisters separated by circumstances of oppression. Through letters Celie writes to God and, later, letters she and Nettie write to each other—expressions of love and desperation that are conveyed primarily in Black Folk English—we follow the two women as they struggle against hopelessness to finally achieve a joyous triumph. *The Color Purple* is a testament to the indomitability of the human spirit, a book that has touched the lives of millions of readers and won universal critical acclaim and countless accolades, including the 1983 Pulitzer Prize for fiction.

Mangled by Hollywood, *The Color Purple* could become an expensive and embarrassing minstrel show. But if brought to the screen with sensitivity, skill and understanding, it might be a film as inspired, inspirational and timeless as the brilliantly crafted novel.

After a great deal of consideration and consultation with friends, Walker decided to sell the film rights to Hollywood producer Peter Guber (*Missing, Midnight Express, Flashdance*) on the condition that she be involved, to the level of her interest, as a consultant. And written into the contract— a rare provision in Hollywood dealings—was the stipulation that half the people involved in the production, apart from the predominantly black cast, would be blacks, women and/or people of the Third World. Walker realized that nothing will change, in Hollywood or society at large, until we create situations in which those changes can occur.

My behind-the-scenes glimpse of the Warner Bros. filming reassured me that Walker had made the right decision, that her work was in good hands. For this was no ordinary film crew and cast that gathered in rural North Carolina during the oppressive heat of summer. It was, instead, a group of immensely talented and dedicated men and women who shared an almost reverent appreciation of the special beauty and powerful message of Walker's book and the determination to do justice to her literary genius.

One major aspect of the production, however, has raised some eyebrows: the decision by Quincy Jones, one of the four producers, to ask Steven Spielberg to direct. Why, wondered many fans and even some detractors of this emotionally and politically charged book, hadn't a black director been selected? And, barring that, why Spielberg of all people? This was a question that could not be easily dismissed. Even the nationally syndicated comic strip *Bloom County* had aimed a barb at the conspicuous absence of blacks in Spielberg's productions. Also, *The Color Purple* requires no spectacular special effects, lovable creatures or fearsome demons. Far from involving extraterrestrial matters, the story in Walker's novel is grounded firmly in the realities of the planet Earth. Despite his undisputed talent, was Spielberg the right director for this challenging job? A fierce sense of protectiveness for Walker's work kept this question foremost in my mind when I went to North Carolina.

As we traveled the highway from Charlotte to Monroe, where the production was headquartered, members of the local citizenry peered curiously into our car. Of course, Claudia Katayanagi, Frances Reid and I hardly comprised an unobtrusive group. We were three women—one Asian, one white and one black, respectively—speeding along in a silver Peugeot, stuffed to the gussets with video equipment. And the entire state was abuzz with the news that Steven Spielberg was in Monroe with a host of California moviemaking types. The locals were on their best behavior—yet there were glints of more than curiosity in the eyes of some. A white van loaded with good ol' boys slowed down alongside, and one yelled something decidedly other than "howdy, ladies" before speeding away.

I was in the South again, and I had to fight a growing sense of discomfort and rage. On my last trip to these parts, I was a fourteen-year-old idealist registering voters and fighting for civil rights. And I wasn't convinced that things had changed.

My mood brightened considerably when we arrived at the Holiday Inn in Monroe, where most of the actors, staff and crew were lodged. I felt immediately at home, in large part because so many people from the Bay Area were involved in the filming. There were Alice Walker as consultant; her companion, Robert Allen, acting as our grip; Whoopi Goldberg, playing her first major film role, as Celie; Danny Glover as Celie's husband, Mister; and Berkeleyan Leonard Jackson as Pa. Costume designer Aggie Rodgers is a San Franciscan, and so was scriptwriter Menno Meyjes, for many years, before he moved to Los Angeles.

Location manager Kokayi Ampah, tall, black and bespectacled, directed us to the principal sets. Ampah spearheaded the preliminary location scouting for the production; his files were crammed with information on schools, churches, villages and farms all across North Carolina and Georgia. "We considered doing the movie in Eatonton [Georgia], Alice's hometown," he told me. "That would have been ideal. But times change. There are a lot of variables to consider." An airplane flying overhead, for example, can ruin a scene that is supposed to take place in rural Georgia in the early 1900s.

Ampah placed most of the sets on a pre–Civil War plantation deep in the countryside and the town set in the tiny village of Marshville, just outside Monroe. Moonsong—the code name for this production—took over a few blocks of the village. Using the existing buildings, production designer Michael Riva and his crew created a turn-of-the-century country town, complete with general store, blacksmith's and tailor's shops, a livery and a bank—a marvel of authenticity and attention to detail. Reportedly, two planeloads of red Georgia clay were flown in to make the dirt streets.

Very early the following morning, this tranquil picture postcard of America's past was a bustling hive of activity. Amid the lights and cameras, a small army of actors, extras and technicians swarmed in what looked like utter chaos. Yet despite the horses and dogs and the children in period costume running through the streets—and the humidity and the temperature that was already climbing to the hundred-degree mark—it all had the feeling of a complex, unchoreographed but very well-rehearsed dance.

The air was filled with the pungent odor of frankincense. Smelling it, Walker and I smiled at each other; we knew that in many religious traditions, frankincense is burned to clear the air of negative feelings and thoughts. Here, however, the device was not a spiritual but a technical one; as a passing grip explained, smoke enhances the image of a crowd scene, and frankincense is an excellent source. "Besides," he added with a grin, "something has to keep the blacksmith's forge belching smoke." Still, another glance from Walker confirmed that whether these people realized it or not, both sorts of purposes were being served.

Assistant director Vicki Rhodes, another black crew member, moved among the clusters of extras, giving instructions for the forthcoming scene. Spielberg, a baseball cap pulled low on his forehead, was talking animatedly with Glover and fourteen-year-old Desreta Jackson, who makes her film debut as the young Celie, while scriptwriter Meyjes, tall, longhaired and with the handsome features of a rock star, stood listening intently. Nearby, Walker was teasing Quincy Jones about his increasing girth.

The unofficial set photographer, Gordon Parks (equally renowned as a writer and film director), moved about the set with a leonine grace, shooting whatever caught his eye. "I don't do this much anymore," he told me. "Only occasionally, for my friends."

I wandered over to talk with Meyjes. A successful adaptation of such a book as *The Color Purple* is a formidable accomplishment. Walker had tried it but finally gave up, exhausted. How did he manage it?

"Alice's novel spoke to me so clearly," he said. "She made my job easy."

But how could he, a white male and a Dutchman to boot, really understand and empathize with the feelings and motivations of black women living in rural Georgia half a century ago?

"The book is so good, it transcends any barriers," Meyjes replied. "While I was writing, none of those things occurred to me. Only when I stopped would I consider the barriers—if they are barriers—of being white, Dutch and a man."

Meyjes worked on the screenplay for almost three months before Jones wrested it from him to show to Walker. While waiting for her reaction, he chain-smoked and paced, never far from a telephone. "I wasn't ready for Alice to see it," he recalled with a laugh. "I was so nervous. I could probably still be working on it."

Alice not only approved the script; she thought it was wonderful. When Meyjes heard the news, he simultaneously felt relief, joy and severe postpartum depression. He became ill and hit the sickbed for a few days.

"Once Alice approved the script," he said, "it was much easier. We could go over dialogue for authenticity. Alice is a great spirit, one of the most extraordinary people I have ever met."

Alice Walker's presence on the set was more than welcomed by everyone involved. Her wisdom and insights were invaluable. She gave set designer Riva a list of the flowers and vegetables Celie would have in her garden. For Jones, who wrote the musical score in addition to acting as one of the four producers, she recorded a gospel hymn remembered from childhood. She worked with costume designer Aggie Rodgers and helped Meyjes fine-tune his script. She was a living link to the past and present-day black rural South.

Many sweltering afternoons on the set, Walker sat beneath a tree giving informal speech lessons. Before a shooting, actors trying to master the subtleties and rhythms of Black Folk English made their way to "Madame Walker's Speech Clinic and Tarot Reading Parlor" to run through a scene.

One of these actors, Akosua Busia, who plays Nettie, has artistic and cultural roots that are far removed from the sultry pine woods of Georgia. Busia is from Africa and was trained as an actress at London's prestigious Central School of Speech and Drama. With Walker's help, she not only mastered the right dialect but also completely confounded local citizens with her ability to switch back and forth between the southern patois and her own impeccable, cultured speech—an English they could never aspire to—and her regal, African-princess bearing.

Busia saw this movie as an ideal project. "I'd been working on a series in London, and when it ended, I told my sister I wanted to go to America and do a Spielberg film," she explained, her huge brown eyes fixed on mine. "The second week I was here, my agent told me to read *The Color Purple*. I stayed up all night reading it. And I prayed for this job. I don't usually call on God for all my parts. But this was special."

She was far from the only person who felt that way. For most of the cast and production staff of this movie, Walker's book provoked such a powerful response that they clamored to get involved. "I fought for this job," recalled costume designer Rodgers. "When I interviewed with Steven [Spielberg], I stood in front of the door of his office, virtually trapping him in there, demanding to know what I had to say to get the job. . . . This was the best project ever for me," she added. "I only hope that Alice is pleased. More than anything I wanted to protect her, protect her work. I read everything she wrote. Just meeting her was enough. If they had fired me the next day, it would have been all worthwhile."

Whoopi Goldberg campaigned for a role before a movie was even planned. Long before the film rights were sold, she recalled, she wrote Walker saying she would "play a venetian blind, if necessary"—just as long as she could have a part in the film, should there even be one. To Goldberg's mind, she and Celie are a match made in heaven. "It is as if Alice had sat down and said, 'I'm going to write this part for Whoopi Goldberg.' She didn't, of course. But it sure fits like a glove," Goldberg added with a grin.

Producer/composer Quincy Jones had a similar matchmaking impulse regarding Chicago talk-show host Oprah Winfrey (whose success is rumored to be a factor in Phil Donahue's leaving the Windy City)—but the character he had in mind for her was Sofia. "I always wanted to act," Winfrey recalled, relaxing in her room at the Holiday Inn, "but I lacked the discipline. Then it just happened.

Quincy was in Chicago on business. It was late, and he was unable to sleep. He tuned in to my show and thought I was the perfect Sofia. Next thing I know, my agent gets a call from [casting agent] Reuben Cannon, and here I am."

Jones saw the movie as ideally suited for his first major feature-film producer's role. "I was waiting for the right one," he explained. *The Color Purple* was it, he decided after reading the novel on vacation (taking it along, he admitted, because "it was the shortest book he had). "Like everyone else, I was deeply moved. I came back from vacation wanting to share the book with my friends and reread it myself."

"Let me do the movie," was Jones' reply when executive producer Guber asked him to write the score. "Knowing this was my first time out," Jones recalled, "I asked him to just let me do it until I made a mistake, then he could come in and clean it up." Jones shared his producer's job with Kathleen Kennedy (whose expertise freed him to concentrate on the score and who was not beyond doing some shooting herself when timing was tight) as well as Frank Marshall and director Spielberg.

Writing the score, Jones drew on more than a decade's worth of research into the history of black music, relishing the opportunity to share the broad range of expression it contains. In general, Jones' enthusiasm and warmth were contagious. Before meeting him, I had only known his reputation—a musical genius who scored more than fifty movies, won Grammy and Emmy and Academy Award nominations and helped bring together the luminaries of rock music to raise millions for famine relief in Ethiopia. I was unprepared for the real man—one of those rare individuals who is really there when he talks to you, with a way of touching people that shows genuine affection. I'd assumed that wealth and fame make people aloof and inaccessible; not so in Jones' case.

"There are some scenes in this movie that I have dreamed about," he declared. "It will be a feast for the eye as well as the mind and spirit. Too many films featuring black actors, or with black themes, were hampered by having too few elements in place. Perhaps it was a great story with mediocre direction. Or tremendous direction and so-so actors. This has everything going for it: great direction, great acting, great story."

It also, thanks to the efforts of Walker and Jones, is a truly racially integrated production—something of no small value to experienced black professionals in the industry. "It feels great," said Willard Pugh, who plays Harpo. "It's good to look up at the end of a scene and not be the only black man on the set." Greg Elam, the stunt coordinator, agreed. "There have been times when I was the only black man for miles around."

Still, the project has a value that goes beyond—and has helped some people look beyond—the issue of race. "*The Color Purple* is not a 'black' story," asserted set designer Riva be-

tween shootings as we sat beneath a stand of trees. "It's a people story. It's about love, hate, fear and dreams. It's universal." Riva is Marlene Dietrich's grandson and designed the sets for *Ordinary People*, *Brubaker*, *Buckaroo Banzai* and *The Goonies*, among other films. Fingering his *Color Purple* baseball hat, the sun and shade playing across his face, he confided he had agreed to work for less pay than he usually commands in order to be part of this production.

But in the more than a year he spent working on authentic sets that would befit Walker's book, Riva discovered that—universality aside—he harbored some disturbing assumptions about black people. "You know, to do justice to this film, I had to confront my own prejudices," he said, gazing at me thoughtfully. "I didn't think I was prejudiced, but I was. I don't even know where it came from. Just growing up in America, I guess." Like most Americans, he had trouble conceiving of blacks prior to modern times as people living a comfortable, middle-class existence; he was used to associating them with poverty and subservience.

Danny Glover also unearthed some prejudices within himself during the filming—not racial ones, but sexual. "Working on this part [Mister] has made me aware of some of my own hostilities against women," he confided. "It's been a growing experience. Everyone working on this movie is growing." So, too, he added, was his own understanding of Mister, and he was reluctant to talk too much about the role. "Mister is in his infant stages. He's growing all the time. Too much talk can stunt his growth." He chuckled and, still a little shy about the artificially produced bald spot old Mister sports, donned his baseball cap.

Walker's characters themselves also undergo a kind of growth. "My characters start generally when they are at the worst places in their lives," she observed as she sat fanning herself on the porch of an old, unpainted house of a neighbor located just off the set. "To improve themselves, they struggle; they struggle to understand their condition. I like that in people. I like to see people pull themselves out of whatever holds them from their best selves. You know, everybody really has a best self and a worst self; some people never fight their way to the best self. That is one of the worst sins in the world—to see the best self, to know it is there and to fail to try to achieve it."

The cameras were ready to roll. "Quiet on the set!" called Rebecca Leventhal, a production assistant who is also Walker's daughter. The scene called for Mister (Glover) and the young Celie (Desreta Jackson) to leave the general store and walk down Main Street. It seemed to go off without a hitch.

Then, during the break, Goldberg and Winfrey wandered onto the set and, armed with cans of purple hair spray, proceeded to adorn the heads of everyone present with purple stripes. Goldberg did the honors for Spielberg personally.

As Jones looked on, beaming like a proud father, I asked him about all the criticism provoked by his choice of Spielberg as director. He grew serious. "I knew I would take heat for it," he said. "But there was never another director for this film. Steven has everything—the science and the soul to make this movie great."

Later, in her hotel room, Winfrey agreed. "Steven is *on* it! He understands. The man has done his homework. When you really see him work, you'll understand."

Glover seconded that claim. "I have these little tests for the directors I work with," he explained. "They don't even realize they are being tested, but they are. I trust [Spielberg]. I don't even look at the dailies."

And Goldberg, uncharacteristically serious, also had nothing but praise. "Steven? You figure a man who can take a rubber monster and make young people, old people, yuppies, duppies and buppies cry has magic. A real touch of magic."

My first real glimpse of Spielberg at work was on the farm set at the former slaveholding plantation, where Riva and his crew had relocated an authentic, small black Baptist church and had built Celie's house, Harpo's house, Mister's house (fashioned by restructuring the back part of the existing mansion) and a "juke joint"—an institution in the black South that was part nightclub and part community center. As I sat under the pines waiting for the shoot to start, Ernie Phillips, one of the set painters, explained that when Sherman's troops passed through here, the slaves told them the old master was still in the house, either asleep or hiding. The soldiers dispensed with this clearly unpopular gentleman and continued on their way, leaving the plantation relatively unscathed. He is rumored to be buried beneath one of the old trees that dot the landscape; I couldn't help wondering if he was turning in his grave.

Spielberg was a moving bundle of energy and intensity. He seemed to be everywhere at once—checking camera angles; talking with actors; joking with the crew; introducing his baby son, Max, to his first movie camera; showering affection on Max's mother, actress Amy Irving—all the while letting nothing go unnoticed. Nothing was insignificant; Spielberg directed the action of each extra or the placement of a farm animal with the same meticulous attention he gave the principal actors.

Watching Spielberg work—his obvious passion, the way he cares about both the magic of moviemaking and the magic of the human spirit—dispelled any doubts about his grasp of the subtleties of Walker's book. Asked if he was ever frightened by his decision to direct The Color Purple, he replied, "I'm still scared"—but, he added, he's been frightened by every project he's worked on. "Fear makes you worry, worry makes you think, and thinking makes you creative." His main worry, Spielberg said, was whether or not he was ready to attempt such an intimate movie. He was, he pointed out, used to doing

"big movies. Movies about out there. I didn't know if the time was right to do a movie about in here," he said, gently tapping his chest.

It was Spielberg who offered my favorite description of Walker. "Alice is like a ghost," he said. "She is otherworldly. And I mean that in the most positive way. She is here, she is real, but she has one foot in the other world."

For Riva, the "other world" of The Color Purple was acutely, addictively real. "The saddest day of my life will be when this film is finished," he mused. Despite the ghastly humidity and heat, the man-eating midges and the long hours? "I'll be tired at the end," he admitted. "You're always tired at the end. But I love Celie and Mister, Nettie, Pa and Harpo and the others. I'll hate to see them go."

During the last weeks of shooting, the farm set's spring flowers and crops were replaced by a covering of "snow," and the actors, wearing heavy winter clothes, valiantly tried to ignore the real-life sweltering heat. Just prior to the shooting of the final scene, a yell went up around the set, and someone broke out the champagne. Toasts were made and seconded. Then, after the final take was in the can, everyone gathered around Mister's back porch to watch a fireworks display against the night sky. "At last," Spielberg noted with a wry smile. "Special effects."

BY ELENA FEATHERSTON
SAN FRANCISCO FOCUS, DECEMBER
1985

THOUGHTS ON THE COLOR PURPLE

The release of the movie *The Color Purple* has unleashed a wide-ranging controversy. Some critics have panned it while others have placed it on their ten-best list. In many parts of the country, theaters showing the film have been turning away people at showing after showing. But in some cities the movie has been picketed because of what some see as its "negative portrayal of Black males." On some radio talk-shows in the New York area that draw primarily Black audiences, callers lined up pro and con on the movie for weeks. A forum on the movie in Chicago drew 600 people, and in New York one drew 200. At the heart of this debate is whether or not the oppression of women as it festers among the oppressed is a fit topic for discussion in a work of art. This debate is somewhat reminiscent of an earlier controversy that sprang up in the late 1970s among the Black intelligentsia focused on Ntosake Shange's choreopoem *for colored girls who have considered suicide when the rainbow is enuff* and Michelle Wallace's book *Black Macho and the Myth of the Superwoman*. But this time around the controversy is more of a mass question.

Those critical of the movie have overwhelmingly zeroed in on the "negative portrayal of Black males" as

their point of assault on the movie (and usually also the book *The Color Purple* by Alice Walker, although there have been a few who separate the two). Different folks have stroked this point differently though. Some have been silly enough to say that the kind of brutalization of women that the film depicts never happened among Black people, or perhaps used to happen but doesn't anymore. Some have even amplified this foolishness with comments like, "My father never beat my mother," or "I never beat my wife." Or even, "My husband never beats me." Setting aside the liars among these people for the moment, such people should be awarded a frog-in-the-well medallion for their additions to this debate.

There are also those who profess to recognize that the oppression of women and the various and brutal forms it takes is an important problem, yet feel the film (and the book) does a disservice to Black people because it raises this problem in an out-of-context, distorted way. They say that by not focusing on the national oppression of Black people *The Color Purple* gives the impression that the enemy is Black men and not the system that oppresses both Black men and women. And that, by leaving out the overall brutality that the system subjects Black men to, *The Color Purple* doesn't show what drives some Black men to the point of brutalizing women. Instead of airing Black people's dirty laundry in public, some propose that this problem (women's oppression among Black people) be addressed by Black people behind closed doors and that putting it out in public in movie form like this panders to racist sentiments and may even stem from a racist motivation to promote negative stereotypes of Black people.

All of this turns things upside-down. First off, the pervasiveness of the degradation and brutality women are subjected to in this society screams out at you from every direction. Rape, women being battered by *their* men, a multi-billion-dollar pornography industry trading in violence against women, millions of women facing raising families on their own. And all of this is a sharper problem for Black women because this all interpenetrates with the oppression they face as Black people. Which is why so many Black women and women in general have welcomed this film, asserting joyously that finally their story is being told on the screen.

The movie has touched a raw nerve. And the fervor of the debate underscored the importance of the questions that have been raised by *The Color Purple*. It is the portrayal of women's oppression and resistance to this that gives *The Color Purple* its power. And it is exactly that that those attacking the movie object to.

As the Revolutionary Communist Party's International Women's Day Proclamation states, "There sits on the backs of women a comprehensive legal, cultural, and political edifice of enormous strength, deep-rooted and constantly bred by the very structure and politics of all class society, so that even her man would become the *reliable agent* of her oppression." And in this sense, it must be said that to fail to recognize this weight upon women; to fail to struggle against this; to uphold the subjugation of women and the male-supremacist outlook that reinforces it, serves only the cause of maintaining the status quo and all the degradation and misery that millions worldwide are subjected to. A movement capable of overthrowing the imperialist rulers and carrying a revolution all the way through to sweeping away every foul aspect of this society is inconceivable without a key part of building that movement being unleashing the fury of women as a mighty force for revolution. This is so because only in this way can you rally all the possible forces for the assault on the enemy, and because even if you could somehow rally the forces to seize power but tried to leave the chains intact that bind women in subjugation, your revolution would only be one that placed in power a new group of exploiters. The way this presents itself to men, and particularly men among the oppressed, is: do you stand with the all-the-way approach to revolution (including its focus on breaking the chains that bind women into subjugation) and work to move it forward? Or do you stand for maintaining at least that one chain of oppression (and ultimately for playing the role of oppressor vis-à-vis *your* woman)? This is why the party says that your stand on the oppression of women is a touchstone question, a dividing line between wanting into or wanting out of the system. And faced with this challenge, many of these guys see a movie that powerfully targets women's oppression and some of them can only cry that it portrayed a negative image of Black men.

But let's look more at some of the points raised by the critics and then later compare that to *The Color Purple.* We've already touched on the pervasiveness of women's oppression. The reality is that there are too many men of all nationalities whom the character of Mister typifies. And there are many more little Misters who, while they might not act out some of the more brutal aspects of how Mister handled *his* woman, do think that their unchallenged right to lord it over *their* women is part of the natural order of things. There is, of course, all the shit that goes on between men and women on the level of "ownership" and who has the say-so over what. And the scene where Mister checks out Celie like he's buying a horse is not all that different from some of what goes on today, especially if you look at what kind of criteria is widely propagated (and accepted) about "what to look for in a woman."

You can't explain this away by talking about the oppression that Black men (or any other men among the proletariat and oppressed peoples) are subjected to—that is, the argument that men become oppressors of women in response to the fact that they themselves are exploited and oppressed on a daily basis. It's true that this is *part* of what goes on. But it's not the essence of the matter. A more fundamental reason for the existence of the oppression of women among the oppressed is the fact that the patriarchy is an integral part of the present system and of all societies divided into classes. Women's oppression is reinforced by the whole superstructure of politics, of culture and ideology generally, of advertising on TV, of education, and in many other ways. The man acting as the lord and master in relation to his wife and children is put forward as the way things are and should be. Oppressed men buy into this too.

We also need to demolish the argument that Black people should deal with this problem behind closed doors. First off, it isn't possible. (Unless people are saying that each couple should deal with this problem behind their closed doors. Of course, the isolation of women behind closed doors with *their* men helps to create the conditions in which their subjugation is carried out and perpetuated.) There isn't any framework through which Black people could collectively confront this question and resolve it without it being seen and participated in by people of all nationalities throughout this society. But even if there were such a framework, it wouldn't be desirable to handle it in that way because the oppression of women does cross boundaries of nationality and class. It is a problem for all those who want to break free from the degradation and misery the system forces millions to endure worldwide. Which makes it a very fine thing that *The Color Purple* has stirred up such broad controversy and drawn such a wide audience.

Now let's get to *The Color Purple* and examine it. In a talk to the National Writers Union, Alice Walker said, "If and when Celie rises to her rightful, earned place in society across the planet, the world will be a different place." The power of *The Color Purple* derives from its depiction of Celie going from just trying to survive in "her place in society" (beneath the heels of several Black men) to a rebellious and absolute refusal to be treated this way. Who can forget the power of the dinner scene where Celie announces she is leaving Mister? There is the rage that comes pouring out as well as the defiance and assuredness of a woman that is clear on what she wants. And then there is the parting curse that Celie puts on Mister as she leaves. "Until you do right by me, everything you touch will crumble," Celie says to Mister. "Until you do right by me . . . everything you even dream about will fail. . . . The jail you plan for me is the one in which you will rot." Celie's curse is not only a promise that she will never again allow Mister to abuse her, but there is also insight here that as long as men

oppress women they will continue to perpetuate an oppressive system. Throughout the story Celie is depicted grappling with degrading brutality (which is not uncommon for women) and the self-doubts and feelings of worthlessness that this treatment engenders (which is very, very common for women of all nationalities. This is why many, many women of all nationalities love this movie).

Very important to Celie's transformation are two women from whom she learns quite a bit and draws support for her eventual step out into the world: Shug Avery and Sophia. Celie's relationship to Shug was central to her transformation. Shug represented everything that society saw as disreputable in a woman. She didn't belong to any man and went where she wanted, for as long, or short, as she wanted. Earning her living performing in the outlaw atmosphere of the "juke-joints," Shug was a scandal for many an upstanding citizen and was quite unrepentant about it to boot. (This was especially so in the book—more on this later.) From Celie's perspective (underneath Mister's boot), all this was both enticing and seemingly beyond reach. Yet it was through getting to know Shug that Celie came alive.

And Sophia, with her determination not to be humbled by any of the men in her life, or by white society either, was in a way everything that Celie wasn't. By interacting with Sophia, Celie first had her eyes opened to the fact that her lot in life wasn't all a woman could hope for. It was also especially powerful later on in the story when Celie's decision to stand up to Mister and leave him brought Sophia back from the effects of the brutality she had suffered in prison and in bondage to the Mayor's wife.

And there are many other strong images from The Color Purple. Especially memorable are how the letters and scenes weave back and forth between the U.S. and Africa, bringing out the international dimensions of both the oppression of women and the oppression of Black people and the links between the two. Remember how both Mister and the African men didn't see the point in women learning to read since they wouldn't need it for the roles their respective societies had for women? And compare that to how the slavemasters made it a crime for slaves to be educated. Also, there was the image of Nettie as the runaway slave, forced to flee because she wouldn't submit to Mister.

It's no surprise that a story like this would be warmly welcomed by those who hate the oppression of women. More than that, if you stand against one section of society lording it over another section in any form, you ought to welcome The Color Purple. It isn't done from a proletarian revolutionary viewpoint, and its approach to resolving the contradiction of the oppression of the women differs from a proletarian revolutionary approach. This is particularly true (of both the book and the movie) in the implied resolution on the level of property re-lations—Celie gets her own house and land as well as her own business. This vision of liberation as a woman having her own property (a democratic right) is not the outlook and aspiration of the revolutionary proletariat. It will take nothing less than the revolutionary overthrow of the imperialists who dominate the globe, and the carrying forward of that revolution all the way to obliterating every foul social relation of this dog-eat-dog setup and every reactionary idea that it has spawned, for the Celies of this world to finally break the chains of women's oppression. But works of art like The Color Purple (both the book and the movie) which typify crucial contradictions of the imperialist system, like the oppression of women, contribute to bringing this about.

From the other side, it should also be said that if you don't want to see forces mobilized to carry out an all-the-way revolutionary approach or if it's OK with you if this chain in particular isn't broken, then you'd hate seeing something like The Color Purple out there and you'd want to rally forces against it. So it comes as no surprise that this movie has met much opposition. But it is quite revealing of the depths of male supremacy in society that many Black men, who being themselves oppressed have every reason to oppose any form of oppression this system dishes out, check out The Color Purple and end up complaining about the male images it portrays.

As for the charge that The Color Purple presents a distorted picture by focusing on women's oppression and not dealing with national oppression, this is just off the wall. Sophia being jailed and beaten was certainly national oppression. As was the lynching of Celie's natural father or Shug Avery and her traveling companion not being able to stop anywhere and rest on long trips through the South. And you could cite many other instances. Those raising this criticism are actually saying something else. They're arguing that The Color Purple should not have taken as its focus the oppression of women as it occurs among the oppressed. Alice Walker never said she was attempting to lay out the whole of the situation of Black people. She said straight-up that she wanted to help an oppressed Black woman find her voice, and she succeeded powerfully.

The portrayal of the patriarchy is especially sharp in The Color Purple. The weight of tradition and the passing down of the "natural order of things" is typified in the relations between Old Mister, Mister, and Harpo. There is Mister's father, the old patriarch-adviser. He objects to Mister's relationship with Shug exactly because Shug is a woman who has not "stayed in her place." And after Celie has left, he advises Mister to simply get another wife (slave) and start all over. Harpo is also expected to assume the patriarchal mantle. He loves Sophia because of her strength and assuredness. But all around him the weight of tradition pulls on him—telling him that his wife should serve him and be kept firmly under his thumb. A very

powerful moment in the movie, illustrating the depth of all this, is when Celie, who still sees her own oppression as "the way things are," tells Harpo that he should beat Sophia, and is in turn confronted by Sophia's defiant rebuke of this oppressor ideology. The scenes of male camaraderie also illustrate another aspect of how the patriarchy is perpetuated and enforced. There is the camaraderie and hierarchy in the relationships between fathers and sons; and there is also the general bond between men. When Shug and Grady come to visit, there is an instant liking between Mister and Grady as they go off, drinking and trading stories.

The movie is generally faithful to the book, and especially so to its main theme, although, as already touched on, the book is stronger in some ways. Some of this seems to stem from the relatively greater freedom that the novel form gave Alice Walker to pursue subthemes which greatly added to the complexity and richness of the story.

But there was one sharp distinction between the movie and the book that deserves mention, and that was the handling of Shug Avery. I'm not talking here about the downplaying of the love relation between Celie and Shug. That was handled quite differently between the book and the movie, but it didn't strike me as a difference that undercut the power of the story. Instead, I mainly mean the insertion of a subtheme of Shug's longing for a reconciliation with her father, who is only mentioned once or twice in the book. In the book, Shug was a "wild woman" and quite unrepentant about it too. She knew that every step of the way her life had been a flesh-and-blood rebuke to everything society had to say about woman's place, and she reveled in that fact. To have this woman come back to the church and into the embrace of her father, the preacher who had done sermons about her lifestyle as sin incarnate, definitely undercuts the rebel image of Shug (which was a big part of what drew Celie toward her) and undercuts the movie's overall strong stand against patriarchy. But, it still must be said that, in spite of this countercurrent, the fact remains that the movie was generally faithful to the book, and especially so to its main theme, and must be upheld.

The need for art like *The Color Purple* stands out even more sharply against the track record of the Black liberation movement of the 1960s (and revolutionary forces of that period generally) on this question. Here I'm not just talking about people like the cultural nationalists who openly promoted the subjugation of women (for example, polygamy, women being unable to participate in political meetings because that was men's role, women walking three steps behind their men, etc.) based on what they called upholding African tradition. I mean the more generally revolutionary forces of that period, who united with and attempted to give guidance to the masses rising up and rocking the

system of oppression. All too often these forces wouldn't go beyond an approach that came down to breaking all the chains of oppression but the one which binds women in subjugation. Many of the revolutionaries of the 1960s saw no problem with defining the struggle of Black people as one for Black manhood. Often when the oppression of Black women was raised as something that had to be dealt with, the response would be that that wasn't a problem among Black people, or that it (women's oppression) didn't exist in the same way among Black people. *The Color Purple* is part of a growing body of works of literature and art done by Black women artists that sharply target women's oppression and do so without apology. And given this historical backdrop (and with the oppression of women sharpening), such works play a very important role and are especially needed.

We also have to touch on the charges that *The Color Purple* disrupts the unity between Black men and women. (Some Black men critical of the movie have even said that they found it harder to get along with Black women after the women have seen the movie.) First off, it's a strange kind of unity that is disrupted by exposure of the oppression of Black women. What the hell is this unity around? Black men being in position to more fully lord it over *their* women? That's a unity that needs to be disrupted. What's really being raised here is some unwillingness to face the prospect of having to change your act as part of dealing with the oppression of women. It's very telling that some who display this unwillingness and raise political justifications for it turn around and attack Alice Walker for her hostility to Black men and her negative portrayal of them. An important though secondary point made in The Color Purple is that there is hope for these men—if they can stop being oppressors of women. The Color Purple clearly shows several of the male characters changing how they dealt with women in response to these women resisting their continued subjugation. This is brought out through Harpo's relations with both Sophia and Mary Agnes (Squeak) and through how Mister begins to relate to Celie after she returns from her trip with Shug.

In sum, The Color Purple is a fine and very much needed piece of art. The stand that it takes on the oppression of women is valuable for all those who want to end the subjugation of one section of society by another in any form. It is a very good thing that it is drawing large audiences and has sparked off controversy broadly. Essentially its critics oppose it and wish to limit its impact lest it contribute to upsetting the status quo that they class sacred. In the face of that, we can only paraphrase the response of one enthusiastic viewer upon hearing of the debate swirling around the movie, "Let the cameras, and the debate, roll."

BY CARL DIX
THE REVOLUTIONARY WORKER

At the time of the film's release, the Bay Area Branch of the Revolutionary Communist Party, USA distributed a leaflet in Richmond, California, calling on proletarians to enter into the debate around the movie The Color Purple. [These are some responses.]

I think the Color Purple was a great movie. It showed how life is now and how it was then. It's facts, it's the truth, I don't think nobody should scorn the movie, I think everybody should be for it. It shows some of the real things going on between people. There's more now of men beating on their wives. What it is, it's more out in the open now. It wasn't out in the open, but now it's even more—maybe because of the way the times are, the way the law is, it's not enforced . . . Where I work there's been a lot of debate over the movie. Some women said you shouldn't show that—that men are not like that, it disgraces the Black man, the male. I and a couple others were saying that if the shoe fits wear it. There are men like that, there are men that do that and there are men that don't. And I figure the ones that are talking about the movie being no good are probably more or less the types that do those things. My husband liked it too. We didn't have too much discussion afterwards, he just said that was a good movie—in fact he cried, it brought tears to his eyes, mine too. In certain parts we were looking at he would grab my hand. It was really when Mister hit Celie and then he grabbed my hand and squeezed it. Now why he did it, I don't know because we didn't discuss that part, but he grabbed my hand and squeezed it. He says that was a very good movie. And there was also two children with us and they said it was good, they cried. It was a great movie. The dinner table scene was great. I feel she spoke up for herself. After all those years. It was something she should have done before, really. To tell the truth she didn't have to take what she took. That was her. As far as the woman (Celie) is concerned, I feel she was stupid herself. No one made her be that way, she was a weak person. She didn't have to take that. That was something she took, because then all of a sudden in life she stood up for herself. She could have did that a long time before that. A woman does this to herself. I mean as long as you got two feet on you can walk if things aren't right. I wouldn't sit and let nobody do me that way. I'm a woman, I'm a human being . . . You got to walk away when things aren't right, you got to show some strength. When it's not "right" in a man's life he walks away—he leaves babies and all. But that was a good movie, one of the best I've seen. Steven Spielberg did a great job. More should be made like that.

A PROLETARIAN WOMAN FROM
RICHMOND, CALIFORNIA

I was really glad to see a movie that spoke to women's oppression and in such an honest way. The movie did make me angry from the standpoint of how long this kind of oppression has been tolerated. It also brought out how ingrained this idea of being a ser-vant to the father and husband is. It's almost like to have a life of your own is not even thinkable at all. At the beginning of the movie, Celie was a lot more submissive and I noticed how it took talking to other women who refused to go along with what was supposed to be so "natural" to bring out that fire in Celie.

I think that this is the effect the movie has on women. There are many of us who bear all this pain and dream of things being different—but these dreams lie dormant because we are not conscious that it is not the "natural" order to take this shit. It does take putting out the rebellious side to bring some consciousness about that the subjugation of women by men is not the "natural" order. In the book—there was one experience that shows how deep this idea is. While Celie's mother knew that there was incest going on between her husband and Celie—she closed her eyes to it and this was like saying to Celie that this was to be accepted and passed on from one generation to the next. I didn't think that the movie was a put-down on Black men. I saw that it was a movie which opens people's eyes to some real things that are happening to women and how sharp it is. While it is true that there is oppression of Black men—the solution is not to enslave a woman at home. I think that the solution lies in getting rid of all oppression for good by getting out the imperialist system altogether. We have to look at who the real enemy is and work to-wards fighting the things that stand in the way of achieving our goal. What really got me was how Mister was treating Celie—like she was some kind of marketable product being judged by how well she cooked, etc. It was like she was not a human being—but something to be bought and sold. I think that these forces who are downing this movie are not that interested in getting rid of this whole system of imperialism. To them—it is just too far out to let loose that fury of women because they would take it too far. It's a terrible thought to them that the "peace" of this existing set-up gets upset to the extent that it could get wiped out all the way.

A REVOLUTIONARY PROLETARIAN
WOMAN

ALICE WALKER ON ALICE WALKER

Elena Featherston: What was it like growing up in the south as a sharecropper's daughter? How does it affect your writing?

Alice Walker: Lots of it was very good, you know. We lived always very far in the country, so that the countryside was wonderful, beautiful. We lived in very shabby houses most of the time, and that wasn't so good. But my parents were both with us and were both storytellers. There was a lot of good . . . I think my mother affected my writing a lot. Being a great storyteller herself, she had an eye for the telling point in a person's character, in a story. Growing up in the South makes me write in settings which are rural instead of urban. I am more comfortable in the country than in the city.

I think I was always trying to hear these other voices. When I was growing up, my sister tells me, from the time I was a little kid, I used to stand on the porch and talk to imaginary people. I would listen to these imaginary people. I think that for me, from the time I was a small child, the universe was peopled with all the spirits I now know are there. . . . I am just one of those people for whom the dead never die.

EF: As a black writer, do you feel you write about the human experience or the "black experience"?

AW: Black writers write about the human experience; anybody writing does. I think that is summed up fairly well by theologian Howard Thurman, who said something I really appreciate. He said that if you go deeply enough into yourself, into your own idiom, it's inevitable, then, that you come up in other people. We have the capability to connect to absolutely everyone and everything, and, in fact, we are all connected. . . . I discover that my family is like any other family in the world of our same class. When I write about my family, about things from the South, the people of China say, "Why, this is very Chinese."

Naturally, I write about the things I know best, from the angle I know best. Black women have a different angle from which to write; they see things from a different point of view. Black women have to look out and through all those people who have traditionally been on top of them: the black man, the white woman, the white man. This creates a different way of looking at reality.

EF: You've won many literary accolades, your novel *The Color Purple* is being made into a film, people clamor to tell you how much your work means to them. What does it mean to you?

AW: I think of my work as a way to make myself well, and to make myself healthy and happy. Almost everything that I do—more and more as the years go by—has an element of joy for me, and if it doesn't I generally don't do it. So I see my work as very organic; it's very central to how I live in the world.

EF: Would you continue to write if no one else read your work?

AW: Yes. It is a very natural way that I've been given to deal with my reality. So I read it, and I'm convinced that, by keeping a journal, I have managed to help myself much more than I will ever help anybody else. . . . I deliberately draw on family and personal history in my work. I am working these things out for myself. There are things *I* need to know, things that trouble me for years. The reader is really second or third.

EF: What would you do, who would you be, if you didn't write? What if that door had never been opened?

AW: Well, it may close, too, you know, and I may not write. But as long as I can operate one member of my body, I will always do *something* just because I like to feel that connectedness to the world around me. I think gardening could easily occupy most of my time, except during the winter months. There is always something. Quilt making, cooking—I am learning to *really* cook, you know.

ALICE WALKER ON THE MOVIE THE COLOR PURPLE

PERMISSION TO USE

First of all it never occurred to me—considering the kinds of films that *are* being made—that anyone would want to do a film of *The Color Purple*. (The first shock was that someone would give it a Pulitzer . . . who are these sweet people? I still don't know.) So I called together a group of friends . . . 5 women including [my daughter] Rebecca, and also [my partner] Robert. We had a meeting to see if we should do it. The first half of the meeting we said, of course not, they never do anything right. This is the reality of living in America—what have they done lately that worked? They have poisoned the water, they killed the fish, they poisoned the air, so why give them anything—we should just run from them. Then someone said, if we always do that, what will we ever get, what will change? We batted it about for a long time. Finally it seemed like something worth the risk.

I remember I was so agonized over the movie at first, that people might be angry at me if it turned out badly. I took it to another friend. She said, "Alice, people are smarter than that . . . they know the movie is not the book." I think what she meant was not quite as flippant as it sounded, but rather that people can understand the politics and they can use whatever happens—whether the movie is great or terrible—as an opportunity to study the contradictions of our racist and sexist society.

I often think of what Bernice Reagon says about coalition: "If you are not threatened to the core, you ain't doing no coalition." I have at various times felt very vulnerable about what would happen . . . But on the other hand—I think it is my Sagittarius rising—I'm a risk taker—I have a belief that people can do really good things, can actually create things, they don't have to always mess up. To be quite honest, I think there is a way in which I have dealt with the whole creation of the book as if it has its own life, and my job is just to move it along. And so that's what I did. I don't feel that attached to it.

When I was in London last year, someone was saying, "suppose it's ruined," and I realized I don't really think that way. It's a movie based on a written story. So I said, if you want to get the real thing, by the end it will be a $3 paperback. Buy it, read it . . . and then you can go to the movie and point out all the things they did wrong. But for a writer like me who writes for a lot of people who don't read, I have to think of visual things, ways of reaching them.

And even if the story is not entirely my vision when it gets to the screen, I think just because of what I have given to the story, it will be progressive enough for people to see some necessary reflections of themselves.

The other thing that was crucial in this decision is that I have seen movies in which there were lines and influences from my work. You know, when something of yours is used you recognize it. I don't mind so much when people do things like this if there is some credit, some acknowledgement that they took it. But there hardly ever is—and this is what has happened to black culture all these years: We produce and produce and create and create and it finds its way into mainstream culture ten years later, white people assuming they are the source of it.* So when I understood that somebody in Burbank wanted to buy The Color Purple and they wanted to actually spend good money to pay for the rights, I had to realize in a sense it was already there and that they would be quite capable of coming out in five years with The Color Turquoise. It would be my story, but it would be about white people, you know? And with no credit—and that would annoy me.

Knowing what we know about the system, to take a chance on having a film based on my story, using just about all black characters and with more of the black story there, seemed worth it.

You know the story I wrote, "1955"—the story about the black woman that a white man hears singing, and then he sings her song and he becomes the star? I'm tired of that story, in real life. If they are going to mess something up I want it to be clear what they've done. But the thing about this film is, unless I'm totally wrong, it's going to be a great movie. I think I'll really enjoy it.

THE SCREENPLAY

You can't put an 8-hour book into a 2-hour screenplay. I think they are *trying* to keep it in its original shape but it will be a movie. That is the first thing I had to realize: it is going to be a movie, and movies have different requirements than novels.

They wanted me to write the screenplay but then they sent me the contract, and it was like a chain: I couldn't write for other publications, for instance, while I was doing it, really like a chain.

Also, I had promised Robert and Rebecca that after I had finished the book, and after they had suffered through the onslaught of people who came after the Pulitzer, that I would be theirs. Writing the screenplay wasn't that important to me compared to their happiness. Rebecca had really missed me. And then the strain of just trying to go on with something I was

*In my opinion, the 1995 movie How to Make an American Quilt (produced by Amblin Entertainment), shows influences from my The Color Purple script. If I am correct, it provides a good example of how black art and culture is transmuted into white.

finished with . . . although the spirits of the book came back to help me along. I was grateful because I had made an agreement with them [the characters in the book] that if I sold the book I wouldn't send them off alone, but at some point I think we all realized they would have to make it on their own and that they could do it. Shug especially was ready to waltz on down to Hollywood. She has that kind of sensibility.

ARTISTIC CONTROL/CREATIVE TRUST

Lots of people thought I should keep some kind of artistic control, beyond being a consultant, which I was, but it was clear to me I couldn't do that. I don't like being controlled. If I could control a creative person they wouldn't be creative enough for me to work with. Steven [Spielberg] is quite capable as a director of really understanding a lot more than people will give him credit for, being white, being a man. Without someone like Steven, all the people who should really see the movie wouldn't see it—it would never reach Eatonton, Georgia, my hometown.

All my life I have been really blessed to meet individual people who seem to have been put in my path to prove to me that they are not the power structure. I'm easily seduced by these people, you know [great laughter]. And I'm also intensely curious about the people who do come across my path . . . I don't take them lightly. I didn't really even know Steven's work. Rebecca took me to see E.T., and then

it just seemed so weird that in should come this person who loves the book, who sits here in my living room and knows every line.

One of my fears was that Hollywood would be so out of touch that they wouldn't even be able to see the people I had drawn—they wouldn't recognize them if they saw them, which means they would cast people who had no resemblance. The thing that scared me was that the people on the screen would be so unlike the people in the book, that when you tried to read the book you'd bring the film characters into it. But I went down to see the people they had chosen; of course, I had picked Whoopi Goldberg to be Celie—and they all looked just like the people I had been writing about. So in a way, no matter what happens with the film, you won't have that problem. Harpo will be Harpo no matter what the actors and director do.

And it was interesting to me to watch what happened to Steven as he was making the movie. He has more ideas per second than anyone I've ever met—it's exhausting. And they are good ideas. They don't always work but they are interesting. What has worked well for all of us has been that there's been a lot of love—a lot of love for the story and for the people as human beings. So this has not been just a business thing, although we do have contracts and all that. But I'm not from a people of contracts. We *feel* our contracts. I listen to them and they listen to me. I'm so happy about that.

MAINSTREAM +
ALTERNATIVES = ?

My function will be to always be on the outside, an alternative, thank goodness. But 20 years from now, if this country is changed sufficiently, I may find myself in what Rebecca's children will think of as American Literature. But what has happened to *The Color Purple* may be a fluke . . . I don't see anyone rushing to buy the rights to *Meridian* [an earlier novel about a woman's struggles in the Mississippi civil rights movement in the 1960s].

With the book I wanted to reach a mass market . . . I wanted to reach the supermarket crowd. They are doing that now [a pocketbook edition] because of the film. The reason the book has done so well up to now is because of the Pulitzer, not because of initial marketing techniques. The high point of this whole business with *Purple* was not when they told me about the awards but when they told me the people on the IRT [NYC subway] were reading it. That was the first time I felt I had connected with my audience.

It is true, I could have waited for a feminist film company to do *The Color Purple*, I could have invested 5 years to raise money, but I really don't have the energy or time. It's funny too. I'm the world's slowest person. I hardly ever run, and I swim slowly. On the other hand, when I have something to give to people I try to give it to them immediately. One of the things I love about life is giving gifts. I *love* giving presents. So that's one of the reasons I wanted to get the movie going now rather than raise the money and take the 5-year plan.

REACHING READERS

I have to think of ways to make readers out of non-readers, to pique their curiosity. I just did a calendar that has pictures and little quotes and wonderful people's birthdays . . . like Fidel [Castro]. [That great laugh bubbles up again . . . she seems to be laughing with Fidel.] I decided that I was really annoyed that I hadn't expressed my love for Fidel because I do love him and I think he's just great. [HN: Have you met him?] No, I don't need to. I've been to Cuba and I meet him every time I walk down the street. I don't need to meet him. He has other things to do, you know, so do I.

We didn't need to meet Alice either. We meet her characters, her compassion, her curiosity, her hopefulness, her genuine respect for human potential in everything she writes— and we receive the gifts she gets such pleasure in giving. We didn't need to meet her but are very glad we did because she has a throaty laugh that has as many words in it as a novel, and in the case of *The Color Purple*, soon to be a major motion picture, as many pictures.

BY HOLLY NEAR, WITH AMY BANK
VOICES, 1985

DEEP
WATERS

May 11, 1984

Dear Rebecca,*

I am sorry if I sprung the notion of Henri**
helping us through this period on you; you and I
should have discussed it thoroughly beforehand.
As the deadline approaches for the completed
screenplay I become more and more panicked that
it isn't nearer completion. The time that I
spend in the city is so filled with all my other
responsibilities that I can't seem to fit everything in. Including the most important: long
talks with you.

*Rebecca Walker Leventhal (who has since changed her last name to Leventhal Walker)
**Henri Norris, an old friend I had asked to accompany Rebecca to a function at school
that I would not be able to attend. Though Henri and Rebecca remain fast friends and
"aunt–niece" today, at the time Rebecca was adamantly opposed to encountering whatever this event was, with a substitute.

I was not only disappointed by your behavior, I was hurt by it. It showed such a lack of understanding of all I am trying to do, and a real misreading of my attempts to do both the best I can in my work and the best I can by you. And these days I have no energy at all to argue—the smallest thing sends me back to bed. But in a month or so we can discuss this in detail. Basically, and even though you are *extremely* helpful and self-sufficient, it isn't easy not having someone to share raising you with—and as you know, Robert at this point is in need of support himself. But even before this I never felt I could really share this with him entirely—though he has always done what he could. I feel bad that I can not be with you on Monday. But this is one of the times you will have to live up to what you say you are capable of doing: handling things by yourself. Henri would be glad to accompany you, if you want her. If not, she won't. It is very draining for me to drive up and down the road so often, which is why I am going to be in the country for longer periods of time. I'm really sorry you hate the country, because you could make this part easier by visiting me, sometimes.

Irregardless, I love you and will always hope you are safe and well and happy.

Mom

March 6, 1986*

Dear Danny,

I have been thinking a lot about you, as actor and spirit, and hoping you are well. In a few days the academy awards nominations will be announced, and I wonder if you will be among those nominated for an award. It isn't that you need the award; you don't. (Except for the difference

*Written in February, typed in March.

it would perhaps make in your public career.) You have, in your acting, reached the level of healer and whether you get the award or not, this capacity to heal through your work will probably always be yours; unless, of course, you spend the rest of your life playing evil detectives and drug profiteers, which you are not doing. On the other hand, for a genuine healer there is even healing power in the portrayal of evil.

Let me tell you a story: When I was a little girl I had a very traumatic experience that meant I could not live with my family for a while. I was sent to live with my grandparents for a number of months. Stories about my grandfather indicated a rather autocratic, wild, renegade outlaw. A man who gambled and drank—and carried a pistol. It was even said he shot someone in the behind. (This was told so that it sounded amusing; it was never said that he shot someone in the back!) There were many stories—that even my barely teenage brothers and sisters knew—about how energetically Papa beat our grandmother, his wife. About how he used to chase her all over the farm, shooting off his gun. Shooting at her; missing only because he was drunk. Chillingly, the stories were told as if this behavior was amusing, and even my parents and the small children mimicked my grandmother's fear; they laughed at how she pleaded for her life, or ran, terrified, through the corn. My grandfather also, always, *all* his life, absolutely loved someone else.

But they were getting old, when I lived with them. The autocratic order still prevailed: He called her "woman" ('oman), she called him "*Mr.* Walker." He no longer beat her. By then I don't think he had to. His word was law.

But in fact, he rarely talked anyway. Rachel, my grandmother, did most of the work—mostly housecleaning, cooking, seeing after chickens and pigs, tending the garden, although he liked working in the garden, too—which he did early, very early in the morning. And I remember long hours of the two of us, my grandfather and I, sitting quietly on the porch or counting the cars that came by. Each of us would choose a color and the one whose color passed by most frequently won the "game."

He was inscrutable, was Henry Clay, and never violent and never raised his voice the whole time I lived with them. And yet, the effects of his violence I could see plainly in Rachel's slavish behavior. It was years later before I realized she was so beaten down that none of us ever knew her true personality, and she had probably forgotten it. So this woman who was literally generous to a fault: she gave things away with an alacrity I've never seen matched; was never able to give herself (we didn't know her, really, at all) because somewhere over the years her self had been lost.

Now, Danny, from playing the role of Mr., some of this will sound only too familiar. But what you might not know—because I wasn't conscious of it for a very long time—is even though I understood on some child's level that he had been, and still was, in many ways "a devil," *I adored my grandfather*.

And over the years I've struggled with this conflict: how to love someone who could destroy another human being. For years I repressed my love, almost as a duty to Rachel. It wasn't until I saw the movie that I fully realized how I had been longing and needing to be able to love my grandfather even as he was when he did the worst things. And the last of the conflict was washed away by your acting. You helped me relive my grandfather's early life, to see him objectively (There he was!), and to take his psyche completely into mine. Unless that had happened, the parts of me that are like him may well have died from their repression, and my capacity to love and understand would have been far smaller.

I will tell you where it happened: When Mr.

runs out of the house, and down the walk, gets on his horse, with his little hopeful bouquet of straggly flowers—that he didn't even plant!—and goes off into the sunset, still trying to court a woman he was too weak to marry and by whom he has three children! And the song "Oh Careless Love" strikes in me the grandfather gene and makes me know that part of the reason I love him so is—he is like me! That in my own way I am renegade and outlaw and there is the same wildness in the intensity of love. But I am not as lazy as my grandfather and I hate violence. I have come to understand that true love means work. Every time I see that scene in the movie I cry the most exquisitely happy tears, for I feel so close to my old confused grandfather. And I can hear him within me saying: "See, it was like this; and just cause I was confused don't mean I didn't love you." Because he *did* love me. We were like twin spirits. But I couldn't accept it if he couldn't love Rachel too. But he just didn't, until, maybe, just before he died.

Danny, I thank you so much for this healing. For your hard work, which just amazed me, and humbled me. Especially when I saw you carrying on, quite heroically, with five (?) children cavorting about the set. My concentration would have been ruined; but somehow you managed to incorporate the tension and distraction into the scenes you played—and they were actually deeper, because of that.

Isn't life astonishing! It is always managing to "hit a straight lick with a crooked stick," which is one of the ways I think about the entire movie experience, which I sense also had very deep meanings and connections for you.

I'm so glad.

With love and thanks, Danny,
Your "granddaughter" and sister,

.

Alice

Feb. 3, 1986

Dearest Barbara,*

I'm *so* sorry you dislike the film! I did too,
the first time; it was a bit like seeing a deformed child and seeing it *as* deformed, rather
than as interestingly, if curiously, different
from what had been envisioned. Now I see its
flaws, but love it for its own sake, and love
the people, too, who made it and made it from
where they are. Doing their very best, for all
that this might appear, to some, inadequate.

It helped me to read somewhere that there are
no mistakes, only lessons. No problems, only op-
portunities, and—from my analyst—that to defend
(one's self, or actions) is to lose. None of this
was about the film, but for me it also applies.

Many, many people, intelligent, sensitive,
wonderful people, do, in fact, love the film.
Many people write to tell me they have felt
healed by it. In any creative collaboration
something is lost, but something is gained, too.
A new creation comes into being—this is part of
the excitement of working with others. If the
book did not exist, or ceased being published, I
would perhaps be more concerned than I am. But
think of the opportunity to study not just the
book *or* the film, but the choices made (and why)
by everyone involved! To do that is to analyze
the whole society!

Why, as a writer, do I need to reach people
who can't read, for instance? Why is it that the
film you described that *you* would have made
would probably never make it to my hometown?

After Rebecca saw the film the first time—and
she had worked *so* hard on it Barbara; all summer, in bugs and heat—she said "Maybe I'll be a
director someday and do the film right."

This was very comforting to me because she

*Barbara Christian

seemed so clear about assuming what will be her generation's responsibilities in the future; as we have tried to assume our generation's responsibilities in the present.

But she, too, has grown to love the film, or at least to enjoy it—particularly for some of the things that are well done: and she loved the actors and their work, which I too think is the best of the effort, perhaps, though my appreciation of Steven and Quincy is also immense. They showed courage, too. A courage the media pretends—from the little I've seen—not to understand, and certainly not to credit.

Some changes I dislike *very* much; some seem hokey, Hollywoodish, juvenile and silly. A *lot* of points were missed.

But, *irregardless*, there's that bouncy, happy kid sweeping across the land, putting out healing and love as well as craziness—at some point you think: why don't more babies have two heads or twelve toes? Or no hair. It's kind of endearing.

But mainly Barbara—let it go. I trust the Universe on this one completely. And it—I feel—is not displeased.

I know your concern is out of love for me and my work, and I love you for that. *But it really is all right.*

Jah knows.

Love,

Alice

P.S. And don't feel bad that you encouraged taking a chance—I'm *very* glad you did. But *I* took it, so you are not responsible.

Four years after the opening of the film:

Dear Steven,

It is the 21st of July, 1989, and I apologize for this raggedy paper and the mistakes. My computer refuses to work, and I've put off writing you for too long, after thinking about you, Amy, and Max, a lot. I was more than sorry to hear that you and Amy are separating, perhaps you have already done so, by now. I hAVE only good memories of the two of you, as many strangers do. However, I am all for divorce when it makes people happier. Also good luck with whatever new love has appeared. This letter is really about Max.

Do you remember, sitting at the big table at Amblin during lunch, we were all talking about ways we could appear in the movie,* our movie, and you asked me if I would appear in it holding Max? I was upset by your question, because of course I could not. There is just too much history for that to have been possible. It's a very long Southern/South African tradition, after all—black women holding white babies. And yet, I felt so sad for us all, that this should be so. And especially moved by you, who had this history as no part of your consciousness.

And then, when we were in North Carolina, I actually met Max. Now here's the odd part. I felt as if I knew him, and had, and that there was a bonding when we looked into each other's eyes. I was shaken by this, and at first thought it came from my guilt over not having been able to hold him for the movie. But the sense that there is a bond between us has never left me. When I heard about you and Amy, my first thought was of that bond. But it seemed crazy to mention

---

*Alice Walker appeared in the movie as a voice in the chorus, singing "Maybe God's Trying to Tell You Something." Steven Spielberg appeared as Harpo's bereft whistling, when Sofia leaves home.

it, and I've put it off and put it off. Besides,
I'm not sure what there is to "do with it."

But finally I decided to trust to the simple.
You know as well as I do that we are living in
extremely perilous times. Somehow, I want Max to
know that there's a friend out there—beyond all
those he knows about in his daily life—who will
help and protect him, should he need it, to the
best of my ability. I thought of sending him a
tiny photograph, so that he can see what I look
like, not to actually remember it, but just to
have my face and being in his consciousness.

That is all. As you can imagine, I feel a little weird writing you this. But I have learned,
with Rebecca, that raising a child really does
require the whole village, and not just mothers
and fathers. She is well, by the way, when last
heard from she and Steven Talmy (they are still
together!) were on an island off the coast of
Turkey!

I saw and enjoyed *Indiana Jones and the Last
Crusade,* though during the violent parts I had
to watch with my eyes covered.

You don't have to respond. And how will you
explain to Max that this person he's never seen
(to remember) will be an underground railroad
for him if he should ever (Goddess forbid) need
it? All I know is it's worth trying.

Alice

RUNNING

THE

RIVER

It was important to me that Celie and Shug be portrayed as the lovers they are in *The Color Purple*. It took a bit of gentle insistence, in talks with Menno, Steven and Quincy, simply to include "the kiss," chaste and soon over as it is. However I was aware, because Quincy Jones sent copies of some of the letters he received, that there were people in the black community who adamantly opposed any display of sexual affection between Celie and Shug. There were also editorials in black newspapers condemning such behavior. Incredibly, love between women was considered analogous to drug addiction and violence.

I knew the passion of Celie and Shug's relationship would be sacrificed when, on the day "the kiss" was shot, Quincy reassured me that Steven had shot it "five or six" different ways, all of them "tasteful."

Although Steven and Quincy refused to meet with Blacks Against the Exploitation of Blacks in the Movies, and other organizations that wished to control certain aspects of the film, there are telling moments in the film when the censor's knife scars the scene. One is when Shug is brought home for Celie to nurse: she would never have been facedown in the wagon like a common drunk. She would have been sick but queenly, for Celie to appreciate. Leaving home, Celie would never have sat in the rumble seat. She had met the woman with whom she would spend the rest of her life: they both knew it. They would have shared a seat, at least.

```
                          Moon Song Productions*
                             September 16, 1985

Dear Alice,

   I've been hoping this would go away, but evi-
dently it won't.**

QJ
```

Most of the letters attached to Jones' note were signed by Earl Walter, Jr., a representative of the Coalition Against Black Exploitation, who did not give permission to have them reprinted here. Well-known activists, psychologists, sociologists and psychiatrists—including Dr. Alvin Poussaint, William Lawson, M.D., Ph.D., and Dr. Wilbert Jordon—are mentioned as members of the black community who have expressed concern that, in the hands of the unscrupulous Hollywood movie industry, *The Color Purple* might be used to psychologically harm black people; this "harm" aparently stemming from how the more "sensitive" areas of my book might be filmed.

Robert Hooks was one of those moved to write to Quincy Jones.

*Spielberg's code name for *The Color Purple* while it was being filmed.
**A note from Quincy Jones that was attached to letters he received from organizations concerned about the depiction of black people in the movie.

ROBERT HOOKS PRODUCTIONS
Los Angeles, CA
August 6, 1985

Mr. Quincy Jones
Los Angeles, CA

Dear Quincy:

   I recently participated in a community event
celebrating the birthday of Nelson Mandela, the
South African leader who is in his 23rd year of
incarceration under that Country's Apartheid
regime. While there, I was approached by several
community leaders who discussed, at length, your
upcoming feature, "The Color Purple," and their
concerns as it relates to the more sensitive areas of Alice's book. I listened and was impressed with the sincerity of these Black
community representatives.

   I was asked by them to send a personal note to
you concerning their desire to meet with you and
talk. I am also enclosing material from the
Coalition Against Black Exploitation, one of the
groups concerned. I have found that it's best to
talk early, rather than late, about such issues.

   I hope all is well with you and yours and I wish
you great success in your producing ventures.

Peace and Love,

Robert Hooks

RH:tp
Enclosure

A letter whose writer could not be found or who chose not to respond to inquiries from my publisher wrote directly to Robert

Friedman, V.P. of Worldwide Publicity at Warner Brothers. She wrote: "The negative portrayal of Black men and Black male/female relationships with the glamourization of lesbianism are themes that too often skew people-to-people relationships in undesireable unfair ways." She goes on to say that "script and story should be carefully packaged with a perspective that uplifts rather than degrades Black people."

A letter from Earl Walter, Jr., to Quincy Jones requests a meeting with the Coalition Against Black Exploitation in order for the Coalition to "ascertain" how some of the "sensitive" areas of the book will be handled.

In a "Viewpoint" article attached to the letter there was a long, thoughtful synopsis of the plot of The Color Purple, until about halfway through when Mr. Walter, Jr., begins to discuss the movie Superfly, a "blaxploitation" film that was produced in the early Seventies. He contends that this movie, with its glorification of gangsterism and drugs, directly encouraged the proliferation of both these plagues in the Black community. "Almost immediately after Superfly's release, the image of the cold, hustling, young Black male, with dark glasses and processed hair, hit the community. In the name of 'trying to get over,' the Superfly image spread throughout the community.

Mr. Walter, Jr., goes on to wonder whether lesbianism, if permitted physical expression and projected from the screen over a high-impact musical score by Quincy Jones, might not run rampant in the community in the same way. From a "collective point of view," he writes, lesbianism is "anti-survival," "anti-productive," and even, at its worst, "genocidal."

Curiously, Mr. Walter, Jr., claims that the Coalition's concern is "not an artistic or creative argument" against my work, nor "a challange to the premises Walker pursues." He says the Coalition's interest is in "separating love from sex in women's relationships. That is, women can and should develop a love relationship with other women, without the need or desire for sexual contact. The same applies to men in their relationships with each other."

Contradicting the Coalition's position in the next sentence—"We are not denying the individual's right for sexual preference"—he concludes his statement by suggesting, chillingly, that gay rights are "negotiable," "subject to collective scrutiny, criticism and control."

In the final paragraph, a boycott of the movie *The Color Purple* is recommended unless "assurances are given in advance that homosexuality is not projected to the masses as a solution to the problems Black men and women face with each other."

TONY BROWN'S COMMENTS

BLACKS NEED TO LOVE ONE ANOTHER

There is a growing inability of black men and women to love one another.

This, you might say, racial divorce is bedded in a strong psychological distrust of and dislike of black manhood. Many males who are black confuse manliness with the ability to act out neurotic feelings. The roots of this pattern of some black men psychologically hating themselves can be traced back to the early 1660s in America when slavery was started.

Slavery was an example of economic racism which I define as the use of the concept of white supremacy for an economic advantage. Example: the security costs of building high fences to restrict escape or sabotage or hiring armed guards to watch the slaves would have reduced the profits of the slavery system.

To avoid these unprofitable methods and to reduce rebellions and escapes, it was far cheaper to rely on restrictions of the slaves' mental and psychological development. Ignorance of who they were as a people was much cheaper—and more efficient—than physical methods of restraint.

African men were assertive by culture and tradition. This made them particularly dangerous. Therefore, the black man's dose of psychological dependency and worship of whites was intensified in proportion to his independence and assertiveness.

Subsequently, he learned to direct his hostility away from the objects of fear and worship, whites, and towards those without power instruments—other blacks, women being the most vulnerable. This phenomenon manifests itself today in the way many black men view themselves and, as a result, what they do to themselves and to those who love them.

Alice Walker brilliantly and powerfully captured this self-hatred in "The Color Purple," a feminist novel. Steven Spielberg adapted it for film. He brought to life, according to TIME Magazine, a black woman's story "both of injustice, at the fists of black men, and of emotional regeneration, at the caressing hands of black women." TIME added: ". . . . Walker's message: Sisterhood is beautiful, and Men stink."

It's the story of Celie (played by Whoopi Goldberg), NEWSWEEK said, "raped by her father at a tender age, abused by her cruel common-law husband, Mr., and brought to life in the embrace of a soulful, bisexual blues singer named Shug Avery. . . . Shug, the catalyst in Celie's journey to self-discovery, ..."

Dorothy Gilliam, a black columnist at THE WASHINGTON POST, wrote that "it is really a film about the purity and depth of love" and "when it concluded, I stood up and cheered." Gilliam was not alone. The "TODAY SHOW" critic said, "It should be against the law not to see" this epic (of beautiful sisterhood and black men stinking).

I'm quoting others because I did not see the movie—and never intend to. If the NAACP had produced it, I would not go to see it. And some who have, have lived what I'm sure my reaction would be. One black man walked out of the Chicago premiere, confronted a black actor in the film, and asked him how a black man could take part in such a degrading movie.

The Coalition Against Black Exploitation said it degraded black men, children and families. A white Los Angeles newspaper said "all that's missing . . . is a shot of Uncle Remus . . ." Willis Edwards, president of the Hollywood NAACP, said it was "stereotypical" and demeaning. Furthermore, the Los Angeles opening was picketed by a host of harsh critics.

While I know that some black men have raped their daughters, I know that the vast majority have not. And although many black men have difficulty loving—period—because much of the love has been drained out by the brutality of a society panic-stricken over black masculinity, enough has been salvaged to make most black women today happy.

And lesbian affairs will never replace the passion and beauty of a free black man and a free black woman. In "Purple," emotional and sexual salvation for women is found in other women. That's not the real world, as some black women, out of frustration, seem to want to believe.

I offer no excuses for the kinds of men that Walker wrote about; they are, for whatever reason, sad examples. But I know that many of us who are male and black are too healthy to pay to be abused by a white man's movie focusing only on our failures.

And because so few films are produced with black themes, it becomes the only statement on black men. "Purple" points us away from the fact that

Nelson Mandela, Martin Luther King and Malcolm X overcame the system's psychological warfare and produced healthy, non-incestuous, non-brutalizing relationships with women. Their women never needed a "Shug."

Furthermore, most of us will be men in spite of white men and women who only publish books by black women or homosexual black men with degrading themes or passive attitudes—and then make them into movies of "the black experience."

And the movie's star, Whoopi Goldberg, TIME said, "hates" being called "a black actress."

She need not worry. With her level of consciousness, she doesn't qualify.

BY TONY BROWN
CAROLINA PEACEMAKER
JANUARY 4, 1986

SCARS OF INDIFFERENCE*

It is difficult to believe, yea, nearly impossible in these state-of-the-art times, that a journalist would attempt to write a critique of a movie without ever having seen the movie, relying as it were on hearsay. An even more challenging task would be to try to respond to such a journalist . . . but one must try:

Show an acutely insecure black man the weaknesses of the sexual awareness of his genre and this is what might happen: He may lash out with every fiber of his being. If you happen to be a black woman he may feel it his duty to somehow make you understand how little you know about your own "emotional and sexual salvation"

and where to find it. He may dare to conclude without an ounce of evidence, not to mention open-mindedness, that a woman can never love a woman with the "passion and beauty of a free black man and a free black woman." One would have to ask what basis he has for these conclusions.

In his article *Blacks Need to Love One Another*, (*Carolina Peacemaker*, 1-4-86), Tony Brown sets forth such ideas as those you have just read in what seems to be a single-handed attempt to slander the basic principle upon which feminism and humanitarianism are built . . . personal freedom— the right to choose. In doing so he reveals that he is among this genre of

*A rebuttal to an article written by Tony Brown and published by the *Carolina Peacemaker*, January 4, 1986.

insecure black men. His tactics are far from unique, we have seen them before. His target is *The Color Purple*, a brilliant novel of black folklore written by Alice Walker, a sensitive, aware black woman. The novel was recently adapted for the screen and since its release has become the subject of much unrest among many black men. Tony Brown, being one of those men, has issued a double-standard, biased, uninformed opinion as to the cultural merit of *The Color Purple*. Simultaneously, he has made evident a serious lack of awareness as to what is happening in the lives of modern black women.

Though it is strictly fiction, Walker's story is about real suffering and its impact is anything but pure imagination. The story is largely about Celie, a young, black woman of the rural South deeply oppressed by the men in her life; first a cruel, incestuous stepfather and later a harshly indifferent husband. The plot unfolds over the first three decades of this century, a very difficult time for Black Americans, especially black women. Walker develops Celie's character from a frightened, uneducated, abused girl to that of a self-assured, strong woman who becomes her own life support system. Celie's growth takes place at the "expense" of a few male egos . . . those of most of the black men in the story and, as it would seem, a great majority of the black men in the audience. If any man viewing the movie or reading the book becomes offended and feels that the message is degrading, perhaps it is because the shoe is such a good fit

that it becomes downright uncomfortable. The shallow images of black men in such supermovies as "Shaft" and "Superfly" warranted protest much more than those of *The Color Purple*, yet instead we were given top-forty songs of worship. Walker's message is clear—oppression is ugly no matter what color it is. In *Purple* it happens to be black, Southern, female and hits home with a lot of people that would just as soon forget. We mustn't forget. We must remember and continue to fight because the ugliness lives on and just as we are, it, too, is breeding.

The Color Purple is not a story against black men: it is a story about black women. The fact that the men in the story are not all good guys needs no justification, for it is not the obligation of any work of fiction to present every possible angle of every possible situation. Walker chose a particular feminist theme and dealt with it, which resulted in many black men protesting and licking their wounded egos. All too often, it is with such dispatch that black men come to the defense of their egos that they fail to realize that they are not the issue at hand.

To quote Mr. Brown: "In 'Purple,' emotional and sexual salvation for women is found in other women. That's not the real world, as some black women, out of frustration, seem to want to believe." Take a good look around, Mr. Brown, there are all sorts of "new" developments. Since the beginning of humankind and in today's real world, women love women, men love men, whites love blacks, and every imaginable variation therein. In the real world, many intelligent, articulate black men are continuing to impact on the women in their lives scars of indifference. Physically invisible yet emotionally devastating, these scars are evidence of the indifferent attitudes and actions of black men who are so busy putting together words to describe how slavery and white supremacy are responsible for their faults, that they are oblivious to the fact that black women, who as a group have always been strong, are now using their strength to better their place in the world. More from Mr. Brown: "And although many black men have difficulty loving—period—because much of the love has been drained out by the brutality of a society panic-stricken over black masculinity, enough has been salvaged to make most black women today happy." In the real world, the time has ended for this excuse—period. The time is overdue for all men to put forth more effort toward learning exactly what makes any woman happy today.

In his article, Tony Brown holds that the assertive African men who were forced into slavery became psychologically dependent on whites and over time this dependency grew "in proportion to his independence and assertiveness. Subsequently, he learned to direct his hostility away from the objects of fear and worship, whites, and toward those without power instruments—other blacks, women being the most vulnerable."

Are we then to accept that today's black men are but modern manifestations of this fear and worship phenomenon which explains why he does the things he does to himself and those he loves? NO!! It is not now, nor has it been at any time in history, justifiable for black men to take the hostility they felt for whites and direct them toward other blacks. Such actions make the black man no better than the white man he blames.

For all the oppression that black men have suffered, black women have suffered twice as much because, as Tony Brown has pointed out, black women had to take it from white society as well as black men. Yet through all of what happened to us then, through all of the present protests and continuing indifference from black men, for black women it is as it has always been—business as usual. We continue to mend our scars, raise our children (with or without the men) and join other women in the fight for our rights as human beings. It's a tougher fight, for the modern black woman is more efficiently armed today than at any other time in history. One of her most vital weapons is the pen, and as Alice Walker has shown, we are ever more skillful in the use of it. Obviously, there are many black men in this country who do not share the insecurities and indifferences that Tony Brown presented in his article, but the fact remains that there are also many who have a job to do if they are to remain in the arena with the new breed of black woman.

Celie summed up a general consensus when she said: "I'm poor, I'm black, I may be ugly and can't cook ... But I'm here."

Amen, Miss Celie, amen.

BY ANITA JONES
CAROLINA PEACEMAKER
JANUARY 4, 1986

SOME

SWIM

ON TEARS

TO BE

WITH US

The letters that follow represent thousands of letters I received, and still receive, about *The Color Purple*, movie and book. Their warmth and sincerity, even when critical, helped a great deal. The final letter, not addressed to me, but to the deceased mother of a friend, captures some of the complexity of the issue of domestic violence and of women's responses to it. It also offers a description of one of the "town meetings" held in many cities about the book, the movie, and me; meetings in which many women and men, like my friend, found it difficult or impossible to speak their own truths.

La Mesa, CA
March 25, 1986

Dear Alice Walker,

I can remember a wintery Friday night in Con-
necticut a couple years ago. The gang from the
paper was headed to our favorite Chinese Restaurant, my boyfriend-then-husband-now had a han-
kering to get his feet on a dance floor and the
heater in my apartment didn't work. But I had to
pass and get home anyway. I'd just made some
friends and they were waiting for me there, beneath the covers of "The Color Purple."

So I grabbed the scrap quilt, sank into the
couch and finished the book.

The moment I was done I wanted to write to you
and say how it moved me, but you know how that
goes, real life steps in and it's on to other
business. I gave the book to my husband, sent a
copy to my mom who gave it to her mom and sister.
I found out that three friends in the newsroom
were reading it and soon everyone was. I even
worked it into a conversation with a 50-ish con-
servative editor, "having trouble with the political piece, and speaking of writing, have you
read 'The Color Purple'?" I'm not sure he ever
did.

Two years pass and I'm in California, reading
Ms. magazine with Whoopi on the cover, Spielberg
at the helm, counting the days til the December
release.

Three or four times later, we're still moved
to tears when Nettie teaches Celie to read, when
Whoopi's eyes grow big as saucers as Shug sings
to her and on and on.

That the movie won no awards last night is un-
speakable. Jealousy speaks loudly I guess and
it's a shame. The Academy obviously lacks all
soul and heart. They who criticized the movie as
a "Disneyfied, safe version of the book" then
picked the safe movie. But the people spoke,

long ago picking the winner and that is what counts. You said you allowed the book to be made into a film to reach a larger audience.

You did:

A man in a blue pinstripe suit sat in front of me during the film. He was obviously dragged there by his wife, ignoring the previews, grumbling, spending time on his soda, staring at his watch. The movie started. Once when I shook myself loose from the grip of the film, I saw his arm draped over his wife. As the credits rolled, she stood and he sat, dabbing his eyes with a napkin. Therein lies the award.

Yours and Spielbergs were masterworks. I hope to one day write something with a smattering of the depth, hope and heart of the story. I would love to have the chance to meet you one day.

Congratulations on winning where it counts.

Sincerely,

Jackie Fitzpatrick

> Derrick Bell
> Stanford University
> Stanford, CA
> February 12, 1985

Dear Alice,

I am teaching here this Spring, but taught in Harvard's Winter Term last month. While in Cambridge, my class and I used the King holiday to see "The Color Purple." We then went to lunch. It was all—the film & lunch—an enjoyable event.

I write in view of the controversy and criticism the film has engendered. In my view, the attacks are unfair. We simply cannot expect one film to save the race from racism. We can hope

that Hollywood will not produce another "Birth
of a Nation" and portray all black folks as
grinning clowns. I thought *Purple* was moving,
entertaining, enjoyable—and not destructive. It
is not all black life—but it represents well
some of black life early in this century.

As for the portrayal of black men, we have
discussed this many times. We need dramatic pre-
sentations of strong black men, but it is not
fair to attack you or the film for not producing
them. Moreover, we cannot have it both ways. Either black males have been the special victims
of American racism as we militants claim and
bear the emotional scars, or we have been lying
all these years. If we have been accurate in our
accusations, then your portrayal should be accepted if not welcomed.

Overall, your book and its transferral into a
very successful film reflects a much deserved
recognition of your enormous talent. Please do
not allow the carping of critics whose attacks
should be aimed at the society and not the ob-
server—to give you pause.

Take Care,
Derrick

                                    March 21, 1986

Dear Alice,

I was, and continue to be, profoundly affected
by your novel, *The Color Purple*. In my own circle, the novel was very well received by women of
all ages—even Catholic nuns!—and caused a lot of
grief to men! (Grief=anger.) You have awakened in
me a desire to know and understand the experience
of Black women. I have read several other of your
works since *The Color Purple*, and was particularly taken with "*In Search of Our Mothers' Gardens*." Like many women, I think, I have

identified with you and welcomed you as a spokesperson for the experience of women. So, first and foremost, I write to thank you for your work and express my appreciation of it. I hope you continue to write for many years to come.

My second reason for writing is because, contrary to public opinion, I was disappointed in Spielberg's interpretation of *The Color Purple*—and I feel like you are a good person to say that to. The question I keep asking myself is, "I wonder what Alice Walker thinks of the film"—despite what's been reported in various magazines, I still wonder what you think.

You see, in my opinion, the "heart" of the novel was left out of the film. Perhaps people have different opinions on what the heart of the novel is. I feel it is the deep relationship between Celie and Shug—and this, I feel, was given only superficial treatment on the screen. I admit such a relationship is difficult to portray in film—but then my question is, why attempt the film at all, if it has to be at the expense of the soul of the book? Spielberg gave us a nice story of poor black folk—but he didn't give us Alice Walker's *The Color Purple*.

It seems to me that Celie found her redemption and healing largely in the intense love relationship with Shug in which they were "erotically bound." I feel one of the central messages of the book was the breaking down of barriers. In this patriarchal and heterosexist society, where most of women's personal, social, political and economic relations are defined by the ideology that woman is for man and takes her identity from man, Celie was aroused to full power through her relationship with another woman. Fairly radical. This you poignantly and sensitively portrayed in your novel. Spielberg, on the other hand, gives us a "nice" friendship with a hint of sexual involvement which was thrust upon us without preparation—so much so that a ripple of disappointment/horror goes through the audience of "Oh my God—they're queer." This does not do the relationship justice. Many people feel the relationship was well presented on the screen—I wonder if they infused the relationship with the depth they experienced in reading the book.

My second major criticism of the film is that it was far too palatable and tidy. The first time I saw the film I was uneasy with it. I couldn't put my finger on it, but it had something to do with the use of music. The second viewing left me feeling manipulated. Did you see *Gremlins*?—that violent little gem shrouded in gaiety? Spielberg is a technical wizard, but, in my opinion, a master at bringing patriarchal values to the screen. In *Gremlins* he gives us horror laced with light, circus-like music—so he has us laughing, for example, while a handicapped elderly woman in a wheelchair is brutally murdered by the evil gremlins. I find this manipulative and irresponsible. (Great values to instill in our children.)

Similarly, in *The Color Purple* we are uncomfortable in spots—but Spielberg does not leave us uncomfortable for long. For example—when Celie moves in to Mister's house—she's hit on the head with a rock (laughter in audience). She cleans up his filthy rat-infested pigsty of a house: whimsical music follows, and a scene from "Joy Dishwashing Detergent"—then Mr. comes and puts his big dirty feet on the table—laughter—. What was the purpose of the "barroom brawl" at Harpo's? Totally unnecessary. Or the dragged-out comedy scene where Sophie's employer can't get the car out of reverse? It is moments like these where I feel the novel was trivialized. Spielberg jerks his audience around from tears to laughter, manipulating for the effect he wants, and finally sending us out of the theatre feeling that all is right and well. The book was not so tidy.

Perhaps my criticisms of Steven Spielberg I should be writing to him—.

As I re-read this letter I am asking myself, "why are you bothering to send a list of criticisms off to Alice Walker? You've been disappointed with a lot of movies, and never done this before—And there are a great number of movies out there that are downright destructive to the human psyche—*Rambo*, for example . . ."

I suppose it has something to do with the fact that, as I said before, I identify with you and love your work. In a way I suppose I feel sort of an "investment" in *The Color Purple*.

Who knows. At any rate, I submit my criticisms of the movie—and my deepest praise for your work.

Thanks for listening.

Donna F. Johnson
CARLETON PLACE, Ontario.

P.S. What *do* you think of the film?!

                    NATIONAL ASSOCIATION FOR
        THE ADVANCEMENT OF COLORED PEOPLE
                       BROOKLYN, NEW YORK
                       BENJAMIN L. HOOKS
                        Executive Director
                          March 12, 1986

PEOPLE
Time & Life Building
Rockefeller Center
New York, New York 10020

Dear Editor:

The NAACP is seeing red over PEOPLE magazine's deliberate exploitation of blacks' sensitivity to *The Color Purple*. The March 10 issue contained a slanted, biased, and unwarranted assault on what we deem to be an outstanding film.

I personally am offended that your magazine chose to take my comments out of context in order to promote increased sales and encourage controversy. I agreed to the interview with a clear proviso that the NAACP was not to be used to denigrate Danny Glover nor any other individuals involved with this movie.

I am disappointed that PEOPLE has chosen to demean the unprecedented success of what may well be a landmark in quality film product involving blacks in major roles. There is too much good in *The Color Purple* to be overshadowed by the bad, and if I am not mistaken, the title was not "The Perfect Color." Now that you've scrutinized and presented the negative, I am hopeful that you will give equal time to exploring the secret ingredients that captured eleven Academy Award nominations.

Not only do you owe an apology to the NAACP, Danny Glover, and Steven Spielberg, but also to all of your readers, whose integrity you have compromised for profit at the expense of one truly "Outrageous Color Purple."

Yours very truly,

Felicia Kessel
Director
Public Relations

FK:jl

NATIONAL ASSOCIATION FOR
THE ADVANCEMENT OF COLORED PEOPLE
BROOKLYN, NEW YORK
BENJAMIN L. HOOKS
Executive Director
March 13, 1986

Ms. Alice Walker
c/o Trade Publicity
Harcourt Brace Jovanovich
250 Sixth Avenue
San Diego, CA 92101

Dear Ms. Walker:

I wanted you to know that contrary to what PEOPLE chose to lead its readers to believe, the NAACP applauds your efforts. "The Color Purple" is a perfect demonstration of the significant contribution that Blacks have been ready and willing to make to the movie industry.

We are hopeful that "The Color Purple" will serve as the turning point for filmmakers, not only to create more films based on various Black American experiences, but to include more Black people both in front and behind the camera in upcoming films.

"The Color Purple" is vibrant, beautiful, and memorable. It's a job well done!

Once again, congratulations.

Sincerely,

Felicia Kessel
Director
Public Relations

FK:jl
Enclosure

Brighton, Mass.
April 13, 1985

Dear Ms. Walker,

I am writing to you out of thanks. I just finished reading your book, *The Color Purple*, and I feel like my chest is about to burst. I almost cried. It made so much sense to me; made me think about my life and the real meaning of love.

My girlfriend and I just broke up. I can't begin to say how much I hurt inside. I feel as if I've lost a part of myself. Sometimes I feel angry; sometimes sad, and other times I'm not sure how I feel. This was my first relationship so I have nothing to compare it to. I lived with this woman for two years I'm not even sure if I loved her. I feel as if I'm a silly little boy who found a substitute for his mother. I was so dependent on her.

All of my feelings became even more mixed-up when she told me that she was coming to the realization that she was gay and was involved with a woman already. I didn't know what to think. I had always thought that I wasn't prejudiced against anyone. I couldn't accept what she told me. Although we had other problems with our relationship as well, I felt rejected simply because I was a male. Other problems we could work out, but I couldn't change the fact that I was a man. I began to doubt my own sexuality. Was it possible for me as a man to love a woman the way she wanted to be loved. All around me I saw men who treated the women in their lives as objects. Was I guilty of that too?

Also adding to the difficulty of separation was the fact that we were living together and still continue to do so because our lease isn't over yet. It has been this way for over a month now. Every now and then I would see her at home. (We are trying to work it out so that only one of us is home at a time. The other person stays at a friend's house.) I would be okay for awhile and then I would get angry, jealous, and sad at the same time. The experiences left me emotionally drained. She still loved me. I didn't know how to respond.

Then she borrowed your book from her friend. She thought I should read it. I wasn't sure. "Was it depressing?" I asked.

"A little," she replied. "A lot of people told me they liked the book though. A friend of mine gave it to her husband. It changed him."

I wanted to believe it could change me. I decided to read it in spite of my discomfort with the main character who falls in love with another woman.

The first time I picked up the book, I read it halfway through. I felt such empathy with Celie that her affair didn't bother me at all. My girlfriend was home the next day when I finished the book. I choked on my tears. All my life I wanted to be loved and to love in return, but my love had too many restrictions—on myself and on those around me. Love is not restrictive; Love frees. Love gives, it doesn't demand, it accepts. From reading your book I learned that all love is good. I learned that I still loved my friend. I could love her and accept her as she is. Thank you so much for teaching me this.

Sincerely,

Jeffrey P. Rowekamp

No. Hollywood, CA
November 25, 1985

Dear Miss Walker,

Twice your book "THE COLOR PURPLE" called to
me when I was at the library. The 1st time I
hadn't been able to even start reading it. When
I saw it again a few weeks after on the shelf, I
figured it was time to try again. How this
lovely work has touched my heart and walked
around my soul. I love to touch the pages as if
they were printed in braille, for there is so
much feeling emanating from the words. Slowly
but firmly did your people rise out of the book
and grab my being. The build was so perfectly
structured that my sorrow and compassion quietly
transformed into a sense of protective love and
admiration [of] your heroine. I laughed and
cried on the same page and celebrated Nettie's
triumphs. How lovely you are to bring these delightful characters into my world. I still carry
them around with me and wonder how they are
finding themselves these days. I loved this book
as a woman and my Child within loved being a
part of the Black world where her friend Lena
came from. Lena was our housekeeper when I was
young. It wasn't till I went thru therapy in the
past several years that I uncovered a heartbro-
ken part of myself, who had felt abandoned when
Lena left our family after a car accident. She
had been my special friend, a mother to me more
than my own mother. I apparently split off from
the memory of that loss at the age of nine, but
kept "Lena" alive subconsciously by taking on
the sufferings and drudgery which she had experienced as a Black servant. Her last name was
Walker, too, and she had a touch of Shug in her.
Our secret times, in the corner of the basement
where she slept, were my only safe times in a
childhood of fear and loneliness. I loved her
hair which she curled with the iron and her "day

off clothes." I always made her go to the town's only drugstore with me so she could see the only other Negro in town—the Cook. My matchmaking was not far off, but no big romance developed. Too soon after that Lena had to quit working for our family, and last I heard she died within that year. I quietly put away my affairs of the heart, locked the door to my memory, and went on my way . . . with only the heart pangs of seeing other Black people to remind me I had once felt something for someone very special.

Now with your books I can leap back into my long-ago world of dark faces, Lena's tales of mystery and romance, and a reunion with a soulmate who protected and loved me.

I'm anxious to see the movie version of your book. When I heard Whoopi Goldberg had been cast I got so excited, because I knew she would be perfect. And I trust Mr. Spielberg will do the story justice with his sensitivity and high imagination.

God bless you dear One, you've given me a great gift with your writings.

Kindest regards,

Ann Clyde
Hempstead, N.Y.

Dear Alice,

As you can see from the article written that criticism of your work abounds. I am saddened and dismayed at the degree to which we befriend ourselves in the quest for true equality, a "fair shake" as it were.

I am a lover, not only of *The Color Purple*, but just about everything that you have written. The depth of sensitivity and struggle that you bring to your characters amazes me still. Your essays, *In Search of Our Mothers' Gardens*, touch me beyond belief. I understand you more as a person, a human being, with every reading.

I also understand what kind of struggle it must have been to trust Steven with your piece, to trust anyone for that matter, black, white or indifferent. *The Color Purple* is a complicated, multi-faceted work yet so simple in its message of hope. The story, unfortunately, cannot be told in two and a half hours. The tapestry of emotional threads that run throughout the story cannot be completely adapted to film.

Yes, Steven did have his work cut out for him.

It's unfortunate, though, that some imaginative, responsible, insightful person of color could not have directed your movie, because it is *your* movie. But then, no one stepped forward, did they? Maybe I'm being presumptuous.

I loved the movie, and I think that Steven did the movie justice within the limits that I'm sure were imposed upon him. But then, I cannot criticize those black folks who feel that they have (especially black men) once again, been slighted, because they have a right to express their opinion. However, my response to these is that whether they like it or not, someone had the courage to adapt the book to the big screen.

To those who criticize the depiction of black men, those kind of black men do exist.

It seems that no matter what we do to uplift ourselves, somebody somewhere is going to tear it apart for some reason.

I could go on forever with this, but I won't because you're probably in the middle of writing yourself. I hope you are resting—you deserve a break.

By the way, you appeared at the Harvard Graduate School of Education in the fall of 1982. You spoke in Longfellow hall. I was a student there at the time. You were just introducing your book and talking about how Celie came into being. That Christmas, I received *The Color Purple* as a gift. I understand that there was a wine and cheese reception for you afterwards, at which I could have spoken with you. Needless to say, I was fearful.

Through your writing, you have spoken to me, and I to you. I do have aspirations of writing maybe an autobiography some day. My journals span many years.

I just want to say thank you for doing your part, for making me proud to be black, to be a black woman and for your contribution. You have done more than some black folks will do in their entire lifetimes. I applaud you.

With Much Love and Respect,

Ann Clyde

Rachel Guido deVries
Cazenovia, N.Y.
9 June 1986

Alice Walker
Wild Trees Press

Dear Alice Walker:

I have enclosed my new novel, Tender Warriors,
which was recently published by Firebrand Books.
Your work has thrilled me with its passion and
vision, and if in some small way this thanks
you, I will be grateful.

I just exchanged books with Charlotte Mendez:
*Condor and Hummingbird** looks beautiful, and I
am looking forward to reading it today.

I've enclosed also a copy of The (latest) Community Writers' Project's brochure, and will ex-
tend another invitation for you to come and read
in Syracuse at The Project. I would of course
love to have you in upstate N.Y., and I have
talked with a couple of other area organizations
about the possibility of co-sponsoring a reading. I realize that you must be inundated with
such requests, but I will continue making what I
am beginning to think of as a yearly invitation.
Sooner or later . . . !

Finally, since I saw *The Color Purple* in the
movies I have wanted to say that regardless of
all the reaction what happened in movie theaters
all over the country was phenomenal: for the
first time in my 37&1/2 years I sat in a fully
integrated movie theater. And the "integration"
was racial as well as in terms of class and age—
I was moved to tears before the movie started
because I was struck instantly by the rarity of
the experience the movie allowed. That is, I am
sorrowfully sure, part of the negative reaction
to the movie. Anyway, I mean that sincerely, and

*Published by Walker's Wild Trees Press.

thank you again. The book—I have taught it several times at Syracuse University, and have students telling me a couple of years after the course that they have given *The Color Purple* to their kids, friends and on and on.

I wish you all the best. And I hope to see you in Syracuse or vicinity sooner rather than later.

With love

Rachel Guido deVries

May 27, 1986

Dear Ms. Walker,

I am writing to you out of my sincere love for your book "The Color Purple" and to thank you for allowing it to be made into a movie. I am not the type of person who writes to actors, musicians, or authors of books, because I am afraid they will not perceive my intentions as being sincere. I was so moved by this particular book and movie I felt I had to write you. I know you are a very busy person and I will try not to make this too long. I believe a person should be told when they have touched someone else in a positive way. I found the address of your publishing company while reading the article "The Making of the Color Purple" in an old issue of *Ms.* magazine.

I have read the book several times, I have the sound track and I have seen the movie 31 times. Now I would usually not tell people that I had seen the movie so many times because I would be embarrassed. I think most people would find it very bizarre to sit through a movie 31 times. I find it strange myself.

The movie touched me in a way no other movie

ever has. The musical score was beautiful, the story was beautiful with emotions which were overwhelming and the acting was superb. I felt some of the best acting was when Celie did not even say anything, her face said it all. I.E., finding the wrinkled piece of paper which said sky and thinking Nettie was dead, going to the mailbox and asking Mr. if there was anything for her, sitting in the jook joint while Shug sang "Sister" to her.

I live in a very stifling city and I was not aware of who Whoopi Goldberg was until this movie, but I loved her so much as Celie, I bought the Broadway album and video cassette. I think she expresses some wonderful and valuable thoughts on life and is the best actor to come around in a long time. I feel she is possibly the most versatile actor around today.

I read every article I see on "The Color Purple" and enjoy talking about it with other people because I feel so strongly about it. I am not apt to stand up for my rights and am easily downed in an argument. I will always, however, express my opinion when discussing "The Color Purple" and express the positive effects it had on me.

I have read many criticisms of the movie and how it portrays black men in a negative way. I get extremely angry every time I read one of these criticisms because I feel these people are not seeing the forest for the trees.

In *Ms.* magazine, Whoopi Goldberg says "The Color Purple is not a movie about race. What happens to Celie is happening to women all over the world of all races and backgrounds, that is the fact. This is a story about the trials of the human spirit."

I am a twenty-seven-year-old white woman who lived in a home where emotional abuse was commonplace. I can't identify with how Celie was physically beaten or sexually abused, but I can identify with her when she was told she had an ugly smile, and that she herself was ugly, and she was a woman and was "nothing at all." I live in a state where incest is rampant, fourteen- and fifteen-year-old girls are forced into arranged marriages through polygamy. Women are made to feel guilty if they are not married with several children by the time they are twenty- five years old. These women are continually sup- pressed and belittled by their husbands and other men. Spouse abuse and child abuse are very common within these homes. All of the polygamist families are white and the incest most happens in white homes. All of the incest cases I have studied have happened in white homes within this state.

During all the times I watched this movie and read the book, I never once thought Mr. was beating Celie because he was a black man. I never tied the beatings or the incest to the black race.

The parts of the movie and the book which im- pressed me were where the love between Celie and Nettie was shown. How they were always touching, loving each other, carving a heart in a tree, playing together in a field of purple flowers and how in the end they are finally reunited along with Adam and Olivia. How strong a woman Sophia was until the white man beat out her strength and crushed her spirit. How Shug showed Celie to love others and herself and sang to her in the jook joint. How after all the years Celie has been abused by Mr. she is able to stand up for herself, the African scenes, the African ceremonial scene, the way Shug feels about God. How it is inside you, how "it pisses God off if you walk by the color purple in a field and don't notice it." These are the parts of the movie I never hear the critics mention.

I have always admired Quincy Jones and am again impressed by his talent on this album. I listen to it all the time. I love what you have to say about the songs. I thought the lyrics in the "Dirty Dozens" were wonderful. I feel every white person should hear why these lyrics were originally written as well as the message in "J.B. King." I also think it is interesting what you say about the songs "Heaven Belongs to You" and "Maybe God is trying to tell you something" because I feel this way about God and Heaven.

In the book, Shug says "man corrupt everything. He on your box of grits, in your head, and all over the radio. He try to make you think he everywhere. Soon as you pray, and man plop himself on the other end of it, tell him to get lost. Conjure up flowers, wind, water, a big rock."

This is how I like to think of God but if I expressed this [way] to the predominant religion in my state of which I am *not* a member, they would be very upset. Their image of God is sexist and racist. He encourages prejudice and discrimination. Our newspaper programs are censored.

I could go on forever about how "The Color Purple" moved me in a positive way. Celie was in such a bad situation and through the help of Shug she was finally able to believe in herself, get out of a bad situation, and make her life meaningful. No one has the right to suppress and abuse another human being or any living creature for that matter.

Thank you Alice for "The Color Purple" and I look forward to reading your other works.

Sincerely,

January 14, 1986
Su Henry
Fayetteville, AR

Ms. Alice Walker
Wild Trees Press

Dear Ms. Walker:

Congratulations on *The Color Purple* becoming a movie! It is one of those books that made me cry more than once during the reading. According to my standards, that is success. That is effective writing. I loved it!

Living in Fayetteville, Arkansas (population 40,000) means that we do not see new movies until they are almost not new anymore. I'm *very* anxious to see *Purple*! If I get anxious enough, I'll drive a few hours to a city to see it. But I can't decide whether to read the book again before or after the movie . . . perhaps before *and* after.

It's exciting to see Whoopi Goldberg starring in the movie. She is an outstanding performer. The pictures of her in *Ms.* (December 1985) make me feel that she has captured the Celie I came to love in the book. I'm glad you two connected. We all benefit from your association.

When I first heard that Stephen Spielberg had directed it, I'm one of those who felt disappointment that you had not had a woman do it. My heart would *love* to see an *all-woman* crew produce this movie, this book about women. But I also understand the reality of that option. As you told Holly Near in the *Voices* (Fall 1985) interview, the 5-year plan would not accomplish your goals. Not only would a feminist film company take longer to reach the people you want to reach, it would also not receive the ravings that *Purple* will get with Spielberg and Quincy Jones working on it. It would not reach as many people. Few hands would hold it on the subway.

Sad but true. Our society just does not support or value women's work and efforts like it supports men's.

As a lesbian, I'm also disappointed that Celie and Shug are not portrayed as lovers. Again, that is evidence that this society does not value women's relationships with each other like it values a relationship between a man and a woman. Their love for each other is just as strong and just as valid as that love between a woman and a man who are lovers. It is also just as important to the development of the characters. The love, affection and sensuality that the two women share is what makes Celie come alive, learn to value herself. She did not receive that from any man in her life. How can that be ignored?

Some comments I have heard concerning omitting the lesbian relationship from the movie vary. One woman wrote to me: "I still maintain that the real basis of their relationship was friendship anyway. (And, what in the hell is wrong with that?)" Another friend responded to that by saying, "And what in the hell is wrong with a woman's sexuality? What is wrong with admitting that a woman could bring Celie alive in ways that a man couldn't?!"

How often I have reminded myself of the importance of friendship as a basis for a lover relationship. How often I have maintained that my friendships on the whole are more important than my romantic inclinations. So I must say now . . . if their lover relationship is implied in the movie, then I am satisfied. If the strength and dedication of their friendship is portrayed in depth, that's what matters. (Besides, I understand that in Little Rock, Arkansas, the crowd gasped when they kissed. Maybe that's all most audiences can handle.) . . . sigh . . .

I bought your 1986 Calendar. It's marvelous! I carry it with me always. The stories you tell with a picture and a few words or verse! I've read through it all and often share appropriate photos/entries with friends for inspiration. I am especially fond of "One of the elders," mid-June. Perhaps I am being somewhat idolatrous . . . but I thoroughly enjoy laying the calendar open to a picture of you while I sit at my desk to write (a daily occurrence).

One summer my lover and I lived next door to her parents. I took upon myself the chore of mowing their lawn for the summer. My favorite smell in all the world is fresh cut grass. They laughed when I moved and clipped around the tiny, purple wild pansies in the front yard under the big maple tree. But it was important to me. That was before I'd read *Purple*, before I knew that "it pisses God off if you walk by the color purple in a field somewhere and don't notice it." Or maybe I did know.

I notice in the back of the calendar that you were unable to find Ida B. Wells' birth date: July 16, 1862 (from *Black Foremothers: Three Lives*, by Dorothy Sterling, The Feminist Press, 1979). The other two women in this book are Ellen Craft and Mary Church Terrell. What an eye-opening book! I feel thrilled to have found this book, these women, and all those lives they touched.

Yet, I can't help but feel angry that we were not taught about these people, about Black struggles and victories in school. Why are these women and men invisible in our history books? I am angry and ashamed. I am 27, colorless (as I was recently referred to in a racism workshop), and grew up in a very white suburb of Houston, Texas. I am often ashamed to be White when I read the newspaper, watch the news, see the blatant racism around me here in Fayetteville. I was attracted to this town by the lesbian community, by my brother who has lived here for years, and by its size and proximity to wilderness. But I miss the dark faces I became used to seeing in Lansing, Michigan, for seven years. The percentage of Blacks and Hispanics here is very low. I miss the cultural diversity. Someday, I'll move on.

Thank you for sharing your talents with me and the world. Thank you for working so hard on the *Purple* script when you were ready to be done with it and turn your attentions to your family. Give Rebecca and Robert my thanks for their patience, love, and support while you accompanied Celie and her friends through their recent movie venture.

With much love and admiration,

Su Henry

P.S. How is Ntozake Shange's name *really* pronounced?

BLACK FILM REVIEW
Washington, D.C.
December 14, 1985

Alice Walker
Wild Trees Press

Dear Ms. Walker:

I wanted to thank you for the interview. I'd hoped the issue would be out by now but I reached an agreement with the Black Film Institute of the University of the District of Columbia to co-produce the next two issues and this is the first issue where I've had to deal with both a typesetter *and* a printer.

One of the interesting things to me as I go around trying to recruit folks to review the

film of THE COLOR PURPLE is their reaction to
the book. I don't remember where I was when it
came out—either in Dayton, Ohio, or Iowa City,
Iowa, at the Writers Workshop. At any rate, it
was a place where more lip service than real attention was paid to black writing and difficult
to find reviews, etc. And by the time I got back
East, people were talking about other books and
other writers.

PURPLE is an interesting book to me because my
great-uncle was a missionary in Nigeria at about
the same time as the characters in your book.
I'm sure you know this already, but the teens to
the 1950s was an unusual period for black Americans to be missionaries in Africa. I'm working—
with my mother—on a biography of my uncle and
have it about half finished, though I am not
sure—because of the kinds of material he left
behind (little self-revelation) whether it will
be of interest to anyone except academics.

On a more personal note, PURPLE (and other
things that have happened more recently) forced
me to take a look at my own feelings towards
women loving women and toward what it is to be a
man. I'd guess that perhaps much of what I am
about to say is old hat to you—you've already
weathered the storm of reviews, if indeed you
read them at all. I've found myself in the position of insisting that my men friends (and many
of my women friends) look to the final scenes of
the novel where everyone comes together, having
come through pain or suffering to some kind of
peace. So many seem to get stuck on the relationship between Shug and Celie.

I suspect that for many men the idea of women
loving women is a difficult one, threatening because it means that women who love women don't
need men in the way that men need to believe
they must be needed. And because it means—on
some level—men compete with women for sex,
which, of course, too many of us mistake for intimacy, friendship, and the things that must be

central to a relationship for it to grow and for both people to be whole.

In my head, this letter was much clearer; now, in the actual writing of this, I find I've lost the thread of what I wanted to say. In the up-coming issue of BLACK FILM REVIEW, the Egyptian director Youssef Chahine says, "My duty is not to let you come away with the American Dream. My duty is to disturb you. I want to make you come away asking yourself, 'What the hell did that son-of-a-bitch Chahine want? I paid good money to go to a film and have him tell me things aren't right?'" He also says, of his most recent film—ADIEU BONAPARTE, that the critical reaction in France was almost divided equally. Which was good, he says, because when people are arguing, perhaps they are also thinking and questioning and therefore no longer accepting the old assumptions.

Ms. Walker, Alice, if I may be so bold, keep on keepin' on. Tell us things that make us un-comfortable and make us think. Ford Madox Ford said that the novel was the highest form of art because it encompassed both ideas and emotion. We need your work at this time, all of us, black and white, Asian and Hispanic, men and women. To make us think. To make us question the old as-sumptions. To enable us to see new possibilities and new ways.

Best wishes for your success in all you do in 1986.

David Nicholson
Editor

Andrew Paschetto
Little Silver, N.J.
January 22, 1986

Dear Ms. Walker,

It's difficult to begin when what I want to say mostly is thank you. Thank you for your wonderful gift! I am well into a third read of *The Color Purple* and have just now come from a second viewing of the film.

For all the valid criticisms of Mr. Spielberg's vision of your work, the characters from the film are who dance through my mind's eye as I read. In the end what I remember is an immense beauty. It is as if all the joy and beauty and vitality contained in the last letter of your book were splashed out over the picture. The characters may not have noticed it, but it was always there, dormant, needing only to be noticed, and believed in, and most important, recognized in ourselves.

All the beauty and joy and vitality and love which your players express is also ours, and, like them, we need only to remember and believe in it. Again, thank you so very much for such a lovely reminder!

With Warmth and Gladness,

Andrew Paschetto

P.S. Please write if you like. I enjoy your calling yourself "author and medium." It's a terrific way to write, by giving interviews to people with stories to tell. Please take care.

Gary Paul Wright
Astoria, New York

Dear Ms. Walker,

I've been meaning to write you for some time now—ever since I read an article about you in *Ms.* magazine. This is the only address I have for you, so I hope this letter reaches you.

As of this writing, much has been written, spoken and debated about your novel "The Color Purple." A lot of it makes me sick to my stomach (not the book, the talk). You didn't ask for my views, but I would love to share my thoughts with you.

I am a 32-year-old black man. I found your book one of the most enlightening stories I've come across in a long time. The arguments that "Purple" demeans the black man are laughable. You tell me what family hasn't had a father, grandfather, uncle, brother or cousin who wasn't the spitting image of Mister ——. You show me *one* family who denies that and I'll show you a pack of liars. Your novel was a slice of life—real life. Black folks are not immune to reality. Many times we (they) have to face facts. Whether good or bad, reality simply *is* . . .

As for the film, it made me laugh, it made me cry. There are many things I felt were contrived and unnecessary. But for me, it did not mar the story, I enjoyed it nonetheless. At no time, I might add, did I ever attempt to compare the movie to the novel. One would be insane to try to do so.

I suppose the bottom line in my writing you is as simple (and as typical) as any fan letter. I just want to thank you for introducing me and the nation to Miss Celie's world and her point of view. It's given us much to think about. You are a powerful, intriguing woman. And I, for one, am proud of you. Keep on keepin' on!!!

Sincerely yours,

Gary Paul Wright

Holding On and Remembering*

BELVIE ROOKS

The night has been a long one. The effort at sleep torturous. I am awake, and as yet there is no sign of dawn. I'm tired and restless and feel as if I have been fighting a cavalry of demons all night and that the demons have won. I recall snatches of a dream and understand immediately that my deceased mother's living spirit is angry. But mostly it is hurt. Saddened. I can feel her disappointment. In the portion of the dream that I could recall I had sat silently, a Peter-like witness to what felt like a public lynching or a witch burning, lacking the courage to stand up (before the hostile audience) for the accused, my mother's memory, or for myself.

The context for the dream is obvious. The evening before I attended, along with Joyce Carol Thomas, my first "community" discussion of the movie version of The Color Purple. The discussion, hosted by the Graduate Women's Forum at Berkeley's U.C. campus, included panelists: Barbara Christian, Luisah Teish, Quincy Troupe, Al Young, and Fran Beale. With the exception of Teish, the other panelists and a good portion of the audience (at least, that portion that dared speak) rabidly trashed not just the film but especially Alice. Throughout the discussion, I thought a lot about my mother. Her voice was conspicuously (and conspiratorially—it seemed) absent, from the panel and the discussion. I left the auditorium wondering what she would have thought about the attack, the discussion, the issues raised in the film and denied by the audience. Later, all night, I had terrible dreams and nightmares of betrayal.

Dear Maxine,

It is about five o'clock in the morning. I understand your anger. Mostly I feel your sorrow and your disappointment. I think the reason that I am writing this, is to let you know that your sorrow, your anger, and your disappointment are but dim reflections of my own

*This appeared in Life Notes by Patricia Bell Scott.

sense of shame and guilt at my inability last night to stand and "bear witness."

I know that a great deal of your disappointment comes from your knowledge that "the accused," in my dream, was one of the few people that I had been able to tell that "my mother was a victim of domestic violence." How statistically abstract and emotionally removed I had managed to make it sound in order to be able to say it at all. What I had really wanted to say was that you were murdered by your Baptist minister husband (my stepfather) and the Celie-like hardships of your life; all of which I knew she would understand. I also knew that I could trust her with my shame, my grief, my tears, and your memory. So, however badly, I had at least managed to get it out. To reveal my deepest and darkest secret.

How hard I had struggled to "control" myself and not cry. Tears were after all a sign of weakness. Painful reminders to me of your weakness. After all, you were dead, they said, because you were weak. You must know, there were so many things about your life—including your death—that frightened me.

I remember (what was for me) the awkward silence following my announcement. Alice, because of my tears, was a watery blur—but she was there. Quietly waiting in her rocker. How hard it had been to continue. But somehow her quiet presence communicated (in a way that I *felt* more than *understood* at the time) that the continuing, the remembering, and the tears were all part of the healing.

I needed to remember how it felt when I received the phone call at Old Westbury, where I was teaching, informing me that you were dead.

"I'm so sorry to have to be the one to tell you this, but your mother has been killed."

A prolonged, shocked, agonizing silence.

"She was killed in a car accident."

A profoundly sinking silence.

"Are you OK?"

And the barely audible, "I'm OK. I'll come right away."

•   •   •

And later on the plane. The numbness. The emptiness. The primordially familiar feeling of complete aloneness. But mostly the frightening familiarity. It was as if all my life I had been holding my breath, waiting for the other shoe to drop—and finally it had.

I remember arriving at the Phoenix airport with dreaded anticipation not wanting to be met by John.* It must have been obvious to you how intensely I had always disliked him. I hope it was also clear how hard, for your sake, I had tried. At the airport though it became instantly clear to both of us, as he reached to hug me and I surprised even myself by instinctively backing away, that with you gone there was no longer any need to pretend.

With what I later understood to be feigned tears and a trembling voice he explained how you had been "traveling too fast on the road and missed the curve. The highway patrol said the speedometer was stuck at ninety . . ."

"Please," I responded, "I don't need to hear the details, I'd just like to see her—alone please."

After your funeral, as we sat around trying to deal with your death, and the brief forty-four years of your life, one of your aunts (your father's youngest sister) said, loud enough it seemed so that I would be sure to hear (and hurt), "Well all I have to say is that anybody that's a big enough fool to drive off a highway and kill themselves, I don't feel sorry for 'em." I sat there stunned and nauseated, beyond shock, waiting for somebody to say something.

Their collective silence I took to be collective assent. Even in death as far as they were concerned you were wrong. A fool . . .

I stormed out of the house in tears. Your friend Miss Mabel** followed me outside.

*Not his real name
**Not her real name

"There is something I need to tell you," she said. "My house is just up the street."

I followed, my only thought being how to get the earliest possible flight back to New York.

Miss Mabel was in her sixties, and when we got to her house, she sat at her kitchen table for a long, long time without speaking.

Finally, she got up and went over to a nightstand and picked up a tin pan with a brownish-maroon-colored facecloth in it and brought it back to the kitchen table where we were sitting. "I'm not sure how to tell you this, or whether I should even be telling you. But your mother was very badly beaten the night she died."

"Beaten!?"

"Yeah, John had beaten her up pretty bad." She said quietly, "She showed up here at about two o'clock in the morning. She was crying hysterically. Really out of her head. Her clothes were all torn off. She barely had on enough to cover her body. Her right eye was practically swollen shut. That poor child, her face looked like a piece of raw steak. This pan was filled with her blood. I had to empty it twice; and I still haven't been able to wash all of her blood out of this cloth."

The other shoe fell, but the edge that I was standing on was falling even faster.

Miss Mabel's voice broke as she gently caressed the cloth, "I begged her not to go . . . you know, I haven't been able to sleep really since she died. I begged her. She was in no condition to drive . . . I don't even know if she saw the cliff . . . she couldn't stop crying . . . she had lost so much blood . . . When she left here she could hardly stand up."

As Miss Mabel talked, I was no longer there. I had gone where you had been. Last week you had been in the same room. Cried in the same room. This week, all that was left of your presence was a tin pan, a bloodied washcloth, some faded bloodstains on the kitchen floor and Miss Mabel's memories.

"I begged her to stay here . . . Ain't nobody gon' mess with you in here I told her . . . I could see how scared she was . . . but she just kept saying how she couldn't take any more, how she had a cousin in Phoenix that would maybe help her . . ."

Suddenly the ledge collapsed completely. And I vomited and retched until there was nothing left. Nothing. No tears. No bruises. No scars. No dried blood. No mangled body. Nothing . . .

This morning I very much need your forgiveness. Please try and understand why I couldn't stand before them last night and argue for your life. I was afraid. Afraid that I would not have been able to do it well enough to make them understand.

I'll ask Alice's forgiveness tomorrow.

And I do think you would have enjoyed the film . . .

MUD

It was nearly two years after *The Color Purple* was released that I began to wonder about my 3 percent of the gross, which was due me according to my contract* with Warner Brothers. Where was it? After receiving no positive response from Warner Brothers' lawyers I decided to write to Steve Ross, Chairman of the Board of Warner Communications, and a friend of Steven Spielberg and Quincy Jones. (Ross is since deceased.) We had met, briefly, on the North Carolina set, and I'd taken to his son Mark, a young man who was working on our film as a production assistant, and who seemed troubled but good-hearted, and definitely in need of the tarot readings I gave him. It was inevitable that I would pursue what was rightfully mine, but after so much sweetness in creating the movie, it was like suddenly getting a bad taste of mud.

*A "deal memo," which was the only contract signed. It was simple, straightforward, and only about three pages long.

October 1987

Steven J. Ross
Chairman of the Board
Warner Communications, Inc.
75 Rockefeller Plaza
New York, New York

Dear Steve,

I don't know if you are aware that I've been trying to get Warner Brothers' lawyers, through my lawyer, Mike Rudell of Franklin, Weinrib, Rudell and Vassallo, to respond to me in a fair way concerning my contract—which I understand is now held by Warner's—for *The Color Purple*, the film.

In agreeing to a 3% share of the gross, after break-even point, naturally I assumed there would be, in fact, a break-even point. Every few months, however, when my quarterly statement comes, I am further away from sharing any profits from the movie than ever.

How can this be?

Legally I'm sure there is some kind of acceptable answer. But morally I just don't see how there can be.

Making the film was, on the whole, a joyful experience for me. I felt nothing but love, concern and care throughout the production from virtually everyone. Even from you, and especially from Mark.

It grieves me even to have to ask about money. But I remind myself that in this case it isn't merely a question of money, but of justice.

Can you help?

Sincerely,

Alice Walker

I enlisted the help of my former husband, lawyer Mel Leventhal, and his best man at our wedding several lifetimes ago, Michael Rudell, now an entertainment lawyer in New York.

October 1987

Dear Mel and Michael,

I am enclosing a copy of the letter I've written to Steve Ross. Please let me know if there is anything you specifically object to.

Mel asked me to write out my expectations based on conversations I had with my agent(s) and with the producers of the movie. I've gone back through my notes and to journal entries and this is basically it: As I say on Steve Ross's letter, when I agreed to 3% of gross profit at break-even point I assumed both these things—a gross profit *and* a break-even point would come to pass. I remember that on the first proposal, which I had from Peter Guber (told to me by Cheryl Peters of Creative Artists), I was offered 5% of the Net. I called everyone I knew who could advise me—Ossie Davis, Gloria Steinem, etc.—and on the strength of their advice said no to Net. They said Net was meaningless, I'd never see a penny. Ask for gross, they said. I did.

At different points during filming I spoke to various agents and producers: What does 3% of gross profit after break-even mean in real terms applied to this picture, I asked. They explained that, first, the picture had to pay off the expenses incurred in making it. *Then* it had to pay for advertising. I was informed that the budget for *The Color Purple* was $15,000,000, and that advertising was another $15,000,000. Break-even, I was told, would not come, therefore, until the picture grossed $30,000,000.

When the movie had grossed over $30,000,000 I was talking to Quincy Jones, who said he under-

stood the break-even point to be $50,000,000.
Soon of course the movie grossed 60, then 70,
then 80, then 90 million. . . . Today I am sure
it has grossed (with video cassettes and foreign
sales) nearly $200,000,000.

I would settle for $3,000,000. I come to this
figure based on my belief that at least
$100,000,000 has been realized in profit and
that 3% of that is due me based on my contract.

I hope this is helpful.

Sincerely,

Alice

Reading these letters now I see the humor in my willingness to
"settle" for three million. Though my lawyer was able to get a portion of the monies I considered due me, as I understood my contract, in the ten years since the movie was released I have received
a fraction of this amount. This sad note explained something that
had puzzled me throughout collaboration on the film. I almost always felt positively about the people involved, the willingness to
work together to produce a wonderful film; still, each time I asked
the tarot (Motherpeace) what was likely to be the most difficult reality to be faced in making the film, the card that consistently
came up was "the Devil." This card, according to Motherpeace,
"symbolizes the 'bondage model' of social organization, the philos-
ophy of 'power over' as a way of life. In place of the natural laws of
the universe, this model establishes dominance and hierarchy. . . .
At the top of the pyramidal structure so loved by Patriarchy is the
Big Man. . . ." Everyone who has ever gone after "net" or "gross" in
Hollywood has encountered this "Big Man," who, in corporate
terms, is the power of the conglomerate, the corporation, to which
the "natural laws" of goodwill, sincerity and honor are sacrificed.

With the money I received from selling the rights to *The Color Purple*, writing a screenplay and being a consultant, I was able to take care of my mother, educate my daughter, make contributions to family, individuals and society I might otherwise not have been able to make. I founded a publishing company, Wild Trees Press, of which my partner was general manager and our friend, Belvie Rooks, publicist. It was successful and often fun. We were in business for about four years and published six wonderful books.

CROSSING
PERSEVERANCE

Journal Entry
February 17, 1990

So much has happened: Nelson Mandela released on the 11th. A tall, trim, beautiful old man. With Winnie beside him looking, above all, *tender*, for him. It was a vision I shall never forget. (As I have never forgotten meeting Dr. King when I was a student at Spelman and marveled at the creases in his immaculate gray "sharkskin" suit.) It was almost too much to take in. To see this man who has been shut away from us for nearly 30 years. And to know he comes back into a world white racists have ruined.

With regard to my books, I had for many years honored the cultural boycott imposed by the African National Congress of South Africa, on all artists and writers, and refused to allow my books to appear there. Increasingly, however, and especially after publication of *The Color Purple*, which many South Africans obtained clandestinely, I was petitioned by university and women's groups to permit my books to be used, in limited quantities, around the country. I was determined not to profit in any way from apartheid, and so, met with ANC officials in London and worked out an arrangement whereby all royalties resulting from the sale of my books, notably those published by The Women's Press in London (and including *The Color Purple*), for five years, would go to the women's section of the African National Congress.

The following documents illustrate the mutual respect, of all concerned, that ensured that *The Color Purple*, the movie, would not be approved for theatrical release in South Africa until after the lifting of sanctions, after the end of the cultural boycott, and seven years after its release in the U.S.; well after the beginning of "a democratic and non-racial, non-sexual, non-homophobic" South Africa, and only with the enthusiastic consent and encouragement of the people themselves. The reception of *The Color Purple*, book and movie, in Africa, China, Cuba and other parts of the world, has been strikingly affirmative, with an understanding of the historical, racial and sexual politics of the work that escaped many of its American and African-American critics.

Though a letter from Steven, to which the following letter responds, pointed to obvious losses to be expected by delaying release, in the end, we waited. I believe, happily.

Alice Walker
January 19, 1987
(Martin Luther King's birthday, observed)

Dear Steven,

I am always happy to hear from you; to know that you and your family are well, and that you are spending months thinking about something. Camus said that each of us will have only (maybe) one or two crucial ideas in a lifetime and we will need the whole of our lifetimes to think about them. This way of looking at ideas relieved a lot of my anxiety when I was a student.

I am more fixed than ever in my position that to permit "The Color Purple" to open in South Africa would be morally debilitating to all those involved in creating or appearing in it, as well as a tactical error on the part of its producers. As you know, there is a black South African initiated cultural boycott of all artistic and entertainment activities by artists from other nations that was voted by the United Nations in 1980 and is still very much in effect. The Organization for African Unity has also recommended that its members not issue visas to performers or other artists who break the boycott.

I grew up in a segregated community/world, so I have a good sense of what passes for desegregation to the average fascist/Nazi racist. I remember myself alone desegregating a restaurant in Greenwood, Mississippi. My husband-to-be was with me, but he wasn't black. In other words, to say that 85% of the theatres in South Africa are desegregated means little if they're in neighborhoods where blacks are not allowed, or if one or two brave or suicidal blacks attend a movie in an atmosphere so tense that they won't even be able to really see it: imagine the fear to laugh, the fear to cry, the fear to respond because you're surrounded by people who obviously

wish you were far away in Bophutatswana or off
the planet. And speaking of Bophutatswana: these
phony "homelands" often don't even have potable
drinking water; the children die like flies from
lack of food. There are *no* movie theatres. And
this is where most of the Native Africans have
been resettled. Think of the Indian reservations: how many movie theatres have you seen on
them? It is exactly the same in South Africa.

Can you imagine how much *I* want to share "The
Color Purple" with my brothers and sisters of
South Africa? How for me it would be like handing my heart and my hand to people who are in-
distinguishable to me from myself? What joy it
would be to imagine Winnie and Nelson sitting in
front of their VCR laughing, crying, smiling,
sighing, or even being appalled. But the reality
is that that is exactly what is not possible until the apartheid regime is destroyed. The Native Africans understand this; on this point
they have been admirably clear. They do not want
to be seduced by bits and pieces of "entertainment" or even "hope" until they can enjoy life
like the human beings they are. So though I want
to give them something that I love and that they
might also be refreshed by, for the time being I
try to offer what they can accept without feeling humiliated—because it is precisely the gift
they asked not be proffered at this time. There
is also this consideration: that the 20,000 or
so brave and/or suicidal blacks who would be
likely to challenge the whites to see the film
at the "desegregated" theatres are in jail.

We *know* the white South Africans steal; and a
pirated version of "The Color Purple" is the
least of it. They have stolen a country, they
have stolen the lives of millions of people,
they have stolen the food and water and education and smiles of generations of human beings.
The only thing they have not stolen is the Native
Africans' ability to fight them in any way they
can. They have asked us, as artists and cultural

workers, to join them in this struggle for their very existence as human beings. What they ask is really very small: keep your gifts to yourself until they can be received in dignity.

So many of the large corporations are leaving South Africa. Why is Warner Brothers still there? That seems a more pertinent question to me than whether "Purple" should open there. Native Africans, or I should say, indigenous Africans, are going to win their struggle against apartheid. How long it will take no one can know. Personally, I think things are moving with a swiftness that truly astounds. When they win, and can accept gifts in their own names, I want "The Color Purple" to go there. And I want to go there myself. And I want to be able to hold my head high. Everything I want for myself, Steven, I want for you.

I will think about you so much while you are making this decision. You are right, I am a "ghost" and I am there everytime you feel I am. It is because we are bound by at least the desire to do what is right, and to express our love and perception of the universe in ways that at minimum will not hurt others. Since we are in the world, however, there are other forces that try to sway us from what we know is just. But justice is our only hope. Continue to think with your heart.

Love and Struggle,

Alice

QUINCY JONES ENTERTAINMENT COMPANY
March 19, 1992
BY FACSIMILE

Ms. Lindiwe Mabuza
African National Congress
Johannesburg, South Africa
RE: *THE COLOR PURPLE*

Dear Lindiwe:

Further to our recent phone conversations, this is to confirm that Quincy Jones and Warner Bros. International would very much like to release THE COLOR PURPLE theatrically in South Africa. We would like guidance from the ANC as to whether or not there are reasons why the film should not be distributed at this time. We look forward to hearing from you.

Thank you for your cooperation.

Sincerely,

June M. Baldwin
Senior Vice President
Business Affairs

JMB:tha

cc: Richard Fox, Warner Bros.
    Quincy Jones

AFRICAN NATIONAL CONGRESS
DEPARTMENT OF ARTS & CULTURE
Johannesburg, South Africa
Fri. Mar 27, 1992

MS June Baldwin
Quincy Jones Entertainment
Los Angeles
CALIFORNIA

Dear MS. Baldwin

RE: "The Colour Purple"

The African National Congress's Department of Arts and Culture has learned with interest of your wish to have the above-mentioned product made available for viewing in South Africa.

Quincy Jones has established himself as an accomplished artist with commitment to the cherished goal of freedom for all people. He has proved to be an unstinting supporter of our struggle in the past by adhering to the policy of boycott of South Africa which contributed to our overall effort to usher in change in our country. Thus this renewed interest in making available "The Colour Purple" to our people cannot but warrant our support.

In line with the resolutions of both the Commonwealth Summit (Harare 1991) on the relaxation of "people-to-people" sanctions and the UN resolutions on Culture 1991 our movement now supports international cultural exchange aimed at strengthening the emerging democratic culture. It is in this spirit that we endorse the position given to you by Film and Allied Workers Organisation (FAWO) and our mission to the USA.

Yours in the struggle,

Wally Serote (Co-ordinator)

FILM AND ALLIED WORKERS ORGANIZATION

Ms June Baldwin
Quincy Jones Entertainment Company
Los Angeles
California

Dear Ms Baldwin

We have been informed by the chief representative of the African National Congress to the
United States, Ms Lindiwe Mabuza, of your in-
quiry regarding the possible release in South
Africa of the movie, THE COLOUR PURPLE.

Let me start by expressing our most profound
gratitude and appreciation for the admirable
stand taken by Quincy Jones Entertainment in observing the Cultural Boycott. As you must be
aware, thanks to your company and others [the
struggle] has reached an appreciably advanced
stage here in South Africa.

Precisely because we can almost see the light
at the end of the tunnel we are now in position
to state categorically that the Film and Allied
Workers Organisation (FAWO) is in favour of having the COLOUR PURPLE released in South Africa.
This is in line with the decisions taken at the
Harare Commonwealth Summit (October 1991). As
well, the United Nations decided to lift the
Cultural Boycott in December 1991.

We believe that such a movie will greatly benefit the people of South Africa as a whole in
exposing [them] to progressive cultural products
particularly of people attempting to overcome
centuries of injustice like yourselves.

An introduction of cultural products of quality like THE COLOUR PURPLE can only inspire our
own artists and, hopefully, further enhance the
process toward the development of a democratic
culture in South Africa.

Yours faithfully,

Willie Currie
General Secretary

QUINCY JONES ENTERTAINMENT COMPANY
April 10, 1992
VIA FACSIMILE

Ms. Alice Walker
San Francisco, CA
RE: *THE COLOR PURPLE*

Dear Ms. Walker:

Quincy asked that I pass on the enclosed letters for your review from the African National
Congress and the Film and Allied Workers Organisation, regarding the theatrical release of THE
COLOR PURPLE in South Africa. With the lifting
of sanctions, Warner Bros. and Quincy feel that
the time has come to plan for the theatrical release of the film. We would appreciate your approval or disapproval by signing in the space
indicated below.

Thank you for your cooperation.

With the greatest respect and admiration,

June M. Baldwin
Senior Vice President
Business Affairs

JMB:gkk

Enclosure

cc: Quincy

THE
RIVER
RUN

Journal Entry
December 13, 1986

Nearly the end of the year and I've written little in my journals. Finally my record of ups and downs with Robert bored me: besides, I began to see that the bond between us remains no matter what temporary problem we have. Even if our relationship as lovers ends, as I feel sure it will, it will be transformed into something else. It was also the year of "The Movie" with tons of letters, the experience of making the movie, the various premieres. I told Robert tonight as we sat in the theater about to see "The Golden Child," which I liked a lot, that it all seems unreal, as if it didn't happen. Or perhaps it all happened, but to someone else. To my sister Ruth, for instance, who seems to have enjoyed every bit of it *thoroughly*.

I am thankful to have been able to return to my former way of life—except that thanks to *Purple* and the sale of my Brooklyn house, I'm in a larger, more beautiful house in San Francisco, and I was able to pay off the mortgage in the country. It is truly wonderful living in a house you like, one that is beautiful. One that perhaps sooner rather than later will be yours. I honestly don't expect to move from here.

My new novel is coming along. Good people, interesting sinners. Sin is a great teacher: and when there's real love, there isn't any sin. I'm enjoying a new freedom in the writing of this book. I let myself go with the voices of the people even when they take me to foreign countries and don't speak much English.

I think learning Spanish, which I'm now doing, is like learning to quilt, for me. Its real function is to further the novel. Ditto the cooking, and that kind of simple, repetitive work is what I must get back into for this last push on the first draft. Odd to think in terms of drafts. *Purple* didn't really require drafts. *Grange* and *Meridian* did though. I think I will call the novel something that came to me in a dream: *The Temple of My Familiar*, and Celie and Shug will maybe drift through, and we can see what becomes of them.

STILL WATERS

Journal Entry
May 4, 1995
So much has happened. It seems quite impossible. Dreams first: I
was walking along a dirt road at dusk. There was a black man—
brightfaced, serious—sitting on the side of the road. Suspended in
a way; sitting, but not on anything. (An angel?) We began to talk.
We disagreed about many things—one of them my notions of how
Steven and Quincy did *The Color Purple*. I despaired of reaching
any kind of understanding. But miraculously, after much discussion, we reached an amicable agreement on the film and on Life in
general. He continued sitting there and I moved on down another
road, my heart light, my arms outstretched, like wings, flying.

I believe movies are the most powerful medium for change on earth. They are also a powerful medium for institutionalizing complacency, oppression and reaction. Steven's feeling about *Gone with the Wind* was so different from mine that when he said he considered it "the greatest movie ever made" I felt the only appropriate response would be to faint. I slept little for several nights after his comment, as I thought of all I would have to relay to him, busy as he was directing our film, to make him understand what a nightmare *Gone with the Wind* was to me. It is a film in which the suffering of millions of black people over hundreds of years of enslavement is trivialized to the point of laughter. It is a film in which one spoiled white woman's summer of picking cotton is deemed more important than the work, under the lash, of twenty generations of my ancestors.

I first saw it as a child, in a segregated theater. My classmates and I squirmed at the heartless caricatures of our parents, still in bondage in the white man's kitchens and fields. Finally we snickered in self-defense, our childish attempt to put distance between us and the fools our ancestors obviously were, according to *Gone with the Wind*, haunting us for the rest of our lives. *Gone with the Wind* might have been a great film if everyone involved in its creation had not distanced themselves from what the Civil War was really about. If they had been able to see themselves, and their own Irish and Jewish and Anglo ancestors, in the characters of the slaves.

I saw it recently on video. The old hurt I used to feel from movies like it was gone; and many were spawned after *Gone with the Wind*: movies that explicitly educated the white public about the kind of "Negroes" who would be permitted visibility in public life. Today it is merely irritating. Scarlett, a pouting, self-absorbed gold digger who never grows up; a woman who verbally and physically abuses a young black girl, Prissy, who, as a slave, dares not defend herself; Rhett, more interesting and better looking than either Scarlett or Ashley Wilkes but with that huge cigar always cluttering up his mouth.

I still have not seen *Jaws, Raiders of the Lost Ark, Indiana Jones and the Temple of Doom* or *Jurassic Park*. I watched fifteen minutes of *Poltergeist* once; I found it terribly disturbing. As I recall, a raw steak began improbable maneuvers around a suburban kitchen: It was not a scene I wanted imprinted on my consciousness. I have seen *Duel, The Sugarland Express, E.T., Close Encounters of the Third Kind**—and recently, *Schindler's List*. All of these movies were thoughtful, challenging, moving, beautifully directed, and new. While *E.T.* remains the character with whom I most identify, as a gardener living in amazement and wonder on Earth in the Western World, I was glad to see how masterfully Steven directed *Schindler's List*, a story which, as a Jew, would have had to be extremely painful, even threateningly so, to him. I wonder if Steven's need to make frightening movies about imagined events will continue, after *Schindler's List*. Somehow I don't think so. What I find as I confront and work through my own fears of what is really true, horrifying though it might be, is that there is less need to make up anything at all, except that which helps the real to be more easily accepted, embraced, understood or changed.

Because I had not seen all of Steven's more popular films, I was unprepared to argue with those who thought that, had I seen them, I would have avoided what was, in their opinion, my dreadful mistake of having allowed him to film my book. There have been times when I've almost given in and gone to see them, just so I would know what so much of the world has seen, enjoyed or hated, and talked about. It is a peculiar stubbornness that has prevented my doing so. Though perhaps I might see them when I am very old. Or perhaps I will take them all out of the video store tomorrow.

It has seemed right to me to base my sense of people on themselves, first—their behavior, their light; and then on that work of theirs that speaks to me in a language I understand with my soul.

---

*I also saw *Indiana Jones and the Last Crusade*, according to a letter I wrote to Steven. However, I recall nothing about it. The films mentioned above left an indelible emotional imprint.

Always acknowledging the imperfections and limitations of persons and of works that is the indisputable sign of being human. Steven is white, and a man. But he is more than that. As I am more than black and a woman. I have thought about this a lot, over the years. For I am moving beyond the need to know myself as "right" or "wrong" but wish rather to know whether I sufficiently understand. If these other movies are so terrible, why were they so popular? Why did everyone who complains go to see them? What is their meaning to the culture at large? Why, if everyone eagerly goes to see them—everyone but me, apparently—is Steven blamed for them? What is the responsibility of the moviegoer?

That I survived the stress of trusting two men I'd never met, with work filled with my own and my ancestors' spirits, is to me the miracle. What made this possible? Was it simply my delight in Steven's boyish chutzpah, which, given Jewish history, is so moving? "What makes this Jewish boy think he can direct a movie about black people?" critics fumed. Well, what did, exactly? It was this that I wanted to know. I thought it might be love. I thought it might be courage. I thought it might be the most wonderful thing of all: Steven had outgrown being a stranger. Was it only the little song "Many Rains Ago" that went out into the world, and into my heart, long before I met Quincy Jones, preceding him like a flag, that caused me, on seeing and listening to him, to feel confident we shared a territory? Quincy says in Elena Featherston's film that what he sees in my work is that God has touched me. I was at first embarrassed, then pleased. It was incredibly affirming to know that what I felt myself was visible to another person, someone who was not uneasy expressing it. I felt the same way about Quincy, and about Steven: that the Universe loves something in the spirits of these men, and for that reason has given each of them enormous power to shift reality in the world.

Quincy and I went back and forth during the filming over which "God" each of us feels, whether Goddess, Nature, Spirit, Mother Earth, the Universe, the God of our ancestors, or people or tribe. I teased him, and he teased back, that if we didn't do the film right,

She was going to be upset. I would often think: whatever the outcome, the Universe will take care of it, and us.

The first picket line I ever crossed was at a benefit showing of *The Color Purple* for the Black Women's Forum in Los Angeles, hosted by Maxine Waters. The second was on Academy Awards night, when *The Color Purple* received eleven award nominations. The picketers were mainly black people, many from the organization Coalition Against Black Exploitation, who made good on their threat to picket the film if the producers refused to meet with their organization to receive its approval of the script. Going into the theater I had a buoyant sense of what battered and burnished warriors we were. By then I knew that almost everyone making the movie had done it, like me, against a personal backdrop of suffering and stress. Marriages were failing, affairs were coming apart, money was tight, physical ailments abounded, households were coming unglued, friendships disengaged. Still, like Celie, we were there. I felt, simply, that the people arrayed against us, shouting or glaring angrily, were wrong, and that time would prove them so. However, they were in complete agreement with the Academy, which gave its approval, and its awards, to the film *Out of Africa*.

Because I know that some of our people wanted awards, for whatever reason, I said nothing about how relieved I was that *The Color Purple* did not receive any. It isn't just that I did not know a single soul making decisions on behalf of the Academy, it was that I was aware of the kind of black characters who had been anointed before. Maids and other white family retainers. I still have not seen any of these judges of the Academy, but my instinct was that they were seriously out-of-balance white men of a certain age, material ease, and social mobility, who would not care for what *The Color Purple* was about, or even, after a lifetime in Hollywood, know. I had read somewhere that perhaps Steven wanted an award; I felt so badly that he might be hurt not to have one, I thought of having one carved. (Though since I think the Oscar, like the American flag, should be redesigned to reflect the reality of the country, I faced a question that could only have a collective answer: What would the new design be?) For me, not getting an award for *The Color Purple*, especially after so many nominations, felt very clean. *Out of Africa* is reactionary and racist. It glamorizes the rape of Africa and attempts to make colonialists look like saviors. To say nothing of how it glamorizes Isak Dinesen's life with the "big game" hunter who gave her syphilis. It patronizes black people shockingly, and its sly, gratuitous denigration of the black woman is insufferable.* But it is a worldview the Academy understood, and upheld. Some black people, outraged that one black woman in *The Color Purple* might physically express her love for another, let this go by without a murmur, as they let go by film after film, decade after decade, by black directors and white, in which women and people of color are insulted, randomly trashed, raped, battered, brutalized and murdered. Or their lives are depicted as empty, comical, devoid of meaning.

How does the heart keep beating? How does the spirit go on? Like my mother, who seemed to switch over to another mode of coping after her body failed her, so that she remained radiant, even though she couldn't move, I felt, after a time of dimness and exhaustion from what seemed like utter meanness of spirit, racism, sexism, homophobia, hypocrisy and craziness, lifted up by an inner

---

*In her book *Out of Africa*, Isak Dinesen (also known as Baroness Karen Von Blixen) writes movingly of her friend, the trader Barkley-Cole, who liked to hang out with "his Somalis" and had a heart condition. One day, she writes, he dropped dead while getting out of his car. In the film Barkley-Cole is shown slowly dying of blackwater fever; simultaneously we are shown, for the first time in the film, the Somali woman with whom he has been living, a relationship quite unknown to Dinesen. The two women stare at each other but don't speak. At the cemetery as Barkley-Cole is being buried, the black woman—who of course in segregated Kenya dares not enter the burial ground or even show her grief—stands silently across the way, appearing like a crow, or perhaps a vulture, on a fence. The assumption of the viewer has to be: blackwater fever, did he catch it from her? In other words, Englishmen like Barkley-Cole don't die of their own disintegrating hearts, as they go about plundering resources and exploiting the weaker peoples of the world; they are ruined by the black women with whom they foolishly sleep.

In addition to this, we now know that the Somali woman represented as being Barkley-Cole's mistress would undoubtedly have been genitally inaccessible to him, because of infibulation. That she was "safely" closed to penetration was probably the only reason she was permitted, by her male relatives, to be Barkley-Cole's servant.

spiritual reserve that I hadn't been sure I had; the assurance that life is grand, no matter what. That suffering has a use; it helps push away the old skin, surely not empathically flexible enough, still clinging to our ankles. That I and all that I love are inseparable forever; and that I deeply love courage and creativity and the boldness to try something new, all of which I experienced among the collective who created our film. That even to attempt to respectfully encounter "the other" is a sacred act, and leads to and through the labyrinth. To the river. Possibly to healing. A "special effect" of the soul.

KATHLEEN KENNEDY, STEVEN SPIELBERG, ALICE WALKER, AND QUINCY JONES ON THE SET OF *The Color Purple*.

INDEX

Alice Walker, winner of the 1983 Pulitzer Prize and the American Book Award for *The Color Purple*, has won international recognition as one of the major writers of the century. She is the author of five novels, including *The Third Life of Grange Copeland*, *Meridian*, *The Temple of My Familiar*, and *Possessing the Secret of Joy*; two collections of short stories, *In Love & Trouble* and *You Can't Keep a Good Woman Down*; two collections of essays, *In Search of Our Mothers' Gardens* and *Living by the Word*; and five volumes of poetry, *Once*, *Revolutionary Petunias & Other Poems*, *Good Night, Willie Lee, I'll See You in the Morning*, *Horses Make a Landscape Look More Beautiful*, and *Her Blue Body Everything We Know*. She edited the Zora Neale Hurston reader, *I Love Myself When I Am Laughing . . .* and her books for children include *To Hell with Dying*, *Langston Hughes: American Poet*, and *Finding the Green Stone*. In the eighties she was publisher and cofounder, with Robert Allen, of Wild Trees Press. More recently she served as executive producer of the independent film *Warrior Marks*, a documentary on the subject of female genital

mutilation. She and the film's director, Pratibha Parmar, also col-
laborated on a companion volume entitled *Warrior Marks*, published in 1993. Ms. Walker's books have been critically acclaimed
and have also been bestsellers. Her novel *The Color Purple* was on
the New York Times Bestseller List for over a year (it was also a film
directed by Steven Spielberg). *The Temple of My Familiar* was on the
list for four months. Her novel of 1992, *Possessing the Secret of Joy*,
spent fifteen weeks on the list. In all, her books have sold nearly ten
million copies and have been translated into over two dozen lan-
guages. Ms. Walker's newest book, *The Same River Twice: Honoring
the Difficult*, will appear in winter 1996.

Ms. Walker's work has appeared in numerous journals and
magazines including *Ms.*, *The New York Times Magazine*, *Harper's*,
Mother Jones, and more. Her short stories have appeared in *The Best
American Short Stories* and twice in *The O. Henry Prize Stories*.

Her many awards and honors include a Guggenheim Fellowship,
the Rosenthal Award for Fiction from the National Institute of
Arts and Letters, the Lillian Smith Award, and the Radcliffe
Medal. Her book *Revolutionary Petunias & Other Poems* was nomi-
nated for a National Book Award. The Newswomen's Club of New
York awarded Alice Walker its annual Front Page Award for Best
Magazine Criticism in 1976 for her essay "Beyond the Peacock:
The Reconstruction of Flannery O'Connor." She has also received
the Townsend and Lyndhurst Prizes.

Ms. Walker's teaching experience includes guest lectureships
and appointments at Wellesley College, the University of Massa-
chusetts, Brown, Sarah Lawrence College, and Harvard. She has
been Fannie Hurst Professor at Brandeis University and Distin-
guished Writer in African American Studies at the University of
California, Berkeley, and Associate Professor of English at Yale.
She was also for many years contributing editor of *Ms.* magazine.

Ms. Walker was born in Eatonton, Georgia. She attended Spelman College in Atlanta and is a graduate of Sarah Lawrence College. She is the mother of a daughter and lives in northern
California.

PHOTOGRAPH AND
TEXT PERMISSIONS

The article on page 223, "Blacks Need to Love One Another" by Tony Brown, is reprinted by permission of Dr. John Kilimanjaro of the *Carolina Peacemaker*.

The article on page 225, "Scars of Indifference" by Anita Jones, is reprinted by permission of Dr. John Kilimanjaro of the *Carolina Peacemaker*.

The article on page 257, "Holding On and Remembering" by Belvie Rooks, published in *Life Notes* by Patricia Bell Scott, is reprinted by permission of Belvie Rooks.

The author also wishes to thank the following people for permission to quote their material: Quincy Jones, Robert Hooks, Derrick Bell, Donna F. Johnson, Felicia Kessel, Jeffrey P. Rowekamp, Ann Clyde, Rachel Guido deVries, Su Henry, David Nicholson, Andrew Paschetto, Gary Paul Wright, and Willie Currie.

Attempts were made to contact everyone who provided material for this book. If anyone was inadvertently omitted, please advise the author or publisher, and acknowledgments, if appropriate, will be included in future editions.